WOMEN'S WORK

WOMEN'S WORK
How Culinary Cultures Shaped Modern Spain

Rebecca Ingram

VANDERBILT UNIVERSITY PRESS
Nashville, Tennessee

Copyright 2022 Vanderbilt University Press
All rights reserved
First printing 2022

Library of Congress Cataloging-in-Publication Data
Names: Ingram, Rebecca, 1977- author.
Title: Women's work : how culinary cultures shaped modern Spain / Rebecca Ingram.
Description: Nashville, Tennessee : Vanderbilt University Press, [2022] | Includes bibliographical references and index.
Identifiers: LCCN 2022005479 (print) | LCCN 2022005480 (ebook) | ISBN 9780826504890 (paperback) | ISBN 9780826504906 (hardcover) | ISBN 9780826504913 (epub) | ISBN 9780826504920 (pdf)
Subjects: LCSH: Food habits—Spain. | Cooking—Spain—History. | Women—Spain—Social conditions—History. | Social role—Spain—History. | Spain—Social life and customs. | Feminism—Spain.
Classification: LCC GT2853.S7 I54 2022 (print) | LCC GT2853.S7 (ebook) | DDC 394.1/20946—dc23/eng/20220215
LC record available at https://lccn.loc.gov/2022005479
LC ebook record available at https://lccn.loc.gov/2022005480

In memory of
Helen Christine Nelms Windham

CONTENTS

Acknowledgments   ix

INTRODUCTION   1

1   Emilia Pardo Bazán: Culinary Nationalist and Ambivalent Feminist   15

2   Frivolous and Feminist: Carmen de Burgos's Culinary-Political Platform   44

3   Mythologies of Culinary Modernity: Gregorio Marañón and Nicolasa Pradera   77

4   Cooking and Civic Virtue: Women, Work, and Barcelona   109

CONCLUSION: Feminist Food Studies and Spain   139

Notes   148
Bibliography   182
Index   00

ACKNOWLEDGMENTS

One summer in the mid-nineties, I was sitting in the air conditioning in my Grandmama's dining room. Calling it a dining room makes it seem grander than it actually was. Her house was a very modest one (the air conditioning was a recent upgrade), originally with only two bedrooms and no indoor plumbing, that she and my grandfather shared with two maiden aunts during the early years of their marriage. The kitchen was galley style. Any overnight visitors were always woken at six in the morning by the banging pots as she put clean dishes away or took them out to get started on the project of the day. Breakfast was usually eggs, a bit of meat (bacon or smoked sausage), and toasted white bread. Grandmama thought it was special to make pancakes for her grandchildren. But I always preferred her biscuits, made with White Lily flour and butter-flavored Crisco. Ingredients were never measured; she made them by feel as her hand combined the flour and the fat and then she added buttermilk a little at a time.

One day that summer Grandmama was cleaning out an old cabinet. She tasked me with coming up with what we should have for supper, something that used what was left of an economy pack of ground beef from the local Piggly Wiggly. Rifling through all the papers and assorted church cookbooks from the cabinet, I came upon a recipe pamphlet that looked old. On closer inspection it was a book of recipes that came with a gas range, one that she and Grandpa had bought new from Sears & Roebuck in the 1960s. Sure that I would find a tasty recipe for something new in that book, I paged through the recipes.

I don't recall details now. But I do remember the feeling of how that recipe booklet and the instructions within it placed me as a reader in a different time. Grandmama and I had a conversation about them. I asked her what she had cooked from it, if anything—she really only followed recipes for baking. We paged through the book. And she reminisced about the new stove in those days, what it meant to be able to buy a new appliance. The cooking she did on it was part of her everyday. It was her daily labor as a rural woman living her life in the post-war Southern United States. She fed her family, preparing special meals for birthdays; she cared for and harvested the crops on the acres surrounding the house; she kept a cow to milk, chickens for eggs and occasionally for the pot, and pigs. These daily tasks were part of the way she sustained her family and community and also produced a small, extra income. It was also a way of life for a woman who was the daughter of white sharecroppers, proud to graduate from high school, but explicitly discouraged from a college education, even when a neighboring family that had recognized her intelligence wanted to make it possible for her to attend the local Bible college.

When I think about how cooking is represented in texts, women's food-work and its intersections with social class, it's impossible for me to separate those interests from what I learned through watching and doing cooking in my grandmother's kitchen. I understood the meanings food could produce and communicate, how foodways could shift over time, for example, with the preference for processed white bread over homemade biscuits or cornbread that were normal during my mother's childhood. Tastes evolved— Grandmama loved pizza and welcomed the visits of grandchildren to go out for it. The modernization of her kitchen meant that I knew it with a dishwasher, a toaster oven, and an electric coffee maker and can opener. Cooking structured her community alongside the local Baptist church. Church dinners featured the dishes each family was known for, vegetables grown in gardens, all served on purpose-built tables outside under the pine trees. Food served as an affective language to communicate love, caregiving, desire for success, and abundance in a life and lifestyle that was shaped by thrift even far long after the need for it was pressing.

My grandmother didn't know much about Spain, other than that I started going there in 1996. But the first and only plane ride she ever took was to come see me in Spain after my study-abroad semester in Salamanca concluded. She approved of the strong coffee even if she added a little hot water to it to suit her tastes. She rode a subway for the very first time. And she appreciated all the gardens and plants we saw on our walks around Madrid, Ávila, and Santiago de Compostela. She disliked ordering two plates for meals—it was too much food!—and I didn't know enough at that point to recommend she order a *plato único* in the restaurants we visited.

When I ask students to think about their food identities in the food studies classes I teach, I do the assignment with them. I think about how my food identities grew from this context and gave the foundation for the questions I ask in this book. For these reasons, I dedicate this book to Helen Christine Nelms Windham.

Women's Work was made possible by support from my home institution, the University of San Diego. My 2015–2016 sabbatical allowed me to complete the archival work for Chapter 4. Faculty research grants from the College of Arts and Sciences gave me extra time for writing, and research support from Dean Noelle Norton sustained the momentum of my work throughout 2020 and through the final stages of completing this book. The USD International Center's award of international opportunity grants paid for several plane tickets so I could stretch limited research funding.

I thank Annabel Martín, with whom I discovered a deep love for research and reading about Spain and its complexities as an undergraduate. She has always been an exceptional role model in this career along with Stephanie Sieburth, who shaped me into the scholar I am today. I will never have a more insightful reader than Stephanie or more supportive mentor. Early conversations about this work with Maite Zubiaurre and Robert Davidson were formative. And later, Roberta Johnson's comments on sections of Chapter 1 solidified certain ideas and opened my eyes to new areas. In the field, there is no better person to know or more insightful scholar of Spain's feminisms and feminist studies. What I have developed here owes an enormous debt to her corpus of work.

I also acknowledge the staff and librarians at the Biblioteca Nacional de España and the Biblioteca de Catalunya. Of special note, the director of the Biblioteca Francesca Bonnemaison, Raquel Muñoz Carrilero, and librarian Maria Oriola Tarragó were instrumental in allowing me access to the archives and materials of the Institut de Cultura i Biblioteca Popular de la Dona in 2015. Moreover, conversations with historians María del Carmen Simón Palmer and Isabel Segura Soriano were illuminating and influential, as is their scholarship.

This work has benefited from a number of interlocutors over the years: Heather Mallory, Zachary Erwin, Virginie Pouzet-Duzer from the early days at Duke. Zack, with the eyes of a "real Pardo Bazánista" read and commented on my Pardo Bazán chapter, for which I'm grateful. Martin Repinecz, my current colleague (lucky me!) and long-time friend, commented on Chapter 3 and improved it tremendously. Liana Ewald and I discussed *Women's Work* and the long nineteenth-century innumerable times, first in San Diego and then via Facetime and Skype. María Paz Moreno and Lara Anderson have been and continue to be exceptional *compañeras* in working to develop food studies within peninsular cultural studies more broadly. I am grateful to them both for their scholarship and friendship.

Jeannette Acevedo Rivera and Susan Larson invited me to speak about this project at their universities, and I appreciated tremendously the thoughtful questions from their students and colleagues. I also thank Eugenia Afinoguénova for her support and her invitation to present Chapter 4 to the colloquium on Gastrocracy, nature, and degrowth that she convened in 2020. The enthusiastic reception of the chapter and questions from participants shaped my revision of that chapter to its current form. Thanks, too, to Suzanne Dunai, whose passion for food history and Spain is always motivating.

I extend a special acknowledgment to the editors and publishers who kindly allowed me to include previously published research in this book. Sections of Chapter 1 were published as "Popular Tradition and Bourgeois Elegance in Emilia Pardo Bazán's *cocina española*" in *Bulletin of Hispanic Studies*. My research on Carmen de Burgos was published in the *Bulletin of Spanish Studies* as "*Escritora-ama de casa*? The Political Tactics of Carmen de Burgos' Culinary Writing." Anja Louis and Michelle Sharp invited me to contribute parts of Chapter 2 for their volume *Multiple Modernities: Carmen de Burgos, Author and Activist*. That book chapter is titled "Bringing the *escuela* to the *despensa*: Regenerationist Politics in Carmen de Burgos's Cookbooks."

John Tallmadge held my hand and helped make sure each chapter says what I wanted it to. USD student Madison Beresford took a first pass with translating quotations in Chapters 1 and 2. Any inaccuracies, and translations in remaining chapters, are entirely my own unless indicated otherwise. And thank you to Sean Grattan for formatting and help with the index.

I am also grateful to my anonymous readers for their close attention and thoughtful comments, and Vanderbilt editor Zachary Gresham's highly motivating enthusiasm has always made opening his emails a delight. I send extra thanks to the Vanderbilt UP crew: Gianna Mosser, Joell Smith-Borne, Jenna Jordan Phillips, Brittany Johnson, and Patrick Samuel for their friendly support, expertise, and vision. To Ana Vega Pérez de Arlucea I extend my gratitude for her cheerful collaboration in sharing contacts for image permissions. Jacobo M. Caridad and Mercedes Fernández-Couto Tella with the Arquivo of the Real Academia Galega kindly offered their digital copy of the image of Emilia Pardo Bazán included in this book. Montserrat Baldomà Soto with the Arxiu General de la Diputació de Barcelona tracked down materials they received from the Biblioteca Francesca Bonnemaison so that images from the Institut could be included. I also thank José

Manuel Lasa Dolhagaray, grandson of Nicolasa Pradera, for sharing his family photos, two of which are reproduced in *Women's Work*.

To my lady locusts Ilana Dann Luna, Rebecca Janzen, Amanda Petersen, Sara Potter, and Cheyla Samuelson: You are wonderful and thank you for having a non-Mexicanist interloper among you. Special thanks to title maven Ilana and sharer of awesome models, Rebecca. Kel Weinhold's coaching and Unstuck program helped me see that I really wanted this book out in the world and the steps I needed to take to get it there. She was instrumental in creating an important community throughout the uncertain early pandemic months of 2020. Fellow Unstucklings and I sustained that community throughout 2021, holding space for the energy and forward momentum of writing group members (special thanks to Miri, Julia, Ali, Liza, and Sarah).

Thank you to Jessica, Neil, and Sheila Ingram, who cheered when I shared good news about *Women's Work* and understood when I didn't want to talk about it. Amanda Petersen and Mike Onofrio helped me feel every success (with champagne!) and are my dearest friends, gin and tonic-drinking companions, and San Diego family. And Keith Lander, my wonderful spouse, with whom I have weathered pandemic uncertainties and more intense together time than we ever anticipated, you make me laugh, you feel proud of me and say it. Thank you.

INTRODUCTION

On December 3, 1916, Emilia Pardo Bazán spoke at the inauguration of the Escuela del Hogar y Profesional de la Mujer in Madrid. Her words, she explained, were not addressed to or about "una mujer ideal y abstracta" (an idealized or abstract woman) but to the woman of today.[1] In what followed, she connected the home, its tasks, and the women who undertook them to the health of Spain and the Spanish race. This modern woman, her home cooking, and feminist politics are not discrete topics; on the contrary, they are ways through which "la mujer debe reclamar el ejercicio de todas las actividades al alcance de su capacidad, y rechazar la suposición de que haya actividades qué le están vedadas por el hecho de ser mujer" (women should reclaim the practice of all activities she is capable of, and reject the supposition that any activities are off limits to her simply for being a woman). She should demand her full rights, both civic and political, or the idea of citizenship is a delusion.[2]

In the midst of World War I, a conflict through which Spain remained neutral while suffering significant impacts on her social, economic, and political life, Pardo Bazán articulated on this single occasion the themes that this book addresses: the roles of women's foodwork in Spanish regeneration and nation-building from the implosion of the empire to the outbreak of Civil War; how women's everyday foodwork connects them explicitly to modernizing practices and ideas; and what makes women, and the working class in general, fit for liberal citizenship in its social, political, and economic valences. Pardo Bazan argued that the home is "la célula de la Patria" (the cell of the homeland) and that women's work within the home, and increasingly outside of it, stimulates the wellbeing of Spain in order prevent its (continued) decadence.[3]

Women's work is a fundamental concept in Spanish feminist theory, even if it has been challenging to define because of the spheres in which it takes place—within the home, on the land, in industry, in intellectual fields, and in the professions—and how it becomes even more ambiguous or "polisémico" in its intersections with social class (118).[4] This book takes on this ambiguity, challenging the notion that women's domestic work is unrelated to broader discussions about modernity, and arguing that foodwork and its representation in culinary discourses has both structured and shifted women's participation in Spain's modernization. Efforts to articulate a new, modern Spain emerged in writing across multiple genres and media. Careful reading of diverse sources—the cookbooks written by the well-known feminists Emilia Pardo Bazán and Carmen de Burgos, the culinary writing of Gregorio Marañón, and *Actas* and archival materials from the Barcelona-based Institut de Cultura—placed in their historical and social contexts yield a better understanding of the roles of food within Spain's uneven modernization process. Further, the book reveals the paradoxical messages that women navigated, even in texts about a daily practice that shaped their domestic and professional lives.

Famous chefs, Michelin stars, culinary techniques, and gastronomical accolades now attract moneyed tourists and media attention to Spain from all over the world. The cuisines and gastronomies of Spain comprise expressions of "banal nationalism"; they also participate in formulations of transnational food identities and patrimonies like those of the Mediterranean diet.[5] Yet, even with this widespread global attention, how cooking became implicated in demonstrating Spain's modernity and, in relation, the roles ascribed to the modern Spanish women responsible for the everyday practices of daily cooking, are areas that scholars have not addressed critically.

On the one hand, this study engages foundational questions about the roles of culinary writing in the oeuvres of key intellectuals like Pardo Bazán, Burgos, and Marañón. Why did they publish in these genres and what do their writings indicate in relation to their other work on modern Spain and its future? On the other, given that culinary discourses, cookbooks especially, were conventionally aligned with domesticity, how do the writers and also the Institut engage women? Are they interpellated in new ways? Does the genre, as one that initiates the action of cooking, also elicit new behavior from women or new thinking about their foodwork? Finally, this study also engages how the study of culinary discourses, the feminist concerns, and the political activities of these writers and the Institut enrich our understanding of first-wave feminisms in Spain and its development toward democracy.

Critical treatment of Spain's culinary discourses is a pressing topic: as María Paz Moreno writes in her study of Spanish cookbooks *De la página al plato*, "un libro de cocina, no es solo un libro de cocina" (a cookbook is not simply a cookbook).⁶ That a number of Spain's leading intellectual figures in the early twentieth century—three of them studied in this book—collaborated in the genre supports this claim. Cookbooks present readers with culinary discourse full of aspirational images and ideas. They serve as containers for memories, paths of connection to other times and communities, and repositories for approximations of the smells, flavors, feelings, and commensality experienced through food. Cookbooks and their recipes offer step-by-step instructions, allude to necessary equipment, and call for ingredients. They tell stories that both clarify and obfuscate processes. Cookbooks are containers of illocutionary acts, given orders that when acted upon facilitate entry into ways of doing and ways of being specific to a community. Their paratextual materials—introductions, prologues, letters to editors—establish the framework of values, ideals, and politics that reader-cooks engage through their practical labor. Culinarity, the activities that surround cooking and eating, exists as a "privileged entry into the social order." Culinary discourse, then, affixes the gestures of culinary practice and converts them into the narratives that generate social meaning.⁷

This study will show how culinary discourse engaged two of early twentieth-century Spain's most marginalized and worrisome groups—women and the working class—at the site of much of their daily labor: the kitchen. During this time Spaniards across the ideological spectrum engaged in serious introspection about what it meant to be Spain after the fall of the centuries-long empire. People wondered what a modern Spain would look like and how it could envision its future while holding on to the identities of its past. Ideas relating to citizenship, work, associationism, and the nation intersected with discourses about modern and traditional cooking, gastronomical identities, and bodily health. Examining the cuisine of this period can shed light on how the accelerating processes of modernization engaged women, both in their domestic and, increasingly, in their public sphere roles. Culinary discourses move the dominant paradigm from eating for necessity to one of agency that allows nascent "citizens" to pick and choose dishes and ingredients in accordance with new ideas of what it meant to be part of a modern Spanish society.

METHODOLOGIES

My approach to these texts is oriented by Susan Leonardi's groundbreaking 1989 article "Recipes for Reading," which shows us how the paratextual elements of cookbooks develop relationships with imagined readers and shed light on the ideological, political, and social purposes that inform writers' interests in cooking and cuisine.⁸ Moreover, an entire cohort of North American feminist historians, anthropologists, and literary scholars, among them Barbara Haber and Arlene Avakian, demonstrate that cookbooks illustrate how women reproduce, resist, and rebel against gender constructions.⁹ They challenge conventional understandings of cookbooks as a genre that reinforces domesticity and the confinement of women to the private sphere, arguing instead that they provide insight into the nature and history of women's modes of production.¹⁰ Barbara Ketcham Wheaton, whose work with the Schlesinger Library Culinary Collection (Radcliffe Institute, Harvard University) has now trained generations of scholars on how to read historic cookbooks considering ingredients, equipment, and people touched by those books. The work of these pioneering food studies scholars and their successors has fostered a feminist food studies approach that is shared by this study.

Critical attention to foodwork reveals complications, complexities, and juxtapositions, according to Psyche Williams-Forson. It forces us to grapple with the hard questions that arise from how power affects people's daily lives through food.¹¹ In their introduction to *Feminist Food Studies: Intersectional Perspectives*, Parker et al. argue that the contexts in which women labor in food systems, food provisioning, and other embodied practices are subject to social and structural inequalities and systems of intersecting oppressions.¹² As one example, the culinary discourses I examine in this book demonstrate that women's foodwork was both acknowledged and institutionalized as part of Spain's modernization even in contexts where hegemonic ideologies would seem to support the persistence of the traditional angel of the house paradigm. Intellectuals and civic institutions framed foodwork as an essential factor in how citizens could develop and thrive in modern Spain. They recognized it as a civic virtue that must be developed outside the home, not merely through the traditional transmission of food knowledges.

And yet such transmissions, which involve interpersonal relationships instead of written texts, must also be accounted for. Along with eating and other types of foodwork, they share an ephemerality that makes their representation in texts incomplete. Giard reminds us that "doing-cooking" is born of ritual, repetition of movements, and motion "rooted in the fabric of relationships to others and one's self [. . .]."¹³ Goody confirms that the practice of cooking can be conveyed only incompletely by recipes; putting instructions into print masks certain kinds of knowledge even as it reveals others.¹⁴ Issues of social class further complicate this representation.

In *The Logic of Practice*, Pierre Bourdieu suggests that the representation of class will always be controlled by the wealthy and powerful, who perpetuate a distorted recognition of how class works and how people of different means contribute to and partake of capital.[15] Given that cooking as a home practice in Spain during this period depended on the labor of two subordinate classes of people—bourgeois women laboring in their own households and working-class or peasant women who cooked as domestic servants, in newly professionalizing contexts, and in their own households—foodwork and its representations were always subject to the interests of the more powerful classes, and any attempt to understand them in relation to Spain's modernization must take this dynamic into account.

In foregrounding how power structures and foodwork intersect, this book understands food as a cultural text, a relatively new view among cultural studies scholars. While not including food as a cultural text, Iberian and Latin-American articulations of cultural studies do not explicitly exclude it.[16] Like other cultural products, food leaves its residue in printed texts; it is performative and produces artefacts; it carries a "sociohistorical symbolic meaning" that is "intertwined with various discursive formations."[17] While the association of food with women and domesticity has discouraged serious consideration, even among feminist scholars who continue to frame the kitchen and food practices as spaces of oppression rather than creativity, ways of knowing that have to do with the body and lived experiences open up new possibilities for considering cooking and thinking, and for understanding food as the hinge between subjects and objects.[18] To understand what food can tell us about Spanish modernization we must endeavor to think about it and with it, and consider the bodies that labor in its production, circulation, and consumption.

A note on critical vocabulary this study adopts from the discipline of food studies: terms like "foodscape," "foodways," and "foodwork" have moved into everyday usage over the last decade, and yet, they have their own genealogies. The term "foodscape" acknowledges food's spatiality, and in this study refers to the environment that determines how people interact with food items.[19] "Foodways" can refer to the eating habits and culinary practices of a community. Rachel Laudan has discussed the evolution from food habits to foodways and pointed out the term's connections with folklore.[20] Carol Counihan defines it as "the beliefs and behavior surrounding the production, distribution, and consumption of food."[21] The term "foodwork" references the labor involved in making meals. My usage also derives from Meredith Abarca's work with working-class Mexican and Mexican American women in her monograph *Voices in the Kitchen*. Abarca observes that Anglo feminist scholarship on knowledge, subjectivity, and agency has little relevance to the daily lives of the working-class women she studies. And yet, their kitchen and domestic practices—their foodwork—reveal a different epistemology, one that "validates the social, cultural, and economic significance of women's household work."²²

CULINARY MODERNIZATION AND ITS CONTEXTS

Spanish modernization in this period dealt with circumstances involving the centuries-long decadence of the empire that culminated in military defeat by the United States in 1898 and the loss of its remaining colonies. There followed a series of profound identity and political crises that, in one form or another, extended into the 1930s and ultimately triggered the Spanish Civil War (1936–1939). Creating what historian Raymond Carr describes as a "complex of pessimism and optimism," political elites and intellectuals struggled to understand why Spain had lost its empire when other Western European nations were building them.²³ Regenerationists, the term applied to those engaged in the work of imagining a modern future for Spain, directed their energies toward political and social reforms.

On the political front, recall the Restoration monarchy's corrupt facsimile of a liberal democracy in the form of the *turno pacífico* (contrived rotation in office) system that kept significant class-based unrest contained. Political leaders and elites had long feared a "revolution from below" by the workers' groups that had begun to organize in the 1840s.²⁴ Plans for political reform were also given urgency by the massive emigration from rural Spain to the cities. Compare the 65 percent of the active population who were involved in agriculture in 1900 with its decrease to 46 percent by 1930.²⁵ This migration added to fears that growing numbers of urban workers would coalesce into an uncontrollable threat to the governing elites. Indeed, only because of state repression and internal divisions among the insurgents was the Restoration able to survive the 1909 Semana Trágica and the general strikes of 1917.²⁶ Following the 1921 massacre of thousands of Spanish soldiers in Morocco (Spain's remaining colonial interest), the spectacle of defeated Spanish soldiers instigated a call for "responsibility."²⁷ Two years later, when the military and king faced a public tribunal for the massacre, General Primo de Rivera called a *pronunciamiento* on September 23. Alfonso XIII soon abdicated, ending the Restoration and establishing Primo de Rivera as Spain's "iron surgeon."²⁸ In 1931, members of the Agrupación para la República, Gregorio Marañón among them, ushered in the Second Republic. Enthusiasm for the arrival of democracy and the prospect that all of Spain's citizens might become participants in the nation's political life signaled the first steps in a radical social revolution. At the same time, however, these social and cultural reforms also threatened Spain's traditional identity.

Primo implemented modernizing reforms throughout Spain, including a network of roads, dams, and irrigation projects.[29] Poor transportation, lack of internal markets, and infrastructure had long isolated rural Spaniards from the practices and ideas of modernization, while cities like Madrid, Barcelona, and Bilbao continued to thrive.[30] They developed consumer cultures similar to those of other European cities, while popular media circulated images and ideas about modern home décor, fashion, hygiene, and cooking.[31] Although such a lifestyle was available only to the urban affluent—Mangien mentions that the cost of a "fonógrafo Quillet" (Quillet phonograph) (350 pesetas) equaled a schoolteacher's entire salary for a month and a half—historians Shubert and Cruz have demonstrated that Spain was already participating in cultural modernity via the normalization of liberal bourgeois ideals, even if capitalist modernization and an entrepreneurial bourgeoisie took longer to develop.[32]

This period also ushered in a fundamental shift in thinking about the roles of women in society. Intellectuals had been obsessed with this topic since the 1840s, and their interest continued through the decades of this study.[33] Women at both the center and the margins of the middle class still functioned largely under the ideology of domesticity; even working-class women had their wages understood as a supplement to those earned by their husbands.[34] Debates about their suitability for public roles and greater access to education engaged women across the political spectrum. Prominent intellectual Margarita Nelken exposed the consequences of this pervasive ideology that forced women to accept exploitive salaries or to depend on marriage or male relatives for financial support. At the same time, debate also swirled around motherhood: would or could a woman's responsibility to educate future citizens within the home limit her contributions as a worker.[35] As a corollary to these debates, a challenging new model of femininity emerged. The *nueva mujer moderna* (new modern woman) offered women a framework for adapting to new social, economic, and demographic contexts and facilitated access to education and the labor market.[36]

Another shift that transformed Spanish society was the increased access to education that made possible an astounding expansion in literacy rates, especially among women, where it rose from 28.8 percent to 52.5 percent.[37] Accompanying this trend, and intertwined with it, was an explosive growth in the market for books and other print materials, including mass-market paperbacks (or "kiosk literature") as well as collections of "classic" texts in the *Nueva Biblioteca de Autores Españoles* under the direction of Marcelino Menéndez y Pelayo, to name two examples.³⁸ Diverse editorial projects including practical manuals, serialized novels, almanacs, and even printed signs engaged new and old readers alike.³⁹

Cookbooks and other culinary writing were very much part of this dramatic expansion. The cookbooks examined in Chapters 1–3 were produced for middle-class women who cooked in their own homes, rather than for professional cooks or those who employed multiple servants. They reached reader-consumers at different levels of education, literacy, and economic means. Given that modernization contributed to a sense of chaos and instability in both individuals and communities, cookbooks and other culinary texts offered assertions of culinary identity and prescriptive models for behavior that allowed readers to respond to new uncertainties.

But even before these new publics arose, culinary writing had enjoyed a long history in Spain. The earliest manuscripts include the thirteenth-century *Faḍālat al-khiwān fī ṭayyibāt al-taʿām wa-al-alwān : ṣūrah min fann al-ṭabkh fī al-Andalus wa-al-Maghrib fī bidāyat ʿaṣr Banī Marīn* (The delicacies of the table and the finest foods and dishes) by Ibn Razīn al-Tugībī and *Kitāb al-tabījfi l-Magrib wa-l-Andalus fī ʿasr al-muwahhudin li-muʾallif mayhul* (The book of cooking in Maghreb and Andalus in the era of Almohads, by an unknown author), the *Llibre de Sent Soví* in Catalan from the early fourteenth, and the Castilian-language *Arte cisoria* from 1423, *Manual de Mugeres* from 1474 to 1525, among others.⁴⁰ Rupert de Nola's *Llibre de coch*, the first cookbook ever published in Spain (1520), and Francisco Martínez Montiño's *Arte de cocina, pastelería, vizcochería y conservería* (1611) were central to understanding cooking and eating in the early modern Spanish court.⁴¹ These and other key texts were reprinted in new editions until well into the nineteenth century, even though they represented the budgets and diets of the aristocracy and high clergy rather than the population at large.⁴² As Pérez Samper has studied, recipe manuscripts also circulated privately among literate women in aristocratic families.⁴³

The earliest cookbooks aimed at the growing middle class date to the nineteenth century and were often translations of French texts, for example, Mariano Rementería y Fica's translation of the *Manual del cocinero, cocinera, repostero, confitero* [s.a.].⁴⁴ Another genre gave instructions for a household cook: examples include *La cuynera catalana* (1837), *Avisos o sian regals sensillas a un principiant cuyner o cuynera adaptadas a la capacitat dels menos instruits* (1860), and *La cocinera moderna* (1888). Social hygienists also treated cooking and nutrition: for example, Pedro Felipe Monlau's *Elementos de higiene privada, o arte de conservar la salud del individuo* (1875) and *Nociones de higiene doméstica* (1897) and later José Garcia del Moral's *La alimentación de las clases proletarias* (1911). Cookbooks and culinary writing also have a precedent in the prescriptive literature that had circulated in Spain since Fray Luis de León wrote *La perfecta casada* in 1583; María del Pilar Sinués de Marco continued in the genre with *El Ángel del Hogar* (1859), *La dama elegante* (1880), and the short-lived magazine version of *El Ángel del hogar*.[45]

Yet, it is with Ángel Muro's "best-selling" *El Practicón* (1884) that a new kind of cookbook emerges in Spain, one that does not assume the presence of a *cocinero* (male cook) or top-notch *cocinera* (female cook).[46] This kind of text addresses a middle-class woman who might instruct a maid and also do some of the cooking herself, and for whom using the food left over from one meal as the base for another is not unthinkable.[47] Muró acknowledges the diverse public for his work: they span from the most hopeless of *cocineras* to the learned academic.[48] He also emphasizes the importance of eating well on a "gasto módico en relación a los recursos de cada cual" (a modest sum according to one's resources).[49] It is in this context that we must understand the cookbooks as the focus of my analysis in three chapters of this book.

Even with this long tradition of culinary writing, scholarship on foodways in Spain has historically been the domain of anthropologists, among them F. Xavier Medina, Isabel González Turmo, and Mabel Gracia Arnaiz. Historians have tended to treat studies of food and foodways uncritically, producing descriptive texts that frame cooking and eating in nostalgic terms without including rigorous bibliographies.[50] Newer work led by historians like Montserrat Miller, Suzanne Dunai, Inés Butrón, and working groups like the Memoria del Hambre project affiliated with the University of Granada indicate a more critical turn toward food and foodways that is complemented by studies from Eugenia Afinoguénova, Eric Storm, and Aitana Guia, among others. Of course, historian María del Carmen Simón Palmer is the exception. Her work has long considered food and food texts critically; among an extensive corpus, her *Bibliografía de la gastronomía española* (1977) has served as a guide into the goldmine of understudied food texts from the nineteenth and twentieth centuries.[51]

Complementing these efforts, food studies scholarship has emerged over the past decade in the fields of language, literature, and cultural studies. Ana Gómez Bravo has explored how foods communicated race, religion, and belonging during the Middle Ages. Her website "The Converso Cookbook" provides a compelling collection of resources for classroom use along with her book, *Food and Culture in the Hispanic World*. Carolyn Nadeau's *Food Matters* offers an extensive analysis of the food practices and meanings represented in *Don Quijote*. Closer to the period of study of this volume, María Paz Moreno's *De la página al plato* serves as a foundational overview of modern cookbooks and culinary writing. She also traces the gastronomical history of Madrid in *Madrid: A Culinary History*. Lara Anderson's *Cooking Up the Nation* documents the construction of a Spanish national cuisine in the period overlapping this study, while *Control and Resistance* discusses the "talk of food" during early Francoism. Anna Riera and H. Rosi Song's *A Taste of Barcelona* details that city's history, cultures, and politics through its cuisine. These monographs are complemented by two special journal issues: "Writing About Food: Culinary Literature in the Hispanic World" in the *Cincinnati Romance Review*, edited by María Paz Moreno; and the issue "Transhispanic Food Cultural Studies" in the *Bulletin of Spanish Studies*, edited by Lara Anderson and myself. Furthermore, the contributed volume edited by Rafael Climent-Espino and Ana Gómez Bravo discusses how food texts and food concerns span economic, environmental, political, and cultural issues, demonstrating that "food is a junction where diverse disciplines in the humanities, social and natural sciences, health and nutrition, and medicine can meet and begin productive dialogues and collaborations."[52] This emerging body of scholarship strengthens the case for a critical reading of culinary and gastronomical writing as well as other food texts that offer new perspectives on cultural phenomena related to nation-building, gender, social class, the environment, migrations, and race.[53]

In its focus on food and culinary discourses, *Women's Work* treats distinctive texts and contexts from a period long associated with the somber philosophical works of mostly male writers like Unamuno, Azorín, and Valle Inclán. Alongside scholarship like Christine Arkinstall's *Spanish Female Writers and the Freethinking Press*, Maite Zubiaurre's *Cultures of the Erotic*, and other work by Maryellen Bieder, Roberta Johnson, Alda Blanco, and Lou Charnon-Deutsch, this study contests the alleged absence of female intellectuals from sociopolitical processes in modern Spain, and pushes this work forward in arguing that women's intellectual work shows up in their foodwork and in their culinary discourse. [54]

Women's Work first addresses the cookbooks and culinary writing of two of Spain's most well-known feminists from the early twentieth century, Emilia Pardo Bazán and Carmen de Burgos, to track how their framing of food, the labor of cooking, and domestic activities cohere with broader debates about the roles of women in Spanish modernization. Chapter 1, "Emilia Pardo Bazán: Culinary Nationalist and Ambivalent Feminist," argues that Pardo Bazán's framing of Spanish cuisine in its traditional and modern forms does important work for understanding cooking as essential to the project of nation building. And yet, she also shows a discordant cynicism toward her ostensible audience of modern middle-class women and toward the modern working-class women who did most of the household cooking.

Chapter 2, "Frivolous and Feminist: Carmen de Burgos's Culinary-Political Platform," shifts in focus to Carmen de Burgos and her three cookbooks: *La cocina moderna* (*LCM*, 1906), *¿Quiere usted comer bien?* (1916), and *Nueva cocina práctica* (*NCP*, 1925). Complicating the prevailing view of Burgos that she published these books to pay the bills, I argue instead that the paratexts in the first and last example show their clear alignment with ideas she develops in her more conventionally feminist works, including speeches given in a number of cities across Spain and *La mujer moderna y sus derechos* (1927). Burgos frames women, their culinary labor, and the meanings associated with cuisine as a meaningful cultural code linked to broader Regenerationist debates. Embedding these ideas in relatively inexpensive cookbooks sold in kiosks allows her to reach women at the site of their labor—the kitchen—and open a space for them to see the culinary as a field of influence and themselves as actors in Spain's modernization.

Whereas the first two chapters focus on feminist-identified intellectuals and their engagement of mostly middle-class women, or those at the margins of this social class, Chapter 3, "Mythologies of Culinary Modernity: Gregorio Marañón and Nicolasa Pradera," turns to the progressive politician and intellectual to explore his framing of well-known Basque chef and restaurant owner Pradera in his prologue to her 1933 cookbook *La cocina de Nicolasa*. Pradera was a working-class woman who achieved social mobility through her cooking and through founding restaurants like the famous Casa Nicolasa. Yet, these changes in Pradera's life, many of them made possible by culinary education and modernization, are erased in Marañón's construction of her culinary persona. Instead, he uses her to create an "authentic" Spanish modernity consistent with how the Second Republic sought to promote tourism for economic development. Moreover, he develops a vision through Pradera that sanitizes the unrest, tension, and instability of the period.

In giving primary focus in the first three chapters to the culinary discourses found in cookbooks by authors aligned with some of the most progressive political and social stances of their times, my analysis looks to the contexts surrounding those books to tease out the meanings generated by how they represent foodwork in writing and also what those representations elide, mask, or erase in relation to social class. Chapter 4, "Cooking and Civic Virtue: Women, Work, and Barcelona," looks to the culinary discourses produced within and about one of the most influential institutions engaged in educating women during this period of study, the Institut de Cultura i Biblioteca Popular de la Dona. A civic institution founded to provide education, dignity, and culture to working-class women, the Institut also attracted more than 40,000 students annually to its cooking classes and served as the institutional home of one of Spain's first celebrity chefs, Josep Rondissoni. Given the enormous responsibility that working-class women had for the foodwork undertaken in Spain during this period, and the degree to which Marañón manipulates the figure of Pradera to suit his own interests, I was drawn to the Institut to understand more about working-class culinary cultures. My analysis of its *Actas*, media about Institut activities and leaders, and its curricula reveal that it was a site of juxtapositions and contradictions, especially in the ways that work, education, and modern cooking intersected with the evolving feminist politics of the Institut and its bourgeois, Catalan nationalist founders. The chapter shows that the organization institutionalized women's foodwork or "cooking right" as one aspect of their social engagement and practices of citizenship. It also reveals that modernizing values enshrined in these culinary discourses also responded to fears that the working class would identify and associate according to class-based interests, in contrast to liberal bourgeois ones. And that cooking right with its basis in scientific, home economics would ameliorate the threat of nutritional and political degeneracy.

Finally, the conclusion summarizes the findings of this study and discusses their implications for how we understand women's foodwork in its intersections with feminist thought during the early twentieth century. It also suggests directions for further research on gender and food cultural studies in Spain.

FIGURE 1.1. Advertisement for MO olive oil, featuring Emilia Pardo Bazán, that appeared in the magazine *Caras y Caretas de Buenos Aires* (after 1890). Image provided by the Arquivo of the Real Academia Galega (RAG) and the Casa-Museo de Emilia Pardo Bazán.

CHAPTER 1

EMILIA PARDO BAZÁN

Culinary Nationalist and Ambivalent Feminist

The role of cookbooks in the literary and intellectual *oeuvre* of Emilia Pardo Bazán has long elicited a range of reactions, from dismissal by contemporary chefs and culinary writers (all male) to uncertainty from subsequent generations of scholars, to surprise from those who do not associate this canonical figure with a genre aligned with the domestic values and ideals that she questioned in her essays and complicated in her fiction writing. Two cookbooks, *La cocina española antigua* (1913, abbreviated as *CEA*) and *La cocina española moderna* (1917, abbreviated as *CEM*), conclude Pardo Bazán's Biblioteca de la Mujer, a series established in 1892 that also includes translations of John Stuart Mill's *On the Subjection of Women* (*La esclavitud femenina*) and Ferdinand August Bebel's *La mujer ante el socialismo*, in addition to works that illustrate important women in history (the Virgen Mary, La Maintenon, Isabel la Católica, María de Zayas).

Many have found it perplexing that Pardo Bazán ended up giving cooking advice to those she wished to instruct about modern feminism.[1] Until recently, the cookbooks received only brief mentions in criticism or surface descriptions in biographies. Having evaded treatment as literary objects, they began to attract renewed attention in 2006 with the publication of María Paz Moreno's article "*La cocina española antigua* de Emilia Pardo Bazán: Dulce venganza e intencionalidad múltiple en un recetario ilustrado."[2] Moreno examines the author's "intencionalidad multiple" (multiple intentionalities), arguing that despite the irony inherent in publishing a cookbook in a series about feminism, the text must be read as consistent with the work of one of the most brilliant minds of the period whose ideas came into conflict with the hegemonic immobility of late nineteenth-century society.³ Lara Anderson examines them in her study of culinary nationalism and fin de siècle Spanish recipe books. More specifically, she demonstrates their commonalities with Pardo Bazán's novelistic production and shows how *CEM* echoes her naturalist writing in the dichotomy it creates between the coarse alimentary habits that signal social decay and degeneration and the "civilizing" culinary practices associated with France.⁴ Exploring Pardo Bazán's use of culinary imagery in models of masculinity and femininity, Kate Good examines her short story "Los huevos arrefalfados."⁵ Hazel Gold argues that the cookbook narratives reflect the sociocultural context of the author.⁶ As a facet of Pardo Bazán's complexity—as an intellectual and manager of her own kitchen—her culinary writing engages gender roles and women's involvement in cuisine as it relates to nation building. Gold, too, notes the "ambivalence" that characterizes Pardo Bazán's address to her readers, but she ultimately frames the texts as largely consistent with the feminist values that Pardo Bazán expresses in other works.⁷

What this framing overlooks, and what other studies have not addressed, is how Pardo Bazán's culinary writing addresses the intersectional dimensions of gender, nation building, and social class. Nor have others accounted for the author's thinking in the culinary writing she published in periodicals, which predates the cookbooks and includes a handful of interventions beginning in 1890 in *El imparcial, La ilustración artística,* and *Nuevo teatro crítico,* in addition to her prologue to Manuel Puga y Parga's (Picadillo) well-known *La cocina práctica* (1905).

This study problematizes the assessment of Pardo Bazán's cookbook project as inconsistent with both her feminist politics and broader body of work. Instead of gendering her work by only reading "seriously" her writing that "effaces its 'feminine' morphology," this chapter argues that these very feminine texts align home cooking—the work of women—with the dominant intellectual projects of the early twentieth century.⁸ The chapter will show how Pardo Bazán legitimizes the culinary as a nation-building discourse essential to Spanish modernization: close readings of the cookbook prologues reveal her rhetorical and conceptual alignment of cooking with other nationalizing discourses, particularly with Generation of '98 thinkers. And yet, her treatment of the women whose labor is represented by the cookbooks and culinary discourse reveals significant contradictions in relation to modern Spanish women and the working class. This analysis will show that the author ultimately displays disappointingly cynical thinking, despite her reputation as one who championed progressive changes in women's education and employment as paths to modernity.

A CONTEXT FOR SPANISH NATION-BUILDING

During the nineteenth century, the development of liberal bourgeois states in some parts of Europe served to catalyze the formation of national identities. However, this process was generally unsuccessful in Spain, where politicians and elites were either unable or uninterested in creating institutions strong enough to integrate citizens both culturally and linguistically. Nationalist movements in Catalonia, the Basque Country, and Galicia worked to establish alternative identities that undermined Spanish national unification and hindered the development of nationwide parties.[9] Moreover, during the Restoration (1875–1923), the *turno pacífico* system effectively excluded both the peasantry (two-thirds of the employed population) and the urban working class from official politics despite universal masculine suffrage enacted in 1869.[10]

Compounding this alienation of the underclasses was the growth of urban Spain and an industrial proletariat in Barcelona, the Basque Country, and Asturias. Between 1900 and 1930, the agricultural sector decreased from two-thirds to 46 percent of the population as peasants moved to the cities, bringing rural poverty and straining the resources of local governments. Proletariat and peasantry alike responded with demonstrations, which intensified during the 1890s and first decade of the twentieth century in the context of Spain's loss of its remaining colonies in 1898 and the Restoration monarchy's crisis of legitimacy. Organizing politically and at the grassroots level, workers escalated strikes and protests to spur the state to create more favorable policies: they rebelled against army conscription for colonial wars (the 1909 Semana Trágica), taxation, and repression and abuses perpetrated by the federal civil guard, particularly in the countryside.[11]

By contrast, outside of the cities, the lack of a transportation infrastructure, the slow progress of modernization, and the weak development of a state-level internal market enabled the survival of traditional identities. Meanwhile, the intelligentsia, concerned by Spain's failure to modernize, called for its regeneration, an impetus that reflected a series of nineteenth-century concerns about what it meant to be both Spanish and modern. As Jo Labanyi argues, intellectuals and politicians effectively wrote the nation into existence, using a newly unified legal code and the creation of a common economic market and currency to standardize national life. After the 1868 Revolution, histories and novels became spaces for debate and negotiation about the complexity of social, political, and economic modernization.[12]

As part of this process, scholars like Manuel Milà i Fontanals, Andrés Bello, and Menéndez Pelayo; Krausist Francisco Giner de los Ríos, founder of the Institución Libre de Enseñanza (ILE) (1876); and Ramón Menéndez Pidal, director of the Centro de Estudios Históricos (1910), created new philological practices to reawaken Spain to its national origins and literary history and to inculcate the citizenry with the proper modernizing mentality.[13] The cultural canons they created would also signal Spain's membership in the group of European states that could trace their national literatures to medieval origins.[14] Additionally, Antonio Machado y Álvarez (*Demófilo*) brought the nation-building practice of folklore to Spain in his monumental *Biblioteca de las tradiciones populares españolas* (1883) to which Pardo Bazán contributed as editor of *Folklore gallego* (first published in 1884).

Nonetheless, as noted previously, to effectively write a nation into being requires a literate community with access to education and printed texts. At the end of the nineteenth century, 55.8 percent of Spanish men and 71.4 percent of women were illiterate.[15] By 1930, following a notable expansion, 37 percent of men and 47.5 percent of women were still illiterate. Those who did not read did not participate in this textual imagining. The idea of an "indivisible national sovereignty" remained illusory for the majority of the population for whom a liberal-national identity had little relevance.[16]

Even still the debates about Spanish identity and modernity appeared in a number of written genres that attempted to impose community and national allegiance and even invent traditions. Pardo Bazán's culinary writing, including her cookbook project, participates in this dynamic. While her construction of Spanish national cuisine has crucial consequences for those for whom the nation, national traditions, and traditional practices are imagined, whose loyalties, political obedience to the nation, and behavior does Pardo Bazán hope to influence through her culinary writing? In the first section, I will detail how Pardo Bazán aligns her culinary project with other nation-building discourses of the period through a series of rhetorical and intellectual strategies meant to engage readers—from middle-class women to her peer intellectuals. From there, I examine how her ideas about Spanish culinary patrimony demonstrate a reactionary perspective in relation to new Spanish citizens. The final section of the chapter considers her contradictory treatment of middle-class women.

PARDO BAZÁN'S CULINARY-NATIONAL STRATEGIES

Historians, sociologists, and literary scholars of different periods and parts of the world have studied the textual and practical developments of national cuisines. While some argue that national cuisines cannot exist except as discourse (Sidney Mintz) or as "products of discursive taxonomies," others including Priscilla Parkhurst Ferguson, Piero Amporesi, and Carol Helstosky have argued that textual representations of foods prepared and eaten by communities serve as instruments of unification during crucial periods of nation building.[17] In the case of France, national cuisine had to be understood in words as well as practices to become meaningful as a national discourse.[18] Sarah Bak-Geller has studied parallel phenomena in the national narratives present in Mexican cookbooks. And, as Lara Anderson details, the serial version of Thebussem's *La mesa moderna* (1888) published in the newspaper *La Ilustración Española y Americana* starting in 1876 began the work of textually unifying the diverse foodscapes of Spain.[19]

Pardo Bazán's cookbooks continue this practice of culinary nationalization with a series of rhetorical and intellectual strategies.[20] As Arjun Appadurai has outlined in his study of cookbooks and Indian cuisine, authors use diverse strategies or "standard devices" in their culinary nation-building. Some "inflate and reify" a particular tradition to serve for an entire nation. Others unify a subjective assortment of recipes under a nationally significant theme or focus on a particular type of food—pickles, for example—and offer recipes from many regions.[21] Pardo Bazán's devices engage already recognized national discourses to convince her readers of the existence and importance of a Spanish national cuisine. Further, these strategies highlight the importance of her own cookbooks, in addition to communicating that her imagined women readers have a role in nation building.[22]

First, Pardo Bazán presents Spanish cuisine as a cohesive, complete, and long-standing culinary system; the books catalogue a "cocina española" (Spanish cuisine) in its old and modern forms. In this way, she continues the work proposed by Thebussem and Un Cocinero, authors of *La mesa moderna* (1888), in their debate about the existence of a Spanish cuisine. The volumes, alongside Picadillo's *La cocina práctica* (1905), introduce books of exclusively Spanish recipes to a reading public, in contrast to nineteenth-century books of recipes that were often translated from French.[23] She also emphasizes the collective Spanish identity of the included recipes, repeating phrases like "nuestra cocina nacional" (our national cuisine), "nuestra cocina regional y nacional" (our regional and national cooking), and "los guisos nacionales" (national stews or dishes).[24] Instead of organizing the recipes by region, she structures them according to general type of preparation or courses. Recipe titles like "Bacalao a la gallega" (Cod, Galician style) or "Morcilla catalana" (Catalan blood sausage) acknowledge how ingredients or preparations may differ according to region. But the volumes' overall organization by type of preparation ("Fritos, frituras o fritadas, y fritangas" [fried dishes] or "Repostería" [Baking]) presents regional recipes as constituting facets of a cohesive and unified "Spanish" cuisine.[25] As Anderson has argued elsewhere, this presentation underscores the unity of Spanish cuisine in its regional diversity.[26]

Important for this argument, Pardo Bazán's organization also idealizes unity across social class divisions. For example, in presenting as one section Spain's "caldos, cocidos, potes, potajes, sopas, migas, gachas" (soups, stews, broths, porridges) she underscores commonalities between the bourgeois *olla* (stew) and the popular *pote* or *caldero*.[27] This collection of dishes derives from the "olla castiza"; they are the nutritional foundation of Spain. Pardo Bazán offers no commentary on quantities of protein that distinguish what bourgeois families can afford to eat in their *olla* from the more modest preparations of popular ones. That said, she does remark on popular dishes that may be suited to "aristocratic tables" ("Sopa de ajo" [Garlic soup]) or recipes appropriate to those of a certain class in which "se observa bien la jerarquía social" (the social hierarchy can be easily observed).[28] Overall, however, she emphasizes national unity built upon a *popular* foundation of Spain's traditional cooking.

In a second rhetorical strategy, Pardo Bazán asserts that Spanish cuisine is not French: the foundation of "nuestra mesa, por ley natural, ... reincid[e] en lo español" (our cooking by natural law ... returns to the Spanish).[29] Her use of the word *reincidir* communicates that Spanish cooking may have strayed toward foreign influences, but that it returns to the traditional.[30] Moreover, women can and should convert French dishes to "nuestra índole" (our style).[31] Writing in *CEM*, she expands on this idea: foreign dishes

> pueden hacerse a nuestro modo: no diré que metidos en la faena de adaptarlos no hayamos estropeado alguno en cambio, á otros (y citaré por ejemplo las croquetas), los hemos mejorado en tercio y quinto.[32]

> can be made our way: I won't say that we haven't spoiled any in the effort to convert them, others (and I give the example of croquettes), we've improved tremendously.

Modern cuisine remains

> española, aún en sus elementos, modificada con aquella que de la extranjera parece imponerse irresistiblemente á nuestras costumbres, y siempre con tendencia á conservar lo bueno de otros días, aceptando lo que, difundido

en nuestro suelo, no pudiera ya rechazarse sin caer en la extravagancia.³³

> Spanish, even in its elements, modified with that from foreign parts that seems to impose itself irresistibly on our customs, and always with the tendency to preserve the good from other days, accepting that in our lands to reject them would be an extravagance.

Her emphasis on "our" customs and "our" lands emphasizes a shared way of cooking. Both her explicit signaling of a national reading and cooking community and her endorsement of adapting and improving upon the foreign elements already present in Spanish cooking entreat her public to participate in her promotion of Spanish culinary nationalism. Moreover, her recommendation that foreign preparations be adapted to the Spanish table does not undermine her cookbook as a national discourse. Reading her perspective with Benito Pérez Galdós's "Observaciones sobre la novela contemporánea en España" (1870) reveals her application of literary nationalism to cuisine. Even though he does not say it in "Observaciones," in practice, Galdós incorporates novelistic models from France and England into his work, a parallel practice to Pardo Bazán's adaptations in her culinary and novelistic writing.

With an additional strategy, Pardo Bazán builds a persuasive case for cuisine's national relevance by aligning it with other nation-building discourses. In a first example, citing poet José de Espronceda, she identifies cooking as an ethnographic document that reveals essential truths about Spanish people: "Espronceda caracterizó al Cosaco del desierto por la sangrienta ración de carne cruda que hervía bajo la silla de su caballo [. . .]" (Espronceda characterized the desert Cossack by his bloody ration of raw meat that boiled under the seat of his horse). The Cossack's preference for bloody raw meat indicates his inherent brutality. The Spartans "concentraron su estoicismo y su energía en el burete o bodrio" (concentrated their stoicism and energy in their soup [of pork and blood]), while "la decadencia romana se señaló por la glotonería de los monstruosos banquetes" (Roman decadence was revealed by the gluttony of their monstrous banquets). These examples illustrate her idea that cooking and cuisine reveal things about a people not observable or quantifiable through scientific reason.³⁴ In addition to their ethnographic nature, the Spanish way of cooking and eating corresponds to "nuestra raza" (our race).³⁵ And in highlighting the national dish, the *olla podrida*, she links cuisine in this statement and in commentary on specific recipes to literature.³⁶

The framework she erects around Spanish cuisine and literature merits additional attention due to ongoing debates of the period about a particularly Spanish literature. Pardo Bazán shows the value of traditional Spanish cuisine through a comparison to *Don Quijote*.

> Olla podrida—Si hay un plato español por excelencia, parece que debe ser éste, del cual encontramos en el Quijote tan honrosa mención, y, sin embargo, se me figura que ya no se sirve en ninguna parte, y que, como las gigantescas especies fósiles de los periódos antediluvianos, se ha extinguido [...] Bien espumado el puchero y añadidos los garbanzos, se echará tocino fresco y añejo, gallina, jamón, chorizo, manos de ternera, orejas de cerdo, una pelota hecha con picadillo, y más tarde patatas, arroz, judías, habas y guisantes frescos. Todo ello ha de cocer cinco horas, y después se sirve ... en las bodas de Camacho.[37]

> Hodgepodge stew—If there exists a Spanish dish par excellence, it seems it should be this one, about which we find such honorable mention in the Quijote, [...] however, it occurs to me that it is no longer served anywhere, and that, like the gigantic fossilized species of antediluvian times, it has become extinct [...] To the well-skimmed broth with garbanzos, one adds fresh and preserved pork belly, chicken, ham, chorizo, veal trotters, pig ears, and a seasoning packet with picadillo, and later potatoes, rice, beans, and fresh peas. All must cook five hours and then it is served ... at Camacho's wedding.

Both emblematic of Spanish cuisine and described here as a relic or fossil of now extinct meals, the *olla podrida* like the *Quijote*, represents the antiquity of Spanish cuisine and literature.[38] In this comparison, Pardo Bazán indirectly nods to both late nineteenth-century literary debates about the French influence on Spanish literature and the omnipresence of French culinary styles in Spain and elsewhere. Despite the "eterno pleito entre la cocina española y la francesa" (eternal feud between Spanish and French cuisines), Spanish cuisine shines "siempre y cuando reúne las tres excelencias de la del Caballero del Verde Gabán: limpia, abundante y sabrosa" (as long as it combines the three excellencies of that of the Caballero del Verde Gabán: cleanliness, abundance, and flavor). Were Spanish cuisine truly inferior, it could not feature a wealth of resources including fish, both freshwater and from the sea, fruits, fowl, Galician and Andalusian hams, and vegetables, which, she comments, "empiezan ya a cultivarse como es debido, [...]" (begin to be grown as they should).[39] This exaltation fulfills an identical function to how critics framed the value of *Don Quijote* in debates about Spanish literature. The former serves as an example of Spain's alimentary "primeras materias" (raw materials) while the latter gives evidence of Spain's seventeenth-century ones in the form of an indigenous literary tradition that proved that Spain could produce contemporary realist novels in the nineteenth century that reflected Spanish national society.[40]

These rhetorical strategies bring to readers' imaginations their shared national community. Pardo Bazán's volumes also participate in a series of intellectual strategies that demonstrate how the culinary exists as another of Spain's cultural canons.[41] John Guillory has studied how institutions participate in delineating the inclusions and exclusions characteristic of cultural canons.[42] In Spain, cultural institutions like the Krausist Institución Libre de Enseñanza and Centro de Estudios Históricos, publishing houses, and their collaborating scholars worked to establish a number of cultural fields that would inform both nation-building school curricula and inculcate citizens with the national ideals appropriate to modernizing Spain. In the literary arena, Menéndez Pidal excavated fragmented pieces of Spain's epic poetry to re-incorporate them "into new and newly-signifying bodies: [. . .] the restored corpus of the 'Spanish Epic.'"[43] The recovery of dispersed and fragmentary pieces of what becomes the foundation of a literary canon suggests a parallel to what Pardo Bazán describes as the work to recover traditional dishes: "Excuso advertir que no presumo de haber recogido ni siquiera gran parte de los platos tradicionales en las regiones. Sería bien preciso el libro que agotase la materia, pero requeriría viajes y suma perseverancia" (I do not presume to have collected even a large sample of the traditional regional dishes. A book with an exhaustive collection would require numerous trips and extreme perseverance). [44]

An additional parallel emerges when comparing Pardo Bazán's culinary project with the practice of folklore. Initiated in 1883 by Antonio Machado y Álvarez, or Demófilo, Pardo Bazán participated as editor of *Folklore gallego* and as the first president of the Sociedad del Folk-Lore Gallego. As a discipline, folklore satisfied an "escape from modernity" and depended upon modern methods of "native cultural discovery and rediscovery."[45] Machado y Álvarez defines the mission of Spanish folklore studies as the discovery of "los tesoros mitográficos" (the mythical treasures) of Spanish regions.[46] Folklore materials, including popular literature, prehistory, ethnography and mythology, and grammar and popular phonetics, are rich and valuable and merit their own archive.[47] For her part, Pardo Bazán stresses that folklore extends beyond erudite specialists.[48] Popular knowledge also exists outside of politics: "El Folk-Lore, por último, no es político, ni religioso, ni revolucionario, ni reaccionario, no tiene color ni bandera, ni más opinión que la de que debe trabajar mucho y desarrollarse y extenderse cuanto le sea posible" (Folklore, lastly, is not political, religious, reactionary, it is not associated with a flag color, or any opinion other than that one must work hard and develop oneself as much as possible). She implies that these lenses would dilute its authenticity. Instead, folklore provides a material link to the customs of traditional life that give *pueblos* "su fisonomía, su carácter, su tipo propio" (their physiology, character, and own type), a way of being that civilization, with its "mano niveladora" (equalizing hand), erases. By amassing collections of popular knowledge and creating an archive, they continue to exist "en un museo universal" (in a universal museum) where the erudite can study the complete history of the past.[49] The threatened loss of traditions that modernity brings, folklore recovers and preserves in a figurative museum, like those for the fossils and sepulchers to which she equates recipes for traditional cooking.[50]

Pardo Bazán aligns culinary practices in *CEA* in ways that echo her approach to folklore. Only a handful of recipes are attributed at all: those that come from historic recipe books by Altamiras or Montiño or others she cites from the cookbooks of contemporaries Picadillo, Muró, Brizuela, Doménech, or Dolores Vedia de Uhagón. Fewer recipes are collected from named individuals at all. Exceptions include those credited to the Condesa viuda de Pardo Bazán or Elena Español. Like the folklore projects that collect popular songs, expressions, and poetry, the collection of recipes is more important than their sources or the individuals who contributed them. In fact, she acknowledges the difficulty of collecting them since "las recetas en las localidades se ocultan celosamente, se niegan o se dan adulteradas."[51]

Second, as with other popular practices, modernity threatens traditional cooking with extinction.

> Hay que apresurarse a salvar las antiguas recetas. ¡Cuántas vejezuelas habrán sido las postreras depositarias de fórmulas hoy perdidas! En las familias, en las cafeterias provincianas, en los conventos, se trasmiten <<reflejos>> del pasado,—pero diariamente se extinguen algunos.[52]

> We must save our old recipes. How many elderly women were the guardians of formulas that are now lost! Among families, in provincial cafés, in convents, these "reflections" of the past were transmitted,—but everyday more become extinct.

The *vejezuelas* Pardo Bazán mentions take recipes to their graves. *Confiterías* and *conventos* may preserve them, but the ephemeral nature of cuisine hastens the disappearance of practices that are not recorded in writing. Pardo Bazán's compilation of Spanish cooking in the two volumes legitimizes them as part of a national patrimony even as the communities that sustained intergenerational culinary practices disperse or break down.

The *vejezuelas*, or elderly women, Pardo Bazán mentions are important. They are the popular class of women who created and sustain traditional Spanish cooking. Further, by designating their "platos de nuestra cocina nacional" (dishes of our national cuisine) as archeological artifacts equal in importance to history's medals, arms, and sepulchers, she connects their culinary labor to Spanish history. Her phrase "Cada época de la Historia modifica el fogón, y cada pueblo come según su alma, antes tal vez que su estómago" (Each period of History changes cooking, and each *pueblo* eats according to its soul, even before its stomach) links popular cooking performed by women to Spanish history and a Spanish soul, inviting a comparison to other Generation of '98 thinkers.[53]

Roberta Johnson, in *Gender and Nation in the Spanish Modernist Novel* (2003), identifies a strong feminine component in both Azorín and Unamuno's conceptions of history. Johnson sees in Azorín a "double-sided temporal edifice," with one side focused on the eternal view and the other giving a view into historical situations and institutions.[54] Azorín identifies occupations related to food provisioning—"aceiteros, vinateros, carniceros, taberneros, bodegoneros, salchicheros, mesoneros, pasteleros" (sellers of olive oil, wine, meat, tavern workers, wine store workers, sausage makers, innkeepers, and pastry bakers)—as the domain of *extranjeros* (foreigners), as Spanish people see them as "bajos y viles" (low class).[55] Poverty, modesty of diet, even hunger are central characteristics of the Spanish soul. Even if Azorín's description of the relative poverty of Spain's alimentary *vida cotidiana* contrasts with the relative abundance necessary to prepare a number of the recipes in Pardo Bazán's cookbook, its focus on the "menudos hechos" (trivial occurrences) that are disdained by history, but which form "la sutil traba de la vida cotidiana" (the subtle obstacles of daily life), underscores the relevance of small, daily events like cooking and eating to his writing on "Spain's eternal soul" and history.[56]

Additionally, in Unamuno's conception of *intrahistoria* Johnson identifies in its alignment with the rural labors of an idealized *pueblo* a space for a female and domestic dimension. Specific dishes are artifacts of Spanish history; they are also the end result of women's culinary labor. Although Pardo Bazán esteems the culinary artistry of men—their cookbooks and expertise are most often acknowledged in *CEA*—she voices the common association of superior cooking with women: "En esta cuestión de la cocina, como en todas las que a la mujer se refiere, la gente suele equivocarse. Sin recorder la superioridad de los cocineros respecto a las cocineras, se da a entender que la cocina es esencialmente femenil."[57] She gives men the upper hand in their *skill* at cooking; but her phrasing emphasizes that, despite their lesser skills, women are commonly associated with cooking because it falls within the sphere associated with their daily, ongoing labor.

It is the practice of cooking that allows women to maintain and transmit culinary traditions. Recalling Luce Giard, "doing-cooking," or "faire-la-cuisine," is a knowledge born of ritual, repetition of movements, and motion "rooted in the fabric of relationships to others and one's self [. . .]."[58] In Spain specifically, popular cooking was transmitted by human mobility, movements from *pueblo* to *pueblo* via migration, through market networks in the patterns of farming, harvesting, and selling produce, and via the women who marry into families from different towns.[59] Pardo Bazán underscores that traditional cooking contributes to a national patrimony. It is a labor overlooked by history books or in the creation of national monuments. Even *recetarios históricos* (historic recipe books) compile the practices of an *alta cocina* (high cuisine) or *cocina burguesa* (bourgeois cooking) rather than popular practice.[60] The female and domestic dimension of popular, daily cooking is what Pardo Bazán transmits in her recording of traditional cuisine in *CEA*.

A second acknowledgment of how women's cooking is implicated in Unamuno's continuity or collapsing of past and present can be seen in how Pardo Bazán discusses her sources for the few attributed recipes in the cookbook. She writes,

> Varias recetas de este libro llevan la firma de las señoras que me las proporcionaron. Cuando transcribo alguna especial de otros libros de cocina lo hago constar; la probidad obliga, —y además, tiene el encanto de lo nuevo, pues generalmente en esta materia, no hay tuyo ni mío—. No es posible, naturalmente, que todas las recetas de un libro sean inéditas . . .; pero si somos dueños de las fórmulas que figuran en cien Manuales, siempre cabe la selección de lo claro y fácil, y hasta de lo ya ensayado.[61]

> Several recipes in this book carry the signature of the ladies who gave them to me. When I transcribe a special example from other cookbooks, I indicate the source; integrity obliges me to do so, —and moreover, it carries the charm of the new, even if generally with these materials, there is no yours or mine—. It is not possible, naturally, that all recipes in a book be unedited

. . .; but even if we are masters of formulas that appear in one hundred manuals, the selection of those that are clear and easy, even those made many times, always belong.

Pardo Bazán's statement that in cooking "no hay tuyo ni mío" (there is no yours or mine) and her description of herself and readers as masters of recipes appearing in one-hundred manuals indicate that popular cooking as a practice belies ownership, unlike the authors or owners of the "grandes hechos" (great deeds) that comprise the written history in books.[62] By identifying herself and readers as *dueños* of the many recipes in the cookbooks, she indicates that knowledge about these practices is already present in the minds and skills of those who carry out work in the kitchen. In this way, she connects herself and readers to those women who labor in the collapsed past and present represented by *la tradición en el presente* (tradition in the present).[63]

These rhetorical and intellectual strategies frame the culinary as an important national discourse. Women—and in the case of traditional cooking, popular women—were creators and the practitioners of traditions that existed outside of text and inform her culinary-nationalist project. Pardo Bazán, then, communicates that the hearth and women's culinary labor is connected to the Spanish soul. Within this framework, Pardo Bazán's cookbook project is consistent with other aspects of her feminist thought. But what happens with Pardo Bazán's culinary-nationalist project when we consider both her modern readers and the modern versions of the *vejezuelas* to whom Pardo Bazán attributes such an important role?

IDEALIZING THE NATION AND THE *PUEBLO*

Pardo Bazán's allusions to *vejezuelas* and other custodians of popular tradition suggest a nostalgic, Romantic understanding of the people, the *pueblo*, one that Inman Fox describes as "a collective imaginative construct organically transmitting a stable cultural legacy."[64] The national legacy that Pardo Bazán's *pueblo* transmits are the culinary traditions that reflect "rastros de nuestra historia, desde siglos hace" (characteristics of our history, from centuries ago), knowledge that should be conserved/archived as what differentiates Spain from other nations.[65] Furthermore, Pardo Bazán implies a synchronicity between different historical periods and the existence of distinct *pueblos* when she specifies that "cada época de la Historia modifica el fogón, y cada pueblo come según su alma, antes tal vez que según su estómago" (each period of History modifies the hearth [or way of cooking], and each people eats according to its soul, even before its stomach).⁶⁶ Her statement acknowledges that the passing of time modifies how people eat, but insists that a *pueblo*'s cooking is tied to an essential identity—"su alma"—more than to literal hunger. Pardo Bazán's *pueblo* is an imaginative subject rather than a political one affected by hunger and scarcity.

Flitter has argued that the understanding of *pueblo* underwent a transition during the nineteenth century from this conservative *Volk* sense to a new meaning as "a pro-active political subject" that offered a focus for ideological radicalism.⁶⁷ The idea of Spain as a democratic, liberal, and modernizing state (as elaborated by the authors of the 1812 Constitution and again during the Gloriosa and Sexenio Democrático) meant that the working classes and peasantry would become "citizens" with the right to participate in official political processes. Democracy would require the restructuring of traditional values and social relationships; accordingly, these manifestations of *pueblo* came into conflict with each other during the Restoration monarchy (1875–1923). Flitter shows that historians responded with organizing notions of "Spanishness" out of fear of widespread working-class revolution. In a similar vein, Pardo Bazán presents the *pueblo* as a powerful force in nation formation. Ultimately, however, this representation serves the interests of elites like herself, namely, those engaged in nation-building projects, and the literate women she hopes will buy her book.

This contradiction becomes particularly apparent when we compare *CEA* to an article she wrote for her "Cartas de la condesa" column in the October 22, 1911 issue of the La Habana newspaper *Diario de la Marina*. She treats a wide range of topics, from Spanish worker uprisings to philology to the *Real Academia*'s dictionary, but she describes as an obligation her chronicling of "la actualidad" (contemporary times), in contrast to her preferred *ensueños* (daydreams) and "curiosidades eruditas" (erudite curiosities). Beginning with a chronicle of social unrest in Spain, she generalizes to the "agitación y ruido hondo" (agitation and uproar) of contemporary life, which has "una cara mucho más fea que la del pecado" (a face much uglier than sin). Her response is to "dar esquinazo a la actualidad . . . de lo que no pesa sobre el pensamiento ni sobre el espiritu" (turn her back on the contemporary . . . toward what does not weigh upon one's thoughts or spirit). She suggests to readers, "Hablemos pues un poco de filología, a propósito de cocina" (let's talk a bit about philology, about how it relates to the kitchen).⁶⁸

This piece was likely inspired by the declaration from the Socialist Unión General de Trabajadores of a statewide general strike in Spain on September 17, 1911, but her description of the "huelgas aquí y acullá, de esas huelgas turbias, con sombrío matiz político y antisocial y revolucionario" (strikes here and there, of those turbulent kind, with their dark, antisocial, and revolutionary political aspect) responds to the more general political and social landscape characterized by working-class and peasant strikes, protests, and violence, which had intensified during the early twentieth century.[69] Pardo Bazán characterizes the strikes as antisocial and revolutionary; she specifies, "revolucionario, sin ideal" (revolutionary, without ideals). While certain revolutions are justified, for example those that helped bring about change, the upheavals occurring in Spain are merely "parodias del monstruoso modelo de la *Commune* francesa" (merely parodies of the monstrous model of the French Commune [Paris Commune of 1871]). Spanish workers are described metaphorically as "una larva que sale de las tinieblas, un espectro que toma cuerpo [. . .] con la forma de horror goyesco que adquiere al mostrarse a la luz del sol" (a larva that emerges from the darkness, a specter that takes shape [. . .] with a form of Goyaesque horror upon showing itself to sunlight). By comparing the protesting *muchedumbres* (masses) to a caricature from thirty years earlier in which politicians were represented as saying one thing while the view into their opened skulls reveals their true ambitions, Pardo Bazán suggests that the working class mask their material desires and violent behavior in the language of revolution.[70] As examples, she notes the 1868 "gloriosa" (Glorious Revolution) and its "reparto de tierras" (distribution of lands); her use of quotation marks communicates her cynicism about the political reforms enacted.[71] Her mention of the judge from Sueca alludes to the murder of a judge and two government officials during the September 1911 uprisings in Cullera. Accusing rioters of taking advantage of "el desorden, con el puñal, con las llamas [. . .]" (the disorder, with dagger and flames), she also refers to the Barcelona Semana Trágica of 1909 and identifies emblematic buildings and women, especially nuns, as innocent victims of the uprising.[72]

This representation stands in stark contrast to the *pueblo* she describes in *CEA*, who perform a central role for the nation as repositories of a culinary patrimony. Pardo Bazán frames the politics of this *pueblo* as illegitimate ("revolucionario, sin ideal" / "parodias del monstruoso modelo").[73] As a frightening mass of dehumanized beings ("una larva"; "un espectro"), they incite terror rather than promote any legitimate social progress. Pardo Bazán even discounts the possibility of hunger, which justified the violence of the Paris *Commune*, as a motivating factor when, in fact, hunger was a chronic feature of the lives of the Spanish working class and peasantry.[74] By indicating that strikers participate in burning works of art and buildings that represent Spain's wealth, she asserts that these protesters do not share her values or those of her readers.[75]

The separation Pardo Bazán constructs between the contemporary *pueblo* and figures like herself and her readers is significant because it signals that this *pueblo* exists outside of meaningful participation in the national liberal project. Their interests are so remote that Pardo Bazán and her readers have no interest or responsibility in responding to the matter: "no nos incumbre arreglarlo [the unrest]." Instead, in contrast to the "tan tristes páginas" (such sad pages) of her report, she proposes thinking about culinary philology, or that which does not weigh upon one's thoughts or spirit.[76]

The focus of this second part of Pardo Bazán's article centers on how the most recent edition of the *Diccionario de la Academia Real* misrepresents the vocabulary of food and cooking. She criticizes lexicographers for their inattention to the nuanced culinary vocabulary of everyday life. For example, they omit references to fish commonly consumed in Spain— "Al 'pargo' no le nombra; la 'sama' sufre igual suerte; la 'lubina' también se la comen, sin salsa" (the seabream they don't name; the bream suffers the same luck; the seabass is also eaten [missing], without sauce). Her quotation marks indicate ridicule of the dictionary's definition of *tortilla* as "una 'fritada' de huevos batidos en aceite o manteca, hecha en figura redonda a manera de torta, y en la cual se incluye, de ordinario, otro manjar" (a fry of whisked eggs in oil or lard, formed in a round shape like that of a cake, in which one includes, ordinarily, another food). By affecting a *casticismo* that alienates speakers of the language, importing Gallicisms for culinary terms that already exist in Castilian, and rendering unrecognizable the language everyone speaks for "otro hablado en la luna" (that other one spoken on the moon), lexicographers leave undefended a *patria* that "se defiende respetando, comprendiendo, recogiendo, depurando y acrecentando con la cultura, el tesoro de su lengua, el gran vínculo nacional" (one defends respecting, understanding, recovering, distilling and growing with culture, the treasure of the language, that wonderful national bond).[77]

In their focus on the minutiae of words, these criticisms reveal a fundamental separation that Pardo Bazán constructs between her readers and the protesters she describes. She assumes that philology, "la preservación de nuestra riqueza filológica" (the preservation of our philological wealth), is a concern her readers share and she invites them to think about how it preserves the national linguistic patrimony as an escape from the turmoil of everyday life and the delinquents who burn works of art and buildings that symbolize Spain's cultural riches.[78] But even as she criticizes philologists for disdaining the culinary vocabulary of ordinary people, she demonstrates that philology is less a refuge from daily life than from a class of citizens who, she assumes, do not understand it and have no interest in safeguarding Spain's cultural wealth.

The only legitimate space for popular interventions in national life, Pardo Bazán suggests, is in texts where the *pueblo* is idealized in contrast to their concrete activity in the streets. She tells readers that it is important that these textual documents accurately reflect words people use; words recorded in the *Diccionario* are "la documentación del archivo, que salvaguarda la hacienda" (the documentation of the archive, which safeguards Spain's wealth).[79] Curiously, she maintains that such archives of popular practices are not political: in her "Dicurso" on folklore she said, "*no es* político, ni religioso, ni revolucionario, ni reaccionario, no tiene color ni bandera [...]" (it is *not* political, religious, revolutionary, or reactionary, it has no color or flag).[80] This assertion stands in contrast to the very political actions of the protesting working class.

Pardo Bazán's stance in this article indicates that the *pueblo* is only relevant to the liberal national project when it is idealized and when its practices are converted to texts. In her discussion of the words that are used to describe foods in Spain and the requirement that writers be precise in their use of those words, she signals that *cocina* itself is a philological project in addition to a folklore one. Consequently, a different group of people will have the key role in practicing the cooking that is significant to the nation. This group, who aspires to or already shares her values, is precisely the target audience for her Biblioteca: emerging or established middle-class women.

If an idealized *pueblo* is central to authenticating traditional cuisine, Pardo Bazán's second cookbook, *La cocina española moderna* (*CEM*), shows middle-class women their centrality to the modern nation. Their domestic activities connect with the ancient traditions presented in *CEA,* and their contemporary practices distinguish Spain as modern nation-state. She arranges the 539 recipes, none of which are reprinted from *CEA*, by major ingredients or preparations (soups, vegetables, *fritos*) into nine sections, including one entirely devoted to *guarniciones* (adornments). As with traditional cooking, the prologue to this volume stresses the importance of maintaining a national culinary foundation—"la base de nuestra mesa tiene siempre que ser nacional"—while also adapting foreign recipes to "nuestro modo" (our way). Whereas the first cookbook was an archive to "recoger las tradiciones" (recover traditions) and "concedía mucho espacio al elemento popular" (granted significant space to popular elements), this second volume aims to educate a particular group of women in the practice of modern, elegant Spanish cuisine, a "punto de honra" (point of honor) for her imagined readers.[81]

Pardo Bazán describes these imagined readers with great specificity. The book is not for those who can pay a *cocinero* or for the "alta cocina" (high cuisine) a male cook would prepare, since the recipes are for those who must limit themselves to "á una mesa hasta casera" (homey or unrefined foods). And households that employ a "docto cocinero" (well-trained [male] cook) even a "cocinera con pretenciones" ([female] cook with pretensions), or "de fuste" (of consequence) are scarce. Instead, the readers who will find her book useful are those who "aspiran [. . .] á que cada plato presente aspecto agradable y coquetón, y á poder tener convidados sin avergonzarse del prosaísmo de una minuta de <<sota, caballo y rey>>" (aspire [. . .] for each dish to be pleasant and charming in appearance, so that guests could be welcomed without the embarrassment of serving dishes of a prosaic nature like those of everyday). The key words *avergonzarse* and *prosaísmo* indicate that Pardo Bazán's intended reader is that woman who, unable to navigate the requirements of a modern, elegant home, might embarrass herself by serving inappropriate dishes to guests. This woman reads and has the money to buy the book, which sold for three and a half pesetas, but she must still think twice about the expense of elegant food. Pardo Bazán informs her, "La comida más corriente y barata admite escenografía. Basta para ello un poco de cuidado y habilidad" (Even the most common and inexpensive foods can be visually appealing. It only needs a little care and ability).[82]

With her insistence that modern cuisine be elegant, Pardo Bazán explicitly links "el que se coma mejor, y sobre todo, con más elegancia and refinamiento" (those who eat better, and above all, with more elegance and refinement) to Spain's modernization: it is one of the "síntomas de adelanto que pueden observarse en España" (symptoms of advancement that can be observed in Spain).[83] Norbert Elias' classic definition of civilization is useful in this connection. Civilization is generally understood to encompass technology, scientific knowledge, religion, and manners, and therefore works to express "the self-consciousness of the West," even national consciousness. As a category of value, civilization indicates a society's superiority over its former primitivity and the primitivity of other societies. It also suggests how a society's manners and conduct can express a distinctive character while rising to a universal level of excellence. Since civilization would tend to diminish national difference to become "what is common to all human beings," the more secure a society is in its identity or nationhood, the more receptive that society is to acquiring the polish of civilization. An elegant modern cuisine would put Spain on equal footing with its neighbors, France and England.[84]

Yet Pardo Bazán's readers are not elegant by default. Instead, they belong to what Noël Valis has described as the difficult-to-define, always tenuous middle class, which signaled in its indeterminacy "a perturbing class confusion" for members of more established groups like the aristocracy, to which Pardo Bazán herself belonged. Middle-classness in Spain was something that could be attained by adopting certain attitudes and lifestyles; in this sense, it often did exist without the financial wherewithal that would support it.[85]

Pardo Bazán acknowledges this aspirational woman interested in adopting the lifestyle and appearance of the middle class in her recognition that inexpensive food can be improved by changing its appearance and also in her lesson about the aesthetics of the foods her readers should serve in relation to their nutrition.

> La función natural más necesaria y constante, es la nutrición. En su origen, se reduce á coger con los cinco mandamientos y devorar á dentelladas, como las fieras, la piltrafa ó el fruto. Lo que ha enoblecido esta exigencia orgánica, es la estética, la poesía, la sociabilidad. Por eso ya no nos basta la olla volcada, ni sufrimos el mantel moreno y gordo de nuestras abuelas, ni nos resignamos á ver enfrente de los ojos un entero queso de bola, que hay que tajar arrimándolo al pecho, ni unas aceitunas flotando en agua turbia y amarillosa. La grosería nos molesta; la suciedad nos horripila; y los manjares queremos que se combinen con tal disposición, que si uno es pesado y fuerte, otro sea ligero y fácil de digerir, y que alterne lo vegetal con los peces y la carne.[86]

> The natural function that is most necessary and constant is nutrition. In its origin, it involves grabbing with the five fingers of one's hands and devouring with one's teeth, like the furies, any scraps or fruit. What has ennobled this organic requirement are aesthetics, poetry, sociability. For that reason, no longer sufficient is the overturned pot, nor do we suffer the dark and thick tablecloth of our grandmothers, nor do we resign ourselves to seeing in front of our eyes the entire round of cheese that one cuts by supporting it against the chest, nor the olives floating in yellowish, murky water. Coarseness bothers us; filth horrifies; and we want that our food be paired in such a way that if one is heavy and filling, the other is light and easy to digest, and that vegetables mingle with fish and meat.

This description of eating and nutrition as a basic fact of human nature evokes animality in contrast to the aesthetics, poetry, and sociability that ennoble the needs of the body, or that civilizes, or makes elegant the daily activities of preparing meals and dining. That the *abuela*'s tablecloth is now intolerable indicates that few generations separate Pardo Bazán's readers from a type of cuisine she describes as repellent; the generalized *abuela* whose table offerings fall short of the tasteful combination of light and heavy dishes could be a family member of any of her readers. For the class-anxious woman two vivid images—the cheese balanced against the chest while being cut and olives floating in unappetizing murky water—represent an imposing culinary standard, which demands an obsession with appearance that Valis identifies as a defining characteristic of the Spanish middle class.[87]

For women whose middle-class status is fragile or those with proletarian finances who aspire to join the middle class, Pardo Bazán's cookbook presents a model of modern attitudes about food and cooking. For example, she discourages serving dishes that might appear prosaic or be identified with a poorer diet: readers will find fewer of the rice dishes so popular in *CEA* since "en mesa un poco refinada, el arroz no puede figurar sino á título de guarnición ó como plato de almuerzo, si los invitados son de confianza" (on a somewhat refined table, rice can only be garnish or the midday meal if guests are intimate friends). While staples like rice and potatoes, the base of working people's nutrition, are marginalized as a garnish or side dish, meats have a central role— "difícilmente se prescinde del plato de carne en comida o almuerzo bien arreglados" (it is difficult to go without a meat dish in a well-organized meal or lunch)—which contrasts with Pardo Bazán's description of the role of meat in traditional cooking as "la parte flaca de la alimentación española" (the skinny part of Spanish nutrition).[88] Additionally, preparing an elegant table implies limiting tasty pork dishes: the "codillo de cerdo" (ham hock) is uncouth if tasty while a ham is the most recommendable.[89]

Although Pardo Bazán normalizes women's presence in their kitchens with these suggestions and even relates that women who pay expensive chefs must "enterarse cariñosamente de cómo anda el fogón" (affectionately keep tabs on what happens in the kitchen), these attitudes suggest that middle-class Spanish families can afford to substitute a ham for a ham hock. Yet, during this period, the diet of the middle class had more in common with that of the working class; the middle class ate more or less the same kinds of food but in greater quantities and with ingredients of better quality.[90] With her recipes and suggestions for serving different courses and dishes, Pardo Bazán offers the modes and manners of the elite for readers to emulate. Those elite ate according to choice or taste; meat was its own dish and not as part of a *cocido* or *puchero*; fresh fish was common on a "minuta bien dispuesta" (well-arranged menu).⁹¹ Thus, practicing modern Spanish cuisine requires imitating to the best of one's ability the culinary choices and practices of the wealthy, which would preclude any integration of marginal middle-class women into identification with the working class.⁹²

Viewed more broadly, Pardo Bazán's modern cuisine could also serve to bolster a sense of national identity as one more project into which the Spanish middle class could channel its energies so as to compensate for a "sense of inferiority (in relation to powers like France and England)."⁹³ At the same time, however, in order to be relevant to the nation, her culinary paradigm would compel its intended audience to strive for impractical levels of domestic elegance.

MODERN WOMEN AND PARDO BAZÁN'S AMBIVALENT FEMINISM

The imagined readers of Pardo Bazán's cookbooks are the same modern women she hoped to convince to take up the cause of feminism, a failure that she addresses in her culinary writing at the same time that she meditates on her writerly and intellectual identity in relation to them. As I mentioned earlier, Pardo Bazán founded her Biblioteca de la Mujer in 1892, a period that biographers have linked to a serious engagement with feminism following the 1889 publication of her essay "La mujer española." That essay serves as the reference point for Pardo Bazán's feminist thought and criticizes the double standard of gender roles in Spain: in that women exist only in relation to the men in their lives while their poor educations perpetuate their inferiority.⁹⁴ Even the most liberal of modern men hold on to a feminine ideal neither from the future nor the present, but the past.⁹⁵ Calling for changes in the social roles accorded to women given Spain's modernization, Pardo Bazán conceived of the Biblioteca to facilitate one part of that education. It would teach Spanish women about feminism and the possibilities of new social roles and appeal to female readerships by including both devotional and historical works, for example, *Vida de la Virgen María* and *Historia de Isabél la Católica*.⁹⁶ But poor sales and lack of interest caused the series to go on hiatus after the publication of *La mujer ante el socialismo*.

The more than twenty years spanning the release of "La mujer española" and Pardo Bazán's cookbooks saw few changes in education for Spanish women. Pardo Bazán reflects on this in her essay about her first cookbook, "Mi libro de cocina" (1913). The state may have created opportunities for women to study in official educational centers, she writes, but social pressures continued to hold women back. Being "allowed" a public career was like being "allowed" to grasp at the moon: "es como si le permitiese coger la luna, porque son escasísimas las mujeres que siguen carrera."[97]

Pardo Bazán resignedly attempts to revive the series with cookbooks, calling the decision the result of "un desengaño ideal" (an ideal disillusion).[98] This framing opens up an avenue to probe both Pardo Bazán's writerly identity in these culinary texts and the inherently contradictory relationships that she and the texts construct with her readers.

In a first example, Pardo Bazán writes that she continues the Biblioteca series with works on domestic economy because "la opinión sigue relegando a la mujer a las faenas caseras" (public opinion continues to relegate household tasks to women).[99] The patriarchal nature of public opinion, she suggests, explains women's previous disinterest in the series and in feminism. And yet, despite this, Pardo Bazán communicates that, like her readers, she has an interest in cooking: she herself plans and prepares meals and collects recipes. In "Mi libro de cocina," she writes:

> Al correr el tiempo, mis cajones iban llenándose y rebosando de recetas recogidas aquí y acullá, y entre las cuales había de todo: platos regionales, otros que son secreto de una familia o de una persona, otros inéditos, que ensayábamos y salían bien y quedaban aprobados; otros usuales, vulgares; alguno más refinado; una pintoresca mezcla.[100]

> With the passing of time, my boxes became full to overflowing of recipes collected from here and there, among which there was a little bit of everything: regional dishes, others that are secrets of families or individuals, others unedited, that we tried out and turned out well and were approved; others common, everyday; some more refined; an eccentric mix.

She is a "modestísima aficionada" (humble amateur), not an expert. Family traditions motivate her interest to have her recipes bound and manageable, especially those of her "familia como de tradición" (family as if of tradition).[101] In this way, Pardo Bazán makes her family situation like that of her women readers. She preserves her family's recipes and domestic traditions, a role belonging to women who "influence" from within the home rather than act outside of it.[102]

Yet even as Pardo Bazán highlights some similarity to her readers, she reminds them of their likely profound differences. Again in "Mi libro," she indicates that her time is valuable, in short supply, and not usually devoted to domestic tasks of managing recipes:

Y el ir archivando tantas recetas me hacía perder el tiempo, un tiempo precioso, no por el hecho de recogerlos, sino porque me pedían copias, y me obligaba a papeleas incesantemente. Si necesitaba una receta, para mi propio uso, el buscarla también era difícil.[103]

And the process of archiving so many recipes made me waste my time, valuable time, not in the work of recovering them, but because people asked me for copies, and incessantly compelled me to complete such paperwork. If I needed a recipe for my own use, locating it was also challenging.

Her pleasure in cooking motivates her interest: "siempre me he preocupado de cosas caseras porque me entretienen" (I have always cared for home tasks because they entertain me).[104] She even misses having time for chores, as she writes in a letter to her friend Alejandro Barreiro: "Por mi parte siempre anduve en guisar, y hasta le tengo afición a estos quehaceres y siento no disponer de más tiempo para practicarlos."[105] Of course, cooking and domestic chores can be a pleasure for Pardo Bazán; she is no middle-class woman with the responsibilities of meal planning, provisioning, and preparation, as well as cleaning, washing clothes, and ensuring that the house has cooking and heating fuel.

Underscoring this difference, in practically every text that mentions the cookbooks, Pardo Bazán acknowledges the surprise others express upon learning that she has written cookbooks. In *La cocina española antigua*, she writes, "y como me han visto aficionada a estudios más habituales en el otro sexo, puede que se sorprendan de que salga de mis manos, o mejor dicho, de mis carpetas, un libro del fogón" (since I am seen as devoted to studies more associated with the other sex, it could be that they are surprised that a cookbook is produced from my hands, or better said, from my notebooks).[106] In the "Mi libro de cocina" article, she writes: "No es descriptible la sorpresa de mucha gente, ante una noticia que, a mi corto entender, no tiene nada de particular" (It's not even describable the surprise of many upon finding out, even if I don't think it's anything special). This surprise underscores the contradictions that characterize her public intellectual profile. She recounts examples of the harassment she received for being a female public intellectual, from being labeled a "fruto de una equivocación de la naturaleza" (the fruit of an error of nature) and "un desaforado marimacho" (an unbridled tomboy) to having the state of her household speculated about during a public lecture: "¡Buena tendrá su casa esta señora!" (What must this lady's house be like!).[107] Yet, these comments on gender norms and her career in relationship to cooking allows Pardo Bazán to make her womanliness a central aspect of this project even as she marks her distance from her readers.

The anecdote from Carmen Bravo-Villasante's biography offers an illustration of the tricky negotiation Pardo Bazán must have managed throughout her career between her interest in possibilities for women (inclusive or exclusive of their domestic lives) and her writerly identity as a woman whose career often rendered her "androgynous."[108] During her 1905 visit to Salamanca in the home of Unamuno, Bravo-Villasante writes,

> como en un momento de intimidad, como mujer curiosa que es, pregunta a la esposa de Unamuno si lee las obras de su marido y ella le responda que no, [Pardo Bazán] decide regalar a la buenísima y hogareña señora un libro de cocina, "La cocina práctica de Picadillo," que acaba de publicarse con un prólogo de la escritora.[109]

> in an intimate moment, and as the curious woman she is, she asks Unamuno's wife if she reads her husband's works and she responds that she does not, [Pardo Bazán] decides to gift this lovely and home-loving woman a cookbook, Picadillo's *La cocina práctica*, that had just been published with Pardo Bazán's prologue.

As Unamuno's intellectual peer, it is understandable that Pardo Bazán might wish to discern the interests of his wife, Concha. Her presentation of a cookbook upon learning that they have no real things in common other than cooking reveals another facet of her contradictory position. While it's possible that Concha could share her intellectual interests, it's more likely that Concha has more in common with the middle-class, female reading public she guides toward elegance in *CEM*.

An additional example of this distance from readers appears in Pardo Bazán's letter to Barreiro about the cookbooks. She writes, "No soy Doctora en el arte de Muro, Dumas, Rossini, Brillat Savarin y Picadillo, pero jamás vi incompatibilidad entre él y las letras" (I am not a Doctor of the arts of Muro, Dumas, Rossini, Brillat-Savarin and Picadillo, but I've never seen the incompatibility between that art and the literary).[110] Pardo Bazán may assess her culinary skills as inferior to those of these well-known culinary writers when she emphasizes, "No soy Doctora en el arte" (I am not a Doctor in the art [. . .]). Yet, she places her writing about food in dialogue with theirs. So it's not that the cookbook project signals a late-blossoming femininity or agreement with gender norms of her period. On the contrary, they contribute to an existing body of writing about food, by men, that has already won public respect.

Joyce Tolliver's work on the gendered dimensions of Pardo Bazán's writing lends some additional insight to these rhetorical gestures. With the focus on her identity in these texts, Pardo Bazán writes "insistently as a woman" as Tolliver found the case to be with her short stories.[111] And yet, Pardo Bazán both undermines and ultimately reproduces aspects of dominant discourses about women's interests. For example, in "Mi libro" she acknowledges social resistance to changes signaled by the Biblioteca: "comprendí también que con el ambiente no se lucha con inmediato resultado" (I understood that in this context the battle does not produce immediate results). She also signals the possibility of adapting oneself to overcome (*dominarlo*) what influences women's interest in domestic rather than public life.[112] Notwithstanding these circumstances, the overall impression Pardo Bazán creates is one of significant difference from the readers she proposed to engage.

In the introduction to *CEA*, she communicates that the imagined readers for the book are at fault for the Biblioteca's poor sales. Continuing the series with cookbooks represents a return to the "senda trillada," or commonplace.[113] To Barreiro she elaborates on feminism's failure to take hold in Spain.

> He visto, sin género de duda, que aquí a nadie le interesan tales cuestiones [el feminismo], y a la mujer, aún menos [. . .]. Aquí no hay sufragistas, ni mansas ni bravas. En vista de lo cual, y no gustando de luchar sin ambiente, he resuelto prestar amplitud a la Sección de Economía doméstica de dicha Biblioteca, y ya que no es útil hablar de derechos y adelantados femeninos, tratar gratamente de cómo se prepara el escabeche de perdices y la bizcochada de almendra.[114]

> I have seen that, without a doubt, that here nobody is interested in these topics [feminism], and women, even less, [. . .]. Here there are no suffragists, neither docile nor brave. Given these circumstances, and not enjoying a battle without support, I have resolved to expand the Section on Domestic Economy of the Library, and since it is not useful to talk about rights or women's progress, I will treat with great pleasure how one prepares an escabeche of partridges and an almond sponge cake.

This cynicism appears later in the *CEA* introduction when she comments that even the small minority of educated women can't be bothered to engage the movement; their interest is "aislado y epidérmico" (isolated and superficial).[115] Although Pardo Bazán places her womanliness front and center in this project, we see in these examples that she participates in a masculinist critique of women. They're insufficiently intellectually prepared to support feminism in Spain and not to be counted on even to read about it.

Despite the important feminist work these texts do—recall that she designates women as practitioners and guardians of a national culinary patrimony and as actors in bringing about Spain's modernization with their adoption of elegant cooking—the overwhelming impression these contradictions leave is one of deep ambivalence. She reveals two additional examples of this ambivalence in the following passages.

First, in her prologue to Picadillo's *La cocina práctica* (1905), Pardo Bazán addresses the reading public for cookbooks—women—and sets up a revealing comparison given the intersections between gender, class, and nationalism that define her cookbook project.

> Hubo señoras que recortaron las recetas, y las discutieron, y las corrigieron, y acabaron por discernir a PICADILLO borla de doctor, máxime cuando hubo probado que unía la práctica a la doctrina. [. . .]
>
> Al consagrar PICADILLO su hasta entonces, si no me engaño, inmaculada pluma, a inundar de saliva las fauces de sus leyentes, a enseñar triquiñuelas y adobos a las guisanderas amas de casa—las cocineras propiamente dichas no padecen la enfermedad de leer, y por eso no miden la sal ni pesan la leche—demostró que conocía donde les aprieta el zapato a los mortales.[116]

> There were ladies who cut out recipes, discussed them, corrected them, and finally distinguished Picadillo with his doctorate in the field, all the more since they ascertained that he united practice with science. [. . .]
>
> Upon devoting his, if I am not mistaken, immaculate pen to making salivate the jaws of his readers, to teaching tips and sauces to cooking housewives—the cooks themselves don't suffer the illness of reading, and so don't measure the salt or weigh the milk—he demonstrated that he knew well the weaknesses of mortals.

Pardo Bazán indicates that cooking and recipes form community; the "guisanderas amas de casa" (cooking housewives) read the recipes Picadillo publishes in his newspaper columns, cut them from the paper, discuss, and critique them. Recipes create and maintain a social network based on cooking and its textual representation that allow literate women with time to read and discuss to erect a taste community that ties them to one another. By contrast, working-class women, those who labor in the kitchen of others "no padecen la enfermedad de leer" (do not suffer the illness of reading), according to Pardo Bazán; they ignore measurements and weights in their cooking.[117] Working women use their instincts to cook; they don't participate in the culinary community of their literate counterparts. This description invokes readers' sentimentality for a pre-modern practice of cooking, a representation of a marginalized working *cocinera* as one who does not challenge the social order. Instead, the female domestic servant exists as a "serio problema social, familiar, hasta higiénico" (serious social, family, and hygiene problem) for not knowing the "guiso más sencillo" (the most simple preparation) or "platos más burgueses" (the most bourgeois dishes), as she writes in 1906 for her "La vida contemporánea" column.[118]

Pardo Bazán invokes a parallel comparison in the final paragraph of *La cocina española antigua*. She advises:

> En las recetas que siguen encontrarán las señoras muchas recetas donde entran la cebolla y el ajo. Si quieren trabajar con sus propias delicadas manos en hacer un guiso, procuren que la cebolla y el ajo los manipule la cocinera. Es su oficio, y nada tiene de deshonroso el manejar esos bulbos de penetrante aroma; pero sería muy cruel que las señoras conservasen, entre una sortija de rubíes y la manga calada de una blusa, un traidor y avillanado rastro cebollero.[119]

> In the recipes that follow ladies will find many that call for onion and garlic. If you want to work with your own delicate hands in preparing a dish, please let the cook handle the onion and garlic. It is her job and there's nothing dishonorable about handling these bulbs with their penetrating odor; but it would be very cruel if ladies had linger, between a ruby ring and the lace sleeve of a blouse, the traitorous and uncouth trace of onion.

Pardo Bazán prescribes feminism and a better education for middle-class women. In the face of their disinterest, she allows for their study of "el arte" (the arts) of Careme and Brillat-Savarin since the study of cooking now substitutes for the piano "esa forma de arte burgués y casero, hoy eclipsado ante la sartén y el hornillo" (this homely and bourgeois art form, today eclipsed by the pan and oven).[120] But the working-class women described in these passages are a problem. Their instinctual cooking keeps bourgeois households from practicing the modern bourgeois cooking that signals Spanish modernity. Their handling of the disagreeable aspects of cooking also serves as a metaphor for Pardo Bazán's position regarding the disagreeable aspects of Spanish modernization—strikes and protests.

CONCLUSION

In examining Pardo Bazán's culinary oeuvre, this analysis shows that she is indeed a culinary nationalist. She aligns cooking with the dominant nation-building discourses of her time in her cookbook prologues. And the culinary writing in her articles indicate that these efforts extend beyond any superficial interest in selling books or as a cynical appeal to women readers. Instead, they comprise a corpus of work in which she outlines how this very feminized practice contributes to understanding Spain in its traditional and modern forms. However, in the same project, the author demonstrates a less straightforward perspective regarding the women whose work her recipes represent and whose contributions supposedly support Spanish nation building.

On the one hand, Pardo Bazán idealizes traditional Spanish women (*vejezuelas*) and the Spanish *pueblo* as a repository of traditions. Yet, this idealization reveals itself in contrast to the frightening political subject *pueblo* she reports on in the "Cartas de la condesa" article and undermines the legitimacy of popular political action in order to foreground a safe representation of the *pueblo* as a guarantor of national traditions. In the same article, she stresses the importance of culinary philology to the nation and signals that cuisine is at least as much about written texts as food, which imposes literacy as a pre-requisite to meaningful participation.

On the other hand, in *CEM*, Pardo Bazán offers the manners and modes of the wealthy for (aspiring) middle-class readers to emulate in order to harness their class anxiety into an unrealistic project of culinary elegance. The comparison of the cookbooks to "Cartas de la condesa" shows that both volumes write the modern working-class completely out of Spanish cuisine and, by extension, completely out of the national liberal project.

As texts that would provide readers with a way to participate in the nation through domestic activities, the cookbooks exhibit an ideological position that furthers the alienation of key populations (women and the working class) from the reality of liberal citizenship. The limitations inherent in the roles Pardo Bazán prescribes for her *guisanderas amas de casa* display a cynical perspective from a writer who in prior decades championed women's education and employment as paths to a stronger and more modern nation, not their cooking.[121] And the supposedly illiterate and instinctual *cocineras* belong to a *pueblo* that does not challenge the social order and remain marginalized as participants in Spain's modernization. That this perspective comes from the writing of one of Spain's most celebrated feminist intellectuals may be jarring. But the ambivalence that Pardo Bazán reveals in this facet of her work and writerly identity reveals the fractures that keep feminism from developing as a widespread political movement in the period of her writing. It also presages the social divisions that would weaken and ultimately derail Spain's early twentieth-century experiment with liberal democracy during the Second Republic.

CHAPTER 2

FRIVOLOUS AND FEMINIST
Carmen de Burgos's Culinary-Political Platform

Known as both a bluestocking and an "escritora-ama de casa" (writer-homemaker), Carmen de Burgos produced a substantial and varied oeuvre during her long career. Her fiction comprises ten full-length novels and more than eighty melodramatic novellas; her nonfiction includes high-profile essays on women's rights, a lengthy feminist treatise (*La mujer moderna y sus derechos*, 1927) and twenty-seven practical manuals on topics ranging from seduction to cooking. Among these were a number of bestsellers that eventually brought her a comfortable income, but tempted critics to impugn both her literary and her intellectual merit. Always marginalized or excluded from the canon, her novels and essays were pulled from library and bookstore shelves during the early days of Francoism.[1] And re-editions of her works remain scarce even today. Nevertheless, beginning with Elizabeth Starcevic in the 1970s, scholars began to question Burgos's reputation as a lightweight writer of sentimental romances by exploring the relevance of her work to the changing cultural and economic landscape of Spain in the early twentieth century.[2] Her popular fiction and essays, they argue, reveal her as one of Spain's most influential early feminists. But her cookbooks, along with the other practical manuals, seem to suggest otherwise, given their commercial purpose and consistency with a domestic ideology that she questions so radically in her other works.

Burgos published three cookbooks: *La cocina moderna* (*LCM*) in 1906, *¿Quiere usted comer bien?* in 1916 and *Nueva cocina práctica* (*NCP*) in 1925.[3] Scholars have tended to understand them as works she used to pay the bills or, alternatively, as evidence of her literary breadth and resourcefulness.[4] Indisputably, the earnings from the cookbooks and other practical manuals helped Burgos make a career out of her writing rather than re-marry or depend upon the teaching of the early days of her career. Yet, neither these practical economics nor the domestic topics of these books discount their role in Burgos's overall effort to align the intellectual, political, and social debates of the first decades of the twentieth century with women's lived experiences.[5]

This chapter complicates prevailing ideas of Burgos's cookbooks as potboilers that reinforce traditional gender roles. I will argue, instead, that her culinary writing is both consistent with her more conventionally feminist works, including feminist speeches given in a number of cities across Spain and the text of *La mujer moderna y sus derechos* (1927). Further, it demarcates cuisine as a feminine field of influence for Spain's modernization, effectively inserting the domestic economy into conversations about wider progressive reforms and understanding women's foodwork as another aspect of the "multiple modernities" that shaped their lived experiences.[6] The paratextual materials published with two of Burgos's cookbooks appear fully consistent with the feminist arguments she contributed to early twentieth-century debates on Spain's regeneration. They are, moreover, characteristic of the expansion of Spain's literary market in the early twentieth century, coherent with the logic of literature as a consumer object, and consistent with Burgos's incursions into this literary scene in her fiction and other works. Their focus—ostensibly the models of behavior and rules readers should follow to prepare and serve elegant meals, or to manage their kitchens and servants—meant that they brought education and new ideas to women inexpensively and at the site of much of their daily labor. They did so in a way that neither alienated the men in charge of the publishing industry nor her readers, who likely identified along a broad spectrum of ideological positions at the time. Moreover, in her essay "De Re Coquinaria" published in the 1925 cookbook, Burgos indicates that cooking and gastronomy are erudite concerns, long featured in historical records and canonical literary works, and responded to politically and socially from pre-history until the present. Knowledge of these learned discourses should influence how women undertake their work in the kitchen. A Spanish sociology of food reveals that women are at its center.[7]

THE BLUESTOCKING *ESCRITORA-AMA DE CASA*

Burgos had more than a passing experience with domestic economy. She followed the traditional path for well-to-do women by marrying at age sixteen. But seven years later, deeply unhappy, she left her husband and birthplace to become a teacher at Guadalajara's Escuela Normal. To supplement her teaching salary, she began to contribute newspaper articles in 1902 and soon became known as Colombine, writing for women on political and social issues of the moment. Not limiting herself to fashion or needlework, Burgos provoked scandal and debate by speaking out on divorce ("El divorcio en España" [1904]) and female suffrage ("El voto femenino" [1906]). By 1908, she was editing literary journals, hosting *tertulias* in her home, and interacting with members of the literary establishment alongside her domestic partner Ramón Gómez de la Serna.[8]

Despite these successes, Burgos continued to face challenges in her career. She was a frequent target of denigration by the male literary establishment, from insinuations of sexual relationships with her editors and peers to ongoing ridicule of her writing.[9] These slanders marred her reputation among contemporaries and successors even though she often focused on themes addressed by established male writers. In just one example, in 1906 she published "La base de nuestra regeneración," an essay that links Spain's regeneration to its education system and condemns religion for creating a stifling anti-intellectual climate. Eight days later, Unamuno published, in the same newspaper, his own article on the role of religion in Spain's modernization, "La libertad religiosa."[10] Nor was she alone in being personally maligned by critics. A number of other female intellectuals, including Margarita Nelken, Federica Montseny, and Concha Espina, were also attacked by male writers who attempted to turn their endeavors into a "national joke."[11]

As an additional challenge, Burgos depended on her writing to earn a living, unlike Emilia Pardo Bazán, who, as a member of the aristocracy, could depend on an inheritance to finance her household.[12] Burgos was a middle-class woman who had left the financial security of marriage to earn her own living in a way that few other women of her class and status would choose. Those who did, according to Margarita Nelken, hid their labor as best they could from the public eye.[13] To do this Burgos developed a career coherent with the dynamic literary marketplace in Spain, which favored inexpensive newspaper formats like *revistas* or the novelette genre to reach a broad, increasingly literate population.

These literary forms belong to what scholars call "kiosk literature." The term refers to texts characterized by their brevity and inexpensive formats that were sold in a network of kiosks to early twentieth-century Spaniards. For those "grappling with instabilities of modern times" these new formats entertained, educated, and exposed readers to a range of ideas and consumer products that reflected the desires and fears of modern society and shaped the development of Spanish modernity.[14]

Burgos's work had a key position among these mass-consumption texts. In her literary works she developed "melodrama with a cause," according to Michelle Sharp. Her fiction allowed her to frame in the forms of parable and cautionary tales the stories that ultimately served as a "pedagogical forum" for her promotion and advocacy of modernizing reforms.[15] Her culinary texts, too, appeared alongside her fiction and shared a number of characteristics that distinguish the kiosk genre of production.

Alongside Burgos nearly all of the notable authors of the day published in these series, including Azorín, Ramón Pérez de Ayala, Valle-Inclán, Unamuno, Galdós, Baroja, Martínez Sierra, and Pardo Bazán. Novelette series, in particular, attracted new readerships: members of the petty bourgeoisie as well as the newly literate working class. Women were also targeted by publishers due to their growing numbers and increasing literacy, even though writers like Unamuno grumbled about the "'señoras y señoritas' que se aficionan a leer las narraciones 'que les dan sus confesores o aquellas otras que se las prohíben'" (women who take up reading those narratives 'given to them by their confessors or those others that they forbid').[16] Yet, it was precisely such readers that publishers like Francisco Sempere and Ramón Sopena hoped to capture by bridging popular and literary works, placing Burgos's practical manuals in their catalogs alongside translations of Kropotkin, Nietzsche, Engels, Nordau, Dumas, Scott, and Dickens.[17] And it is to these women readers that Burgos directed much of her writing, including both her fiction and her cookbooks.[18]

Burgos reached her female readers in the newspapers with which she collaborated, advising them about skin care or fashion in one article only to follow it with another on divorce.[19] In a collaboration spanning 1905 to 1928, Sempere published Burgos's *LCM* and the *NCP* as part of a series aimed at female readers, the Biblioteca de la Mujer, in addition to hardcover editions of her short stories, novels, and versions of her feminist speeches. This diversity of editorial projects suggests that her writing engaged women at different levels of education, literacy, and economic means. The market for these inexpensive texts allowed her ideas to reach reader-consumers who might not have encountered them by attending her feminist speeches or by seeking out her overtly political writing.

The dual challenges of gender-based slander and a money-earning career focused on producing kiosk literature for women readers have conspired to marginalize Burgos in literary history.[20] Because both her intellectual and popular texts all circulated together, the line between "serious" and "frivolous" writing became blurred. The "reproduced" nature of her practical manuals was a more general characteristic of kiosk literature as Larson has explored.[21] The cookbooks' listing as *arreglos* (arrangements) in the publicity materials included in each volume distinguishes them from the listed speeches, translations, novels, and studies she authored. Their "reproduced" nature, suggested in this designation, separates them from her completely original writing. Furthermore, the relative absence of Burgos's authorial voice in the recipes supports the view that they were largely borrowed from others, or, as Carmen Simón Palmer speculates, copied directly from French cookbooks.[22] The texts also feature what some would describe as self-plagiarism or revisions of previous work under modified titles, an additional characteristic of the kiosk format.[23] Given these details, it is entirely plausible that Burgos was one of those writers who, by virtue of having to earn a living, obliged editors with whom she had long-standing relationships by lending her name to works to further their marketability, and that the cookbooks were envisioned by her editor as such.[24]

These practices certainly contributed to the exclusion of her culinary writing from literary and political conversations and cast a shadow over her writing in genres conventionally understood as "serious," such as her 1927 essay *La mujer moderna y sus derechos* or her critical monograph about Larra's life and work, *Fígaro* (1919). The mixing in the marketplace of all of these works presented male writers with fuel for their rejections of her intellectual work, and, even today, the mixture continues to challenge attempts to classify her.

Yet, while the market gave critics license to dismiss her work as unimportant and frivolous, Burgos exploited its appeal and availability to women. For example, in the prologue to *El arte de seducir*, re-issued in 1924 under the new title *Tesoro de la belleza (arte de seducir)*, she shows her awareness of her tenuous hold on literary circles and the contradictions generated by the varied writing she had published:

> Cuando algún imbécil pretende hacerme de menos, me llama la ilustre autora de *¿Quiere usted comer bien?* [. . .] Por cierto, puede usted decir que un fabricante de Algemesí incluía en los saquitos de arroz que vendía una receta tomada de mi libro culinario para hacer la paella. Me pidió permiso y se lo di. Y el hombre me obsequió con unos cuantos saquitos con lo cual estuve una temporada dedicándoles a mis amistades saquitos de arroz en vez de libros.[25]

When some fool attempts to denigrate me, he calls me the illustrious author of ¿Quiere usted comer bien? [...] Absolutely you can say that the producer of Algemesí [rice] put the recipe for paella from my cookbook on the packets of rice. He asked my permission, and I gave it. And he presented me with a number of packets, so many that for a whole period I dedicated those to my friends instead of books.

Burgos names as *imbécil[es]* (fools) those who attempt to dismiss her as a mere author of cookbooks. Yet instead of trying to downplay the genre, Burgos invalidates the criticism by noting proudly that her *paella* recipe was so good that it was included with the rice packets sold by the rice producer. Her playful presentation of the issue, in which she equates the bags of rice sold with her recipe to the books she dedicated to friends and acquaintances, reveals Burgos's awareness of her role in the literary marketplace. Just as her recipe for *paella* circulated with bags of rice, so her writing circulated in the weekly novelettes for women. Literature is a commodity; books are little different than bags of rice. But by refusing to take seriously her critics' discounting of her intellectual status, she mocks those who might be tempted to do so.

The dismissal to which Burgos responds both sarcastically and playfully is implicitly based on her gender. In the same text, she writes that her practical manuals represent an obligation—"un deber"—assigned to her as a woman. Yet, she defends their usefulness to her readers, noting that the texts "con su apariencia frívola y ligera, encierra[n] conocimientos útiles para la cultura de la mujer" (with their frivolous and insubstantial appearance, contain useful knowledge for women's culture). Her role in creating them "es una obra social" (is an act of social work), and she is not "arrepentida de haber escrito estos libros tan sencillos, tan femeninos" (regretful for having written such simple, feminine works).[26] If Burgos considered her cookbooks to be simple and frivolous in their concern with feminine topics, why would she stress that this is merely their appearance?

Kate Cairns and Josée Johnston, in their study of "food femininities," articulate a useful paradigm for Burgos's culinary project. They write,

> Food femininities are enacted through embodied interactions in everyday life [;] these interactions unfold in specific socio-cultural contexts and involve a complex interplay of cultural schemas and material resources. [...] In certain settings, we may be able to redo gender in ways that deviate from dominant cultural schemas about femininity (e.g., at a potluck with women's studies

students). In other contexts, compliance with dominant expectations may be required to establish an accountable gendered self.²⁷

This analysis will show how Burgos complies *superficially* with dominant expectations for women's interests and concerns in early twentieth-century Spain. However, she takes advantage of the setting of a women's inexpensive practical manual—a genre that conveys specific behaviors and embodied interactions—to articulate ideas about cuisine and gastronomy that deviate from dominant cultural schemes about femininity.

Scholars have tended to assume that Burgos consented to producing practical manuals only during the early part of her career and for purely economic reasons. Though Burgos published her first cookbook, *La cocina moderna*, in 1906, her involvement with these texts continued for another two decades. She published her second cookbook, *¿Quiere usted comer bien?*, in 1916, and she released the third, *Nueva cocina práctica*, in 1925 as part of her *Obras completas*, a re-issue of her twenty-seven practical manuals in a series that did not include her fiction.²⁸ In the 1925 cookbook, she updates the "Carta-Prólogo" with several precise edits. She also incorporates the 1906 introduction, weaving pieces of the earlier essay verbatim into a new one, expanding it significantly from seven pages to sixty-four. This essentially new essay, named for the recipe collection attributed to Apicius, demonstrates her ongoing involvement with the cookbook project years after the early part of her career with its economic pressures and when, according to Catherine Davies, she was making a good living.²⁹

It is true that Burgos wrote for money and according to the interests conventionally associated with women, but at the same time she attempted to build a place for herself in the intellectual life of early twentieth-century Madrid. While her fiction, essays, and articles examine the position of women in a modernizing Spain, they also entertain readers and present them with feminist arguments. Scholars have already collapsed the dichotomy between Burgos's "serious" or intellectual work and her mass-market writing by reading her novelettes as some of the most important work for feminism created in Spain during the twentieth century.³⁰ If in these works she "constructs proximity and interaction between intellectual debates and women's lived experiences" and gives voice to Spanish national anxieties in a discourse ostensibly about domestic concerns, why would she abandon this practice in practical manuals like her cookbooks? I argue that she did not. Burgos capitalized on their mass-market nature and their frivolous appearance to inoculate these texts with a feminist agenda. She was nowhere more clear about that agenda and her

FIGURE 2.1. Cover of Carmen de Burgos's *Nueva cocina práctica* (1925). Image provided by the author.

tactics for disseminating it than in the "Carta-Prólogo" she included in two of her cookbooks.³¹

BENEATH THE MASK OF CHATTER

Burgos's "Carta-Prólogo" is ostensibly an expression of her interaction as a woman with the established patriarchal order. With obsequious yet warm formality, she addresses editor Sempere as both her *estimado* (esteemed) and *querido* (dear) friend and closes the letter with formal affection: "Y expresando á usted en estas líneas mi ideal sentir, accepto el encargo de arreglar el libro de cocina que me indica. Deseo que el público lo acoja con el mismo placer que los escribe su amiga y s.s.q.s.m.b., Carmen de Burgos" (And expressing to you my best possible feeling, I accept the assignment of arranging the cookbook you indicate. I am hopeful that the public embraces it with the same pleasure in writing them as your friend and most faithful servant, Carmen de Burgos).³² Burgos's rhetoric expresses her assent to Sempere's request and acknowledges the gender-determined hierarchy that defines their relationship. This primary dialogue reflects the established order between a powerful man and a less powerful woman and works with the genre of the text to support a conventional association between women and domesticity.

Burgos's description of her imagined readership also appears to uphold convention. She identifies her audience as women who strive to emulate the "muchas grandes damas y mujeres de buena posición" (the many great ladies and women of good position). For those possessing both education and means, cooking may be an interest rather than a necessity, but the price of the book, a mere 1.25 pesetas, meant that anyone aspiring to middle-class elegance could also afford it. She reassures her readers that their interest in cooking need not condemn them to laboring in the kitchen like servants: "si no manejan por sí mismas el sopillo y el mortero" (if they don't handle themselves the bellows and pestle and mortar). Rather, knowing about cooking would make them better directors of their kitchens and households. By using "the many great ladies and women of good position" as the model, Burgos presents her cookbook as a textbook that offers "cuanto á la buena dueña de la casa pueda interesarle" (all that could interest the good mistress of her home) to become one of those grand women, from all the details of the kitchen and dining room to ideas about nutritional hygiene).³³

However, within the primary dialogue with Sempere, Burgos creates a secondary dialogue with her readers that offers an alternative model of femininity and illustrates the expectations that structure both her relationship to Sempere and her role as a middle-class woman.³⁴ While Burgos's intellectual chops threatened the literary establishment, her writing in cookbooks and other genres with a primarily female readership would not challenge the dominant gendered hierarchy that marginalized or excluded women writers.[35] Paradoxically, this discrimination created a rhetorical space that Burgos used to advantage by practicing what Maite Zubiaurre describes as "double writing," a tactic that enabled her "to speak meaningfully and to consistently undermine patriarchal beliefs, while at the same time faking harmless chatter."[36] In their focus on Burgos's sentimental novels, Ugarte, Louis, and Johnson analyze how she conceals subversive ideas about women, their careers, and their social rights in fictional texts that, on the surface, pose no threat to the established order. Likewise, in her articles she might advise readers about skin care or fashion, while planning another piece on divorce, only to follow with "an enchantingly frivolous article about the Spanish royalty."[37] Similarly, her cookbooks appear to conform to generic expectations even as they offer a critique of the ideology of domesticity that confines women to their homes. By drawing attention to her writing and her public career Burgos's deferential letter to Sempere actually disputes the traditional, restrictive model of femininity outlined in practical manuals. Thus she establishes two kinds of dialogue: one with her editor, who represents the literary establishment; and a second with female readers constrained by gender expectations.

Even in the first sentence of the "Carta-Prólogo," she calls into question the expectations of Spanish society regarding women's roles and capabilities, pointedly reminding her readers that the idea of the cookbook project did not originate with her. Rather, her participation is a simple acceptance of Sempere's *demanda* (request). She reassures him that it is not inappropriate to ask this of a woman; writing a cookbook "no [. . .] realiza nada de extraordinario" (is no extraordinary achievement). Clarifying that her interest in her own subsistence spurs her participation—"trabajando como obrera" and "para ganar el sustento" (working like a laborer and to earn a livelihood)—she emphasizes that the cookbook is her work. She is a worker (*obrera*), and her tool is her "pluma aguja" (sharp pen).[38]

In the version of the letter that appeared in the later cookbook, this sentence differs in two words from the earlier version.[39] She adds the verb "acceder a" (accede) to Sempere's *demanda*, indicating her acquiescence to the request and reflecting, perhaps, a cynicism about their publishing relationship. This small change shifts the sentence from a commentary about the requests appropriately made of women—to write on topics related to domesticity—to a commentary about the requests made of Burgos specifically and the roles she fills as a public writer.

In both versions, Burgos's rhetoric illuminates how she makes her intellectual credibility as a writer central to the cookbook project while it acknowledges the public identification of cooking as a "natural" part of women's work. Burgos works to denaturalize this association: she emphasizes her *arrangement* (*arreglar* in the 1906 version, *hacer* in the 1925 version) of the cookbook and her *writing* of the introductory essay, a choice that distances her from the recipes. She does not write them, but simply arranges them. The introduction, however, she takes credit for: "[...] tenga usted paciencia para leer los párrafos que siguen como muestra elocuente de mi culinaria erudición [...]" (have patience to read the following paragraphs as an eloquent demonstration of my culinary erudition [...]).[40] Her request for readers' patience backhandedly acknowledges the possibility of their exasperation at the same time that she sassily informs them that her cookbook introduction will impress with its erudition.

A delightful example of double writing occurs in the second sentence of Burgos's letter. She warns Sempere that she could have responded with anger to his request that she, an established writer, produce such an insignificant or anachronistic work, if not for his redeeming generosity and good nature. Yet, Burgos masks this warning in a convivial narration of her alternative response:

> Fuera genio al uso, y mi sorpresa llegaría al enojo, capaz de romper la antigua y leal amistad, asombro de autores que no conocen editor tan rumboso y campechano: mi sorpresa ha sido de otro orden; me ha obligado a exclamar: —¡Diablo de Sempere! ¿Cómo ha adivinado que guiso mejor que escribo?[41]

> Deviating from my typical demeanor, my surprise could become anger, capable of breaking our longstanding and loyal friendship, to the astonishment of writers who know no editor so generous or good-natured: my surprise was of a different nature; it obliged me to exclaim: —That sly Sempere! How did he guess that I cook better than I write?

She agreeably acquiesces to the request since, she takes care to stress, Carmen de Burgos cooks even better than she writes. With the question "¿Cómo ha adivinado?" (How did he guess?), she pretends not to see the gendered assumptions that Sempere makes. Her phrasing both confirms her culinary abilities and raises the possibility of a negative outcome to his request, given Burgos's status as a professional writer. In the later version, Burgos pushes the point further, substituting "as well" for "mejor" (better): "¡Diablo de Sempere! ¿Cómo ha adivinado que guiso *lo mismo* que escribo?"[42] By comparing her cooking and writing skills, Burgos questions the assumptions that undergird Sempere's request. Equating them emphasizes that cooking and writing are both skills rather than qualities determined by gender. The comparison dismantles the idea that either practice inherently links to gender. Furthermore, the assessment of her cooking skills as *equivalent* to her writing skills is an ironic comment about the publication of the cookbook, given that by 1925 her reputation as a writer was so established that Sempere was republishing her cookbooks as part of her *obras completas*.

Burgos goes on to invite her readers' complicity in a secret that she confesses to Sempere: "Le confieso á usted en secreto que á veces dejo la pluma porque siento la *nostalgia* de la cocina" (I confess to you in secret that sometimes I leave my pen because I feel the *nostalgia* of the kitchen).[43] Framing this confession as a secret is the most visible marker that Burgos has written something radical. By characterizing the kitchen, cooking, and domesticity as sites of nostalgia, she suggests that the idea of the domestic space as the place of women belongs to an old social configuration. Burgos may identify "ocupaciones caseras" (household tasks) as fundamental to women's nature, but at the same time she casts doubt on the "naturalness" of this interest by describing it as an inheritance from the past: "Largos siglos de herencia marcaron en nosotras sus huellas, y nuestra naturaleza nos inclina a ocupaciones caseras, del mismo modo que a buscar las alhajas y los encajes" (The inheritance of long centuries left in us [women] their traces, and our nature inclines us to household tasks, in the same way as we seek precious adornments or lace).[44] In the present, for Burgos, cooking is optional; it becomes part of the affective sphere of the home in which she participates in caring for her family. The tools of the kitchen do not replace her tools as a writer.

This rhetoric presents Burgos's work in the public sphere as routine; her description of cooking as something she does out of wistful remembrance takes for granted that her work is acceptable, a radical notion given the strength of the dominant ideology surrounding traditional women's role in the home. Margarita Nelken's classic study *La condición social de la mujer en España* (1919) shows bourgeois marriage as a prison both for the woman who had to marry, or "vende[rse] legítimamente" (sell herself legitimately), and for the man who became financially responsible for his wife and any unmarried aunt, sister, or niece. And yet, the idea of a middle-class woman working outside the home "aparece todavía, a la mayoría de las gentes, como una cosa insólita [. . .] que debe ser ridiculizada" (still seems to most people like something unheard of [. . .] that should be ridiculed).[45] This deeply entrenched attitude, which Nelken criticizes, limited women to domestic chores and maligned as immoral the women who had to work out of financial necessity.[46] In the context of Nelken's analysis, Burgos's description of her own work makes activity in the public sphere seem not shameful, but an object of pride.

In additional examples Burgos continues to dismantle the restrictive prescriptions for women's domestic activity. She specifies a social and biological role for cooking, arguing that its role in the broader community and women's responsibility for it justify a formal culinary education for them.[47] She also links cooking to the public sphere by connecting praise for her cooking to her work: "Le aseguro a usted que, á veces, viendo el gusto y apetito con que los rebaña mi familia, he sentido el mismo asomo de vanidad que experimento cuando alguna persona *que no los ha leído* me elogia mis artículos" (I assure you that seeing the enthusiasm and appetite of my family who clean their plates, I have felt the same hint of vanity that I experience when someone *who has not read them* compliments my articles).[48] Burgos describes the pleasure that comes from having a dish complimented, but she keeps her work as a woman writer on the same table with the dishes. This statement also reveals a cynical criticism of her public, expressed in the modifying clause "que no los ha leido," which is omitted from the later version of the text. By describing the individuals who praise her as not having read her writing, Burgos nullifies the praise she attributes to her cooking and backhandedly criticizes Sempere for exploiting her public reputation to sell books, a reputation she earned first in 1904 as a consequence of her work on divorce. The disparagement of those individuals who know of her but neither read nor purchase the texts she writes also suggests the circumstances that make her publication of practical manuals like the cookbooks an economic necessity. Both interpretations make clear Burgos's desire to be recognized as a writer even as they show how she grapples with the tension between her gender, her public career, and her dependence on the literary marketplace.

Near the conclusion of her "Carta-Prólogo," Burgos may emphasize that the most important part of the cookbook is her *elocuente* introduction; she also designates it as an example of her "deseo de que la mujer no desdeñe las ocupaciones del hogar, cualquiera que sean su intelectualidad y su posición" (wish that women do not disdain household occupations, whatever their intellect or position). This emphasis complicates conventional understandings of how domestic chores support the ideology of domesticity. It also complicates her subversive message regarding the artificiality of limiting women to the private sphere and its domestic chores. With the example of her own career, Burgos challenges society's structuring of women's interactions with men, and she criticizes the social control exerted by an ideology of domesticity that restricts women from playing greater roles in the public sphere. At the same time, she argues for biological and cultural importance of cooking as one of the "ocupaciones del hogar" (occupations of the home), presenting it as both the provision of needed nutrition and as a noble art form.[49] This framing makes it not merely another invisible household chore but a form of what feminist historian Gerda Lerner calls "practical knowledges," bodies of knowledge that come into being when groups of individuals, like women, are excluded from institutional or structured power.[50] The practical knowledge of marginalized populations is central to the social lives of individuals and their communities; the "ocupaciones del hogar" of cooking and childrearing are critical for the life of the community.[51] In other words, it is the fact of women's confinement to the home and to domestic roles to which Burgos objects, not the domestic tasks women perform.

So, Burgos encourages her women readers to imagine themselves in the *foro* (debating forum) and in the *Parlamento* (Parliament) but tempers her call for a radical reorganization of women's roles by also emphasizing women's kitchen responsibilities: "¡Yo no me opongo á que vayan al foro y al Parlamento [. . .] despúes de haber dispuesto la cocina en su casa!" (I don't oppose that women go to the forum or Parliament [. . .] after having taken care of the kitchen"); "¡Yo deseo que vayan al foro y al Parlamento [. . .] después de haber dispuesto la cocina en sus casas!" (I want women to go to the forum and Parliament [. . .] after having taken care of the kitchen). The *foro* is for after the cooking is done.[52] In another example, Burgos suggests that women, following her example, can balance their responsibilities within the home with careers outside of it: "Porque yo, querido amigo, creo y practico que la mujer puede ser periodista, autor y hasta artísta, sin olvidar por eso los pequeños detalles del hogar para su acertada dirección, guarda de la salud, la paz y sosiego de la familia. ¿Por qué negarlo?" (I, dear friend, believe and practice that women can be journalists, authors, and even artists, without forgetting the small details of the home that with their able attention remains healthy, peaceful, and calm for the family. Why deny it?).[53] She does not tell her readers that the things women do in their homes are unimportant. On the contrary, these two examples demonstrate the importance she places on those tasks, her belief that women should not be limited to them, but should be able to contribute in the public sphere as legal and social equals to men.

FEMINISM FROM WITHIN THE HOME

In the "Carta-Prólogo," Burgos confirms the conventional functions of a cookbook and the expectations that structure her relationship with the patriarchal literary establishment at the same time that she creates a secondary dialogue with women that encourages their awareness of the artificiality of their gender-determined limitations. This dynamic may affirm that Burgos participated in cookbook writing as part of a transactional relationship with Sempere and his publishing house. But Burgos's paratexts in these cookbooks invite us to examine more closely the feminist agenda that she embeds for her women readers behind the "chatter" that would seem to render the cookbooks frivolous and unimportant.[54] The 1906 prologue, specifically, echoes ideas in two of her feminist speeches, *Misión social de la mujer* and *Influencias recíprocas entre la mujer y la literatura*, that she gave just a few years later, both of which highlight the connections between Spanish women, the home, and national progress.

Before treating those speeches, it's important to acknowledge that Burgos's feminist activity found a number of other fora and audiences during debates about the new social and political order of a regenerating Spain. For example, in her speech delivered to the Italian Asociación de la Prensa in Rome on April 28, 1906, Burgos presented an exhaustive analysis of the situation of Spanish women. Later published by Sempere under the title *La mujer en España*, this tract linked women to her hope that the Spanish *pueblo* in its infancy would "saber dirigir y aprovechar nuestras fuerzas" (know how to direct and take advantage of our strengths) in order to arrive to its "juventud potente" (powerful youth).[55] Similarly, in a series of articles published in the Valencia newspaper *El Pueblo* and writing under the pseudonym Gabriel Luna, Burgos subsequently linked Spain's regeneration to its educational system and condemned the persistent anti-intellectual influence of the Church for stunting Spain's growth and ability to modernize.[56] Likewise, the 1906 articles for her column "Femeninas" in the *Heraldo de Madrid* displayed for her readers women's activity throughout Europe as writers, artists, scientists, workers, and housewives, touching on the roles of women in their homemaking, child rearing, and education.[57] In response to Finnish women winning suffrage in June 1906, Burgos solicited participation in a survey, titled "El voto femenino," about the preparedness of Spanish women to obtain voting rights (November 25th *Heraldo de Madrid*). With only 922 respondents in favor, in contrast to 3640 against, she remarked, "el pueblo español, comparado con el de otras naciones, sufre un notable atraso; es aún mayor el peso de los atavismos que la fuerza del progreso que lo impulsa. La mujer necesita en España conquistar primero su cultura [. . .]" (the Spanish people, compared to other nations, suffer a notable backwardness; even greater is the weight of the atavisms than the force that drives progress. In Spain, women need to first conquer their culture [. . .]).⁵⁸ If Spanish women need to "conquer" their culture, to rise up against the weight of traditions that weaken progress, how might they go about doing so in a way that would prepare them for the obligations of citizenship? We find clues to Burgos's ideas about this in *Misión social de la mujer* and *Influencias recíprocas entre la mujer y la literatura*.

In *Misión social de la mujer* (1911), Burgos articulates a vision of feminism that rejects a popular definition of "mujeres masculinizadas que abominan del amor y del hogar" (masculine women who detest love and the home).⁵⁹ Fearful of the "delirios y desequilibrios" (delusions and instabilities) associated with this version, Burgos specifies her idea of the ideal modern woman: "dulce y fuerte, que ama y piensa, con perfecta consciencia de sus derechos y deberes. Una mujer muy tierna, muy amante del hogar, algo coqueta (en la acepción del deseo de agradar) jamás masculinizada" (sweet and strong, who loves and thinks, with perfect awareness of her rights and obligations. A very sweet woman, very devoted to the home, somewhat flirty [in her desire to please], never masculinized). By rejecting a radical and alienating idea of feminism that is strongly at odds with traditional femininity within Spanish culture, Burgos makes feminism moderate and accessible, which allows her to present stronger criticisms. For example, exposure to culture does not masculinize women, nor do myths or biology justify ideas of their inferiority.⁶⁰ Instead, insufficient education is the root of the issue, not just education for a job or a career, but an education for the "vida práctica" (practical life) within the home. If, by the wayside, this home-oriented, practical education based on cooking, hygiene, and child pedagogy also allows a woman to find work outside the home at a time of "desgracia" (misfortune), all the better. Burgos presents women's welfare and education as key to the "engrandecimiento" (aggrandizement) of Spain. From the home women fight alcoholism and tuberculosis.⁶¹ The mother cares for and nurtures the seeds of Spain's future in her children. Matrimony benefits both husband and wife so that he does not seek happiness outside of it and she does not become its martyr. An independent woman does not need to marry but can choose it freely and consciously. Progress accompanies the abolition of "la esclavitud femenina" (feminine slavery); comprehensive education prepares for equality.⁶²

In the later speech, *Influencias recíprocas entre la mujer y la literatura* (1912), ostensibly an analysis of how literary history represents women, Burgos connects the great transformations in politics, science, and industry to an important evolution in the lives of women. By presenting as "abandonados" (abandoned) the outmoded ideas about male superiority, Burgos proposes instead that women and men are "dos sexos llamados a complementarse en una común y diferente misión" (two sexes called to complement one another in a common if different mission).⁶³ She writes, "nadie niega las facultades femeninas que se desenvuelven en las ciencias, en las artes y en el trabajo. Nadie duda de que la mujer, sin dejar de ser mujer, de ser madre, esposa ejemplar, hija sumisa, puede tomar parte en las lides del saber" (nobody denies women's abilities in sciences, art, and the working world. Nobody doubts that women, without ceasing to be women, mothers, exemplary spouses or submissive daughters, can take part in the battles for knowledge). This "nueva mujer" (new woman), according to Burgos, is the "*compañera* culta" (erudite partner; italics in original) of her spouse. She neither succumbs to "los delirios de un feminismo antipático y masculinizador" (the delusions of a disagreeable or masculinizing feminism) nor finds refuge in the "adormecimiento de la hembra, sin aceptar su parte de responsabilidad en las grandes obras sociales" (women's complacency, without accepting her duties to social change). Instead, the equal—"a la misma altura"—of her spouse, she receives "todo el apoyo de hombres cultos que sienten la necesidad de regenerar la verdadera patria y saben que sólo puede conseguirse educando a la mujer" (all the support of learned men who feel the responsibility for recreating the true nation and know it can only be achieved through educating women).⁶⁴ Burgos's feminism does not alienate women from the tasks of traditional domesticity—the home and children. Instead, without abandoning their homes, women must "hacer una obra de extensión fuera de él [. . .] e intervenir en la vida pública" (extend themselves outside of it [. . .] to take part in public life). Women fulfill their social obligations to the nation by opening their homes to new ideas, "las auras frescas y vivificantes que vienen a oxigenar los cerebros" (the fresh and invigorating air that oxygenates minds).⁶⁵

Given the role Burgos accords to the home in these speeches, it should come as no surprise that the essays in two of her cookbooks sustain a corresponding feminist platform. Indeed, as she states in the introduction to her *Las artes de la mujer* (1911), "los libros escritos para la mujer no pueden mirarse con desprecio" (books written for women should not be looked down upon) since "desde muy antiguo ha dominado en las escritoras, aun las más varoniles, la tendencia de hacer libros para su sexo" (for a very long time women, even the most manly, have tended to write books for their own sex).⁶⁶ She frames domestic obligations as the "naturales ocupaciones" (natural occupations) of women and warns against a version of feminism that would have women renounce or despise them.⁶⁷ Instead, the cookbooks promote ideas that Burgos frames as essential to women's evolution as capable members of society and future citizens.

Burgos begins the introductory essay to *LCM* in the same "double writing" style used in her "Carta-Prólogo." She invites the male establishment to understand her work in the cookbook as trivial, imagining that even her favorite poet Heinrich Heine would ridicule her method of historicizing even the "cuestiones más baladís" (the most trivial subjects) like cooking.[68] But she justifies this approach since it will be most appealing to what she insinuates is an unsophisticated female readership of aspiring "bellas elegantes" (elegant beauties). In this example, Burgos uses a recognizable model also employed by María Pilar Sinués de Marco, the nineteenth-century author of women's conduct manuals, to make her prologue sound conventional and consistent with the texts middle-class women supposedly find entertaining. By calling attention to the fact that aristocratic or royal historical figures cooked "como cualquier simple mortal" (like any other simple mortal), Burgos indicates that her easily impressed women readers will imitate them.[69] The aristocratic women she names as models cohere with stereotypical notions of women's interest in aping the practices of the aristocracy.[70] By aligning herself with those who might criticize the text and its purpose, Burgos renders it unthreatening in its consistency with hegemonic domestic ideology and the prescriptive texts that uphold it.

Burgos may present her work disarmingly, but her dismissal of the text's importance masks a number of features it has in common with her more overtly feminist work, specifically her tendency to historicize the topic at hand. Michael Ugarte analyzes how Burgos traces women's issues through Greek and Roman mythology, theology, science, legal codes, art, literature, and philosophy in her *La mujer moderna y sus derechos*. Her style, he notes, synthesizes the work of diverse thinkers and scholars to present their ideas in a readable fashion and to comment on them as "Colombine, her writerly persona."[71] In her speeches, she presents readers with a primer on each topic at hand: she names relevant data, reviews the history of the issue, and draws comparisons with other nation-states. These displays of erudition function to assert her prominence and legitimacy as a commentator, as Ugarte has argued. Additionally, in the case of her cookbook prologues, she embeds within these history lessons a reframing of how her readers should view their roles as women in relation to these topics. She establishes a recognizable context that demonstrates commonalities between her readers and the topic at hand in order to challenge the social role conventionally ascribed to women.[72]

For example, Burgos begins the body of the 1906 prologue by historicizing the role that cooking and food have played in the West, from the consumption of the "frutas de paraíso" (fruits of paradise) that motivated Adam and Eve's fall from grace to the "héroes de Homero reunidos alrededor del carnero ó del puerco entero" (Homer's heroes gathered around an entire mutton or hog) to sixteenth-century excess, in which "la cantidad se apreciaba más que la calidad" (quantity was appreciated more than quality).⁷³ Burgos brings Spain into this gastronomical history by comparing the excess of Louis the Fourth's court to the Bodas de Camacho episodes in *Don Quijote*. Accordingly, when she transitions from describing the role of cuisine in western history to naming the "elegant beauties" of Europe who take an interest in cooking, she casts these women in a historical-political light. She indicates at the beginning of the essay that she lists these women to impress her readers with their aristocratic status. But, more than merely elegant, she gives examples of powerful women with political roles in the public sphere. Their interest in food she connects to some of the most influential culinary and gastronomical innovations in the West. For example, Catherine de' Médici "fué la primera mujer que se interesó oficialmente por el arte culinario y la que divulgó el uso de los tenedores" (was the first woman who officially took an interest in culinary arts and who circulated the use of forks). Madame Dubarry and Madame de Pompadour invented dishes, such as "los filetes de truchas" (filets of trout) and "los *filets de volaille*" (filets of chicken). Madame de Sevigné and Madame de Pompadour collaborated with famous chefs of the day (Mouthier and Vatel) and played a part in the conversion of chefs into representatives of "el renombre culinario de Francia" (France's culinary renown). Contemporary sovereigns "no desdeñan ocuparse de cocina" (do not scorn kitchen work).⁷⁴ For example:

> la emperatriz María, viuda del zar Alejandro III [. . .] preparaba ella misma los alimentos[;] la reina Alejandra de Inglaterra posee talento culinario y la difunta reina Victoria se ocupaba mucho de la mesa real desde el punto de vista de la higiene[;] la emperatriz de Alemania prepara con frecuencia el desayuno de su marido, y en cuanto á la reina de Italia, todo el mundo sabe que uno de sus placeres es hacer platos de su país, muy del gusto del rey Víctor.⁷⁵

> Empress María, widow of czar Alexander III herself prepared meals; Queen Alexandra of England possesses culinary talent and the deceased Queen Victoria took responsibility for the royal table from the perspective of hygiene; the empress of Germany frequently prepares her husband's breakfast, and, in the case of the queen of Italy, everyone knows that one of her pleasures is making dishes from her country, much to the taste of King Victor.

Female political figures demonstrate that food preparation is a meaningful social practice, not merely domestic labor that belongs to women of inferior status. Paradoxically, this discourse normalizes the idea of women laboring in the kitchen while at the same time it converts cooking into a social practice that shapes politics. For example, after listing the culinary activities of women of the past she writes, "La cocina francesa fué un Napoleón que conquistó el mundo: hoteles de todas las naciones, y hasta las mismas cortes, comen con arreglo á sus preceptos" (French cuisine was a Napoleon that conquered the world: hotels from every nation, even in their courts, eat according to French precepts).[76] She reinforces the point more directly by quoting French gastronomer Jean-Anselme Brillat-Savarin: "Concedo a la cocina un gran papel social. Dime lo que comes y te diré quién eres" (I grant cuisine a significant social role. Tell me what you eat and I will tell you who you are).[77] In opposition to Spain's domestic ideology, Burgos redefines cooking as a female activity that has consequences for the public sphere. These "bellas elegantes" (elegant beauties) may attract the interests of *cursi* middle-class readers, but Burgos's tactic shows them how the culinary innovations of the powerful women she describes are a public discourse with political stakes for their nations.

Everyday cooking like that represented by the recipes in Burgos's cookbooks conventionally belonged to the private sphere of the home, in contrast to public-sphere gastronomy or cooking for monarchs, nobles, or powerful church leaders. In relation to Spain, Victoria Enders and Pamela Radcliff demonstrate that the public-private binary, which designated the private home for women and public spaces for men, persisted well into the twentieth century and pervaded the homes of working-class, peasant, and middle-class women to different degrees.[78] As Burgos suggests as well in *La mujer en España*, women traditionally counted only as homekeepers, not as citizens. The work of nineteenth-century hygienists like Pedro Felipe Monlau framed housekeeping as the "natural" domain of women. Even progressive thinker Gregorio Marañón, who in the 1920s and 30s argued for the equal social status of men and women, substituted a biological essentialism for women's "nature." Activities outside the home were permissible as long as they did not interfere with childbearing and rearing.[79] The social control exerted by these gendered spheres defined women as naturally apt for motherhood and the home, while the public arena suited men's biological and psychological characteristics. Any challenge to these ideas implied defying nature.[80]

By linking everyday cooking to public women and culinary innovations that shape politics, Burgos involves an idea of cuisine as a meaningful cultural code. Priscilla Parkhurst Ferguson defines this process as one that "systematizes culinary practices" and transforms "culinary gestures" into "a stable cultural code," often via print text. When culinary labor is represented in print, cooking becomes something societies think with and about in the public domain.[81] Examples include the invention of French cuisine, its export abroad, and its centrality to French national identity, in addition to nineteenth- and early twentieth-century debates about a parallel, autochthonous Spanish cuisine.[82] While Burgos is not concerned with defining Spanish national cuisine, her framing of the commonalities between her readers and powerful women opens a space for understanding women's cooking labor in their homes as relevant to the public sphere. In this way she deconstructs the binary between cooking as a private-sphere practice and its public-sphere socio-political impact, an implicit challenge to the entire construct of "women's nature."[83]

An additional challenge emerges from Burgos's call in these prologues for women's culinary education and its social impact. She notes that "todas las hijas de la reina de Dinamarca" (all the daughters of the queen of Denmark) in addition to "todas las princesas hijas de Eduardo VII" (all of the princess-daughters of Edward VII) of Britain received a formal education in how to run a home and cook. These examples demonstrate the need for state-sponsored culinary education.[84] Curricula for female education designed in the nineteenth century focused specifically on household chores to the detriment of building skills in reading or writing. Teacher-training programs (the Escuelas Normales) created in 1858 covered "los principios de higiene doméstica y labores delicadas" (principles of domestic hygiene and delicate needlework) since domestic competence was essential to women's "careers" as wives and mothers.[85] By 1906, little had changed, so what does Burgos's proposal signal specifically?

The culinary education she proposes closely resembles feminist efforts elsewhere in the West to re-define domestic tasks into the field of home economics. As Sarah Stage and Virginia Vincenti have observed, the turn of the twentieth century marked the politicization of domesticity as women in the United States were urged "to use their skills in 'that larger household in the city.'"[86] As I examine in Chapter 4, home economics allowed women to assume a professionalized role outside the home and gave them a role in public policy, expanding their housekeeping from the home to social and municipal contexts. Similarly progressive, Burgos's proposal to make cooking part of education reform would create a domain for a professionalized workforce of women; cooking instructors would form "un cuerpo especial de profesores, tan bien considerados y bien retribuídos como los de las otras materias" (a special group of professors, as well considered and compensated as those of other subjects).[87] Like the US-American home economists, Spanish women would be prepared to address cooking and nutrition as part of social policy, by working to improve "las condiciones materiales de la vida de la clase popular" (the material conditions of the popular class). In this context, cooking becomes a social practice with relevance to national health. Providing women a culinary education, Burgos argues, has the potential to strengthen the nation's public health and hygiene and improve the material conditions of Spain's working class.[88]

Burgos may be promoting the Escuela de Artes e Industrias, where she accepted a lecturer position in 1906.[89] But her writing on these topics connects her cookbooks to two major political concerns of the early twentieth century: first, that of Krausist-influenced proposals to educate the masses into a socially responsible and modern citizenry; and second, to improve their nutrition. Progressive liberal Joaquín Costa, also a member of the Institución Libre de Enseñanza, acknowledged the importance of food and nutrition in creating a modern Spain when he endorsed the slogan "Escuela y despensa" (School and pantry) to describe necessary reforms to improve productivity and competence as part of a broader program of economic modernization.[90] Krausist philosophers (including, for example, Fernando de Castro) identified women as central to modernization since women were the formative agents of the future citizens on whom the nation's progress would depend.[91]

By mentioning the possibility that culinary education for women would improve the nutrition and material conditions of the working class, Burgos frames culinary education as a way for women to be active participants in Spain's regeneration. Her example of North American women who "se intentan en muchas partes las cocinas ambulantes para llevar la enseñanza á los pueblecillos rurales" (try to create mobile kitchens to take teaching to rural towns) suggests that women's role in the modern nation transcends their roles as mothers and caretakers in the home and influences political policy. Her praise for the culinary education women receive in England, Switzerland, Belgium, Scandinavia, France, the United States, Denmark, and Finland sets up the recurring comparison of Spain to its already modernized neighbors.[92] It also highlights those states' investment in the education of women, one lacking in Spain and still a contentious issue in 1906, in addition to setting up as models states that offered greater support for women's rights.[93]

"DE RE COQUINARIA": BURGOS'S SOCIOLOGY OF SPANISH CUISINE

Burgos's expanded 1925 introduction to *NCP*, "De Re Coquinaria" integrates this focus on women's education as a path toward rights into what becomes a much more comprehensive essay. Its title alludes to the Roman collection of recipes attributed to Apicius, an intentional choice given how she connects contemporary concerns related to food to the Classical world and other scholarly discourses.[94] In the essay, Burgos covers topics ranging from the antiquity of culinary arts to the culinary writing of famous chefs throughout history, culinary literature in Spain and Europe, cuisine's role in diplomacy, its role in Spain's "classic" literature, in addition to the history of Spanish cuisine, among other topics. The essay intersperses commentary in her own authorial voice with extended quotations from male authorities and their works, which range in genre from the literary and critical to the medical and gastronomical. This patchwork functions to entertain her readers; recall that it is also a recurring strategy she uses to legitimize her thinking, per Ugarte. Burgos makes a comprehensive case for cooking and eating as social and cultural discourses that are serious, intellectually rigorous, and essential to women's work in the kitchen. Women's influence—their labor in the kitchen preparing the recipes included in the book—ultimately informs a sociology of a particularly Spanish cuisine.

Sharp has argued that Burgos's practical manuals are examples of the Victorian encyclopedias of feminine knowledge most famously represented by *Mrs. Beeton's Book of Household Management* (1861). The "encyclopedic" nature of *Mrs. Beeton* meant that it was envisioned to instruct middle-class women in everything they needed to know about managing a household.[95] In this vein, it makes sense to consider another of the manuals produced in Spain a few years after Burgos's publication of *NCP* that carries the "encyclopedia" marker in its title. This book, *Encyclopedia Culinaria: La cocina completa* by María Mesteyer de Echagüe, otherwise known as the Marquesa de Parabere, was first published in 1933. Parabere later became the owner of the high-end Madrid restaurant El Parabere in 1936.

According to Lara Anderson, Parabere's book is essentially a manual of French culinary techniques that acquires its encyclopedic status due to the structure the author imposes on how culinary information is communicated.[96] In the first few chapters of the text, Parabere informs readers about the ideal kitchen, its location, and essential tools; table manners and settings; details about different foods including their proper names and the parts of different animals. These foci are quite similar to other culinary practical manuals published in France, Britain, and Spain. And yet, Burgos's paratextual materials for her two cookbooks distinguish her contributions to the encyclopedic practical manual genre. We see this most clearly with the "De Re Coquinaria" essay.

Instead of focusing exclusively on the practical or utilitarian aspects of running a kitchen and a household, in addition to recipes, Burgos's essay demonstrates how the culinary and the gastronomical are intellectual fields throughout history that manifest distinction in ways similar to other scholarly discourses. For example, the appearance of lentils prepared by the Biblical Rebeca confers an "aristocracia histórica a los desdeñados potajes de bodegón" (historic aristocracy on the disdained stews of the tavern), an inversion of the humility associated with the dish in Spain.[97] Culinary discourses also characterize both the writing and social dynamics of the Classical world. Roman emperor Antonio was so satisfied by a meal, he presented his daughter to the cook, demonstrating in Burgos's words, "¡Era mejor ser cocinero que ministro!" (It was better to be a cook than a government official!). Further, cooking and its discourses are erudite: "Platón equiparó la cocina a la oratoria elogiando por igual <<los que guisan y presentan bien las ideas y los alimentos>>." (Plato found cuisine to be the equal of oratory [;] 'those who cook and present well ideas and foods'). Greece so esteemed its "siete cocineros" (seven cooks) that they were accorded the same status as "los siete sabios" (the seven sages).[98] And "[T]odo un libro de *Epigramas* de Marcial está consagrado a celebrar lo que se come y lo que se bebe" (An entire book of Martial's *Epigrams* is dedicated to celebrating what one eats and drinks). She also affirms that politics and shifting social values transform culinary practices, from the "grandeza culinaria" (culinary superiority) that disappeared during the French Revolution to reappear under Napoleon I and an "arte culinario" (culinary art) that "se democratiza" (becomes democratic), as demonstrated by the publication of the cookbook *La cocinera repúblicana* with its recipes for "manjares modestos" (modest delicacies).[99]

As a further indication of the seriousness of culinary discourse, Burgos includes an entire section dedicated to "Personajes que cocinan" (Noted figures who cook).[100] Among them are the aristocratic women mentioned in the 1906 version of the prologue and other monarchs. But in this version, she also underscores important literary figures, all of them men, with the exception of Mme. de Sevigné, who esteem cooking for themselves, lending their names to recipes, or inventing them. In addition to these monarchs and writers, Burgos informs readers about the great *cocineros* of France and Spain: Careme, Taillevent, Brillat-Savrin, in addition to Roberto de Nola, Francisco de Ardit, and Carlos Cuesta.[101] Her point: these figures, most of them men, are significant contributors to cuisine and gastronomy, fields that possess social and intellectual prestige.

The cookbooks of these individuals also legitimize cuisine, from Apicius to mostly French works from the middle ages to more modern ones.[102] Spain's contribution to this archive includes the *Sent Soví* from the twelfth century, in addition to the *Arte Cisoria* by the marqués de Villena, which gives instructions on how to set a table, a topic presented by a noble man of status long before it became associated with the domestic space of women.[103] Moreover, Burgos highlights that Spain's cultural and intellectual institutions recognize cookbooks as significant discourses:

> Nuestros autores de libros de cocina se preocuparon tanto de la parte literaria de sus obras, que la Real Academia Española coloca en su *Catálogo de Autoridades del Idioma* (1874) al lado de los grandes escritores, a Diego Granado, por su *Arte de cocina a la usanza española, italiana y tudesca;* a Martínez Montiño, por sus escritos sobre *Pastelería, bizcochería y conservería,* y a Roberto de Nola.[104]

> Our authors of cookbooks gave such care to the literary nature of their works that the Real Academia Española listed in their *Catálogo de Autoridades del Idioma* (1874), alongside the great writers, works by Diego Granado, for his *Arte de cocina a la usanza española, italiana y tudesca,* by Martínez Montiño, for his writings about *Pastelería, bizcochería y conservería,* and Roberto de Nola.

Burgos's comment indicates that the literary nature of these works explains their status. But, in this multitude of examples, she makes clear that cooking is not merely a practice that belongs to the vulgar and uneducated. Instead, it has long influenced social, cultural, and historical thought.

If we understand Burgos's essay as part of a larger goal affiliated with her practical manuals, to inform women of everything they need to know about a given topic, her essay presents a distinct vision of what she thought women needed to know about gastronomy and cuisine. Culinary history along with the interconnectedness of food and other learned domains are essential knowledge for her readers. These areas, in their practical applications and their erudite ones, apply to women and should influence their work in the kitchen.

In addition to indicating that cuisine and gastronomy are intellectual fields that should inform women's culinary work, Burgos also presents an extensive argument for a sociology of food, especially as it relates to Spanish modernization and women.[105] She opens the section titled "Influencia social de la cocina" (the "Social influence of cuisine") by affirming that "la cocina tiene gran influencia en la suerte de los pueblos. Los pueblos que comen mal son pueblos tristes, faltos de energías, de inventiva, que se empobrecen y degeneran" (cuisine has a significant influence in the destiny of [distinct] peoples. Communities that eat poorly are sad, they lack energy, initiative, they become impoverished and degenerate).[106] To elaborate on her point about the relationship between food and the health of the nation, she quotes extensively from Portuguese writer José María Eça de Queirós's essay "Cocina arqueológica."[107] Queirós links the "carácter de una raza" (character of a race) to a nation's cooking, which "hace comprender tal vez mejor las diferencias intelectuales [of different nations] que el estudio de sus literaturas" (makes more understandable the intellectual differences of nations than the study of their literatures). He asks why the "estudio práctico de la culinaria grecolatina" (practical study of Classical cuisine) has been neglected.[108] In parts of her essay that follow, Burgos answers this question in relation to Spain. Her rhetorical move here is consistent with other gendered strategies in her culinary writing: she affirms the validity of her argument in advance by using the writing and ideas of a male intellectual.

Burgos's sociology of Spanish cuisine advances a theory of taste in relation to Spain based on Spanish culinary history and national literature.[109] She criticizes Spain's ignorance of the importance of food as a social discourse, by citing Un Cocinero de su Majestad's 1876 letter lamenting the Spanish monarch's preference for Parisian preparations over products from Spain, and comparing Spain's "Sent Soui" [sic], or Sent Soví, which documents the ways of eating in the territories belonging to the Crown of Aragón, to the better-known culinary manuscripts created in France where "se ha desenvuelto este género más [. . .] porque en ninguna [otra] encontraron un ambiente tan apropiado" (this genre has been most developed [. . .] because in no other locale has there been found a context as appropriate).[110] Not until the nineteenth century, she argues, did Spanish writers foreground food and cooking. Fernanflor, Ossorio Bernard, Dr. Thebussem, Angel Muro, Adolfo de Castro, and Francisco María Montero all wrote in the "secciones gastronómicas" (gastronomical sections) for magazines like *La Época*, *El Liberal*, *Blanco y Negro*, and *La Ilustración Española y Americana*.

Spain's supposedly characteristic sobriety in areas of cooking and eating are partially to blame for this ignorance, a temperance rooted in Catholicism and in response to "las costumbres disolutas en la Edad Media" (the dissolute customs of the Middle Ages) and the Inquisition's attention to gluttony as indicative of sin. Popular knowledge enshrined a longlasting attitude that "Para ganar el cielo había que comer mal, y aun sigue esa teoría en personas supersticiosas" (To go to heaven, one needed to eat poorly, and this attitude persists among the superstitious).[111] Eating well was "una especie de crimen que había que hacer sin que nadie lo viese" (a kind of crime that had to be done out of sight) or something that only the "grandes y príncipes de la iglesia" (powerful or princes of the church) participated in openly. If austerity in cooking and eating marked the chastity of society in this religious framing, modern hygiene embraces similar ideas in Burgos's time: "Los naturistas y vegetarianos ya no hablan de abstinencia desde el punto de vista moral sino del higíenico" (The naturists and vegetarians no longer speak of abstinence from the perspective of morality, but from that of hygiene).[112] These are just two different ways of making identical judgements about the social meanings of food and cooking. Burgos further affirms that "Las comidas sobrias del pueblo español lo son solo en apariencia, pues se emplean en ellas grasas y cereales en abundancia. [. . .] La característica verdadera de nuestra cocina fue la abundancia, sin preocuparse mucho de la delicadeza" (The plain meals of the Spanish people are only that way in appearance, since they contain fats and grains in abundance. [. . .] The true feature of our cuisine has been abundance, without giving too much attention to delicacy). With this comparison, Burgos shows that sobriety in matters of food is not an inherent national characteristic; instead, it is a social construction that shifts according to the dominant epistemological paradigm. In what follows, she looks to literature and legal and historical data to show that abundance has always been a "característica verdadera" (true characteristic) of Spanish food even as "delicadeza" or polish have not.[113]

Spanish literature shows that canonical authors use food to reveal characteristics of social strata in different time periods. Juan Ruiz, Arcipreste de Hita, was "el primer ingenio que se ocupa de la cocina" (the first writer/creator to treat cooking). His *Comedia Humana del siglo XVI* informs readers of the delicacies made by nuns and the "guisos populares" (popular dishes) of the period, in addition to revealing the sensuality of food long associated with characters doña Cuaresma, don Carnal, and don Amor.[114] Cervantes also "nos hace una pintura tan exacta de su época" (gives an exact representation of the time) and its foods. *Don Quijote* illustrates the eating customs of *pastores* and *jornaleros* (quesos de cabra, migas, gazpachos, aceitunas, in addition to the *olla* or "huevos de torrezno" [eggs with pork belly]); poor *hidalgos* and clerics and their *sota, caballo y rey*; in addition to the delicacies consumed by the bourgeois and aristocrats.[115] In her analysis of these authors' literary uses of food, she stresses that they "no desdeñaban comparaciones que caen dentro de la coquinaria" (they did not scorn comparisons that relate to the culinary).[116]

Historical data also chronicles how people ate and what that meant about their social roles. Burgos writes, "Desde muy antiguo los legisladores se han ocupado ya de Re Coquinaria, y aparecen sus prevenciones en le Fuero Viejo de Castilla, el Ordenamiento de Alcalá [. . .] y las Viejas Ordenanzas de diferentes ciudades de la Península" (From antiquity and onward lawmakers have taken into account [D]e Re Coquinaria [On the Subject of Cooking], and it shows up in their legal warnings in the Fuero Viejo de Castilla, the Ordenamiento de Alcalá [. . .] and the Viejas Ordenanzas of different cities of the peninsula). This framing indicates that the topic of her essay "De Re Coquinaria" is one long addressed by officials of the state. They document how dishes presented to the King must be "BIEN ADOBADO" (well marinated), or the "abuso" (abuse) committed against subjects in the fourteenth century whose homes were burned and farms razed when they were unable to provide the necessary tribute to supply the opulent feasts of traveling monarchs.[117] She also reviews archival documents from the eighteenth and nineteenth centuries that detail the meals that could be purchased for specific amounts of money. Her point in sharing this data is to demonstrate that historical texts already chronicle how people ate and attitudes toward those ingredients and dishes. They reveal how ideas about Spanish foods acquired certain meanings over time.

In offering such details, Burgos is working toward her own framing of a concept of taste in relation to Spain. She writes, "El espíritu nacional, exaltado, apegado a lo antiguo, abominando todo lo que venía de Allende el Pirineo, hizo que se perpetuasen los platos antiguos sin que la cocina progresase" (The national spirit, impassioned, committed to the traditional, hating all that came from Beyond the Pyrenees, has perpetuated traditional cooking without allowing cuisine to progress).[118] The development of taste is allied with modernization and progress, while preferences for traditional dishes signaled by a rejection of mayonnaise, *fois gras*, or roast beef, for example, are allied with the past or a position that rejects progress. She cites a series of popular *dichos* (sayings) about the poor quality of Spanish food, which Larra (Fígaro) crystalizes in his writing. She further highlights the "pobreza disimulada" (dissimulated poverty) in epigrams by Jacinto Polo and Miguel Moreno and the formation of a gastronomical mindset aligned with farcical gastronomical societies that turned dishes and banquets into jokes.[119] In giving these examples, Burgos creates a discourse about taste, food, and progress that is embedded in a Spanish social and political context that her readers might recognize.

Burgos returns to *Don Quijote* and uses Sancho Panza as a key example of her point:

> Creo que con todo lo expuesto queda demostrado que no es la sobriedad la característica de nuestra cocina. Sancho Panza, que encarna el espíritu popular, es un comilón tremendo al que no le duele tanto que le den de palos o lo manteen como "beber mal y comer peor."[120]

I think that with all that has been explained it is clear that sobriety is not the [dominant] characteristic of our cuisine. Sancho Panza, who incarnates the popular spirit, is a tremendous glutton for whom a beating is not as painful as "drinking poorly and eating worse."

When Dr. Pedro Recio de Tirteafuera prescribes privation and an austere diet for Sancho as governor, Sancho renounces his greater social status to return to his role as a servant but one who can eat according to his own desires. About this situation, Burgos comments,

> Estas palabras encierran todo el secreto. Es el afán de estar a la *pata la llana* lo que hace a *Sancho-Pueblo* no pensar lo que come, con tal de no verse sujeto a reprimir sus naturales inclinaciones de falta de cortesía. La cocina española adolecía de falta de buen gusto.[121]

> These words capture the entire secret. It is the eagerness to embody the popular, [those without class privileges], that make *Sancho-Pueblo* not think about what he eats, so that he never is subject to repressing the natural inclinations of the impolite. Spanish cuisine has suffered from the lack of good taste.

Good taste—and elevated social status—would seem to require that Spaniards think about what they eat and deprive themselves of both tasty dishes and satiety. Instead, Burgos's reading of these examples leads her to propose a social theory of taste linked to progress and modernization, one that puts women and their culinary work at its center.

In a first example, Burgos indicates that women, in their control of household spending on food, contribute to the degeneracy of national cuisines:

> Según todo esto, yo creo que las mujeres puedan ser las que causen la pérdida de las naciones sometiéndose a los regímenes más severos para estar esqueléticas. Las francesas dejan decaer la tradición de su cocina nacional. Hacen buena la frase de la criada que se despide de la casa donde no hay compra y por consiguiente falta la *sisa*. "Usted, señora, no necesita una cocinera, sino una vaca."[122]

> According to all of this, I believe that women could be those who have caused the downfall of nations since they subject themselves to severe diets to be skeletal. The French are allowing the tradition of the national cuisine to decay. They make true the saying of the maid who leaves a house that can't

pay for groceries and thus lacks provisions for servants. "You, ma'am, don't need a cook but a cow."

Burgos clarifies that the *sisa* is the "gaje *legal*" (legal bonus, italics hers) of cooks and what sustains their work in the homes of their employers and their own larders.[123] Women's decisions about food purchasing don't just affect the private household economy but serve as an almost legal bonus that contributes to the salaries of the servant class.

Additionally, Burgos attributes to the lack of women's engagement the fact of Spain's impoverished cuisine and, by extension, backwardness: "En España faltó más el gusto que el dinero. Un escritor autorizado en coquinaria afirma que en España el abandono e indiferencia en material de alimentos y el ocuparse sólo de política origina el atraso" (In Spain taste has lacked more than money. A writer well-versed in cuisine affirms that Spain's neglect and indifference in relation to foods and only focusing on politics gives cause to its backwardness). The reason, Burgos argues, "es el haber hecho que las mujeres desdeñen el ocuparse de la cocina, creyendo que es una cosa inferior" (having made that women disdain kitchen work, believing that it is inferior) when cuisine, as she demonstrates in this essay, is a key cultural discourse.[124] By linking the priority given to politics, Spain's *atraso* (backwardness), and the attitudes women were conditioned to assume, Burgos insinuates that the practice of marginalizing women from the discourses that shape the nation is the reason for Spain's backwardness and, by extension, Spain's slow modernization. Consequently, the supposed poverty of Spain's cuisine is a contributing factor to Spain's degeneration as is the marginalization of those individuals responsible for creating it—women. Given that the practice of cooking is seen as women's work, cuisine and the development of a Spanish "buen gusto" (good taste) must begin with women.

Thus, Burgos's essay, as she states explicitly, functions to develop those talents among her readers.

> He tratado de recoger todo lo Bueno de nuestra cocina y lo mejor de la extranjera para ofrecer a las lectoras en este este libro, del que espero saquen el fruto y satisfacción que yo les deseo. No se debe olvidar que para guisar se necesita talento, gusto y sentimiento del arte culinario. No basta entregar el libro a una cocinera cualquiera. Hay que mirar cada receta como una partitura. Sólo las virtuosas de la cocina sabrán interpretarlas bien. ¡Bien provecho![125]

> I have attempted to gather all the Good of our cuisine and the best offered by foreign ones to offer the [women] readers in this book, that they learn

from it and find the fulfillment that I hope for them. One should not forget that to cook one needs talent, taste and a sense of the culinary arts. It's not enough just to give the book to any cook. One must look at each recipe like a musical score. Only the most talented will know how to interpret/perform them well. Enjoy!

The "sense of culinary arts" she offers in this volume educates women that their kitchen work, though ostensibly private-sphere and caretaking, in actuality links them and their daily labor to the most vital of public, social discourses. Cooking is not merely a practice that belongs to the vulgar and uneducated. She gives evidence for understanding its art and intelligence in this comprehensive essay.

By 1925 when the essay was published, Burgos was a well-known author and intellectual whose books sold well. In underscoring the intellectual qualities of discourses widely associated with femininity and domesticity, Burgos also makes a statement about her own writerly identity. As a woman Burgos encountered resistance to her authority, both intellectual and social. Each time she wrote, she had to assert her legitimacy as a thinker to counter the pervasive maligning of her work and her reputation. Only by putting her knowledge on display so exhaustively (in a sixty-four-page essay introducing a cookbook!) could Burgos combat criticism of her person and writing and thumb her nose at those very critics.[126] In commenting about her recipe for *paella*, Burgos underscores the dynamics at play:

> una buena Paella es una especie de poema sinfónica en el que han de estar bien afinados todos los instrumentos para producir el gran acorde, deleite del paladar y conforto del estómago. [. . .] Yo confieso que he tenido el mismo asomo de vanidad que cualquier *bas-bleu* laureada por la Academia haya podido sentir, cuando los grandes arroceros de Algemesí, señores Ferragud y Compañía, me pidieron permiso para poner en sus sacos la receta de Paella que di en la primera edición de este libro, y que ahora reproduzco.[127]

> a good Paella is like a symphonic poem in which all the instruments have to be well tuned to produce the great chord/agreement, delight of the palate and comfort to the stomach. [. . .] I confess that I have experienced the same hint of vanity as any bluestocking honored by the Academia might have felt when the great rice producers Algemesí, the men of Ferragud and Compañía, asked my permission to include on their rice packets the recipe for Paella that I gave in the first edition of this book, which I have reproduced.

Burgos equates the esteem and recognition of her *paella* to the approbation one might feel upon admission to the Real Academia Española. The comparison connects the culinary and her writing; it also makes a veiled, ironic reference to the fact that, as of 1925, neither Burgos nor any other woman writer had been admitted to the Real Academia.[128] In this context, any vanity Burgos might feel as a result of the Academia's approval must be illusory; the only lasting vanity left to her as a woman writer is that of the *arroceros* who recognize her recipe for *paella* as a work of art, even if the literary establishment refuses to give her intellectual work credit.

CONCLUSION

In the paratextual materials included in her cookbooks, Burgos advances a series of surprising arguments about the roles of women and their activities in a modernizing Spanish society. The fact that she wrote cookbooks ostensibly to direct women's activity in their homes may seem to confirm the most cynical representations of her as merely an *escritora-ama-de-casa*. Yet, she uses this mass-market text to reach her women readers in their homes. Under the clever mask of a primary dialogue with her editor, Burgos performs compliance with the food femininity expected of women by upholding conventional expectations about women in relation to a patriarchal literary establishment. But she also creates a secondary dialogue with her women readers that deviates from the dominant cultural schema applying to women, food, and domestic concerns, and instead encourages their awareness of the artificiality of their gender-determined limitations. In her 1906 introduction, she may begin by insinuating that readers do not take her writing work seriously, but in brief pages she re-defines the daily labor of many women as a meaningful cultural code. She connects cooking to education reform and the expanding social roles available to women as part of a modernizing agenda. And she gives women and their everyday expertise an important role in improving the material conditions of people's lives. As with the feminist speeches she offered about women's roles in literature and their social mission, Burgos connects the domestic economy of the home to Regenerationist debates about the roots of Spain's backwardness and wider progressive reforms.

Given how Burgos connected her ideas about women to the social structures created by the Church and men—rather than ascribe them to "natural" circumstances—it should come as no surprise that she connects the most erudite of intellectual figures, movements, and ideas to the everyday practices of cooking. In this reconfiguration of the genre of encyclopedic culinary knowledge, she identifies women and their work as central to a sociology of Spanish cuisine and taste. She enacts a "food femininity" that complies with dominant expectations of the women to whom her writing was directed. At the same time, she also "re-does gender" in a way that deviates and challenges the norms of her times. Carmen de Burgos was marginalized from literary history as a direct consequence of one of the most basic and most revolutionary things she did: she made a public career as a woman writer. Had her oeuvre not been completely banned with the onset of Francoism, it's entirely possible that the strategies for engaging women she demonstrates in her culinary writing would have allowed her to enact and model femininities and feminisms with long-lasting consequences for modern Spanish women.

CHAPTER 3

MYTHOLOGIES OF CULINARY MODERNITY

Gregorio Marañón and Nicolasa Pradera

This chapter brings together two figures, Nicolasa Pradera and Gregorio Marañón, whose lives and ideas about cooking in 1930s Spain come together in Pradera's 1933 cookbook *La cocina de Nicolasa* and Marañón's prologue of that book. We know relatively little about the woman, Pradera. We know a lot about the man, the famous endocrinologist, intellectual, and statesman of the Second Republic, Marañón. Both figures, famous for excellence in entirely different fields, exemplify different threads of how Spanish modernization was unfolding in the 1930s. One was a highly educated scientist and intellectual whose ideas and actions ushered in Spain's Second Republic; the other was a working-class woman who ascended to culinary fame and economic success through her cooking and founding of one of the Basque Country's most well-known restaurants, Casa Nicolasa.

Nicolasa Pradera was born in 1870 in the Vizcayan village of Markina and died in 1959 in Madrid. Employed as an "ayudante de cocina" (kitchen assistant) at a young age by the Gaitan de Ayala family, Pradera followed their daughter to San Sebastián upon her marriage to take charge of the kitchen.[1] At some point, Pradera undertook training with well-known chef Ignacio Doménech.[2] Through her daily shopping Pradera met her future husband, Narciso Dolhagaray Picabea, owner of a prestigious butcher shop.

They married and opened Casa Nicolasa in 1912, which became successful due to the growing tourism industry in San Sebastián. After its sale in

FIGURE 3.1. Portrait of Nicolasa Pradera and her husband Narciso Dolhagaray Picabea (1935). Image printed with permission of grandson José M. Lasa Dolhagaray.

FIGURE 3.2. Portrait of Nicolasa Pradera (1948). Image provided by Ana Vega Pérez de Arlucea and printed with permission of her grandson José M. Lasa Dolhagaray.

1930 or 1932 for the significant sum of 40,000 pesetas, Pradera opened the restaurant Andia in San Sebastián and, in 1940, Nicolasa in Madrid.[3]

Gregorio Marañón was born in 1887 to a bourgeois Madrid family with both a significant library and connections to leading intellectuals of the period, including writers Benito Pérez Galdós, José María de Pereda, and Marcelino Menéndez y Pelayo.[4] A doctor of medicine, Marañón researched human sexuality, emotion, and temperament and belonged to a cohort of scientists, physicians, and intellectuals who applied scientific modes of understanding to art, history, and literary criticism.[5] Socially he moved among both the highest and the lowest classes in Spain: he treated patients belonging to the court of Alfonso XIII, in addition to artists, politicians, and journalists; and researched populations affected by hunger and poverty.[6] Politically, Marañón identified as a liberal. He remained distant from active politics until 1922 when he visited Las Hurdes with the king.[7] Then, in 1926, a month-long imprisonment for alleged participation in the Sanjuanada political coup against Primo de Rivera supposedly served as the catalyst for his direct engagement with political life.[8]

This engagement came first through Marañón's writing: in a series of prologues to political essays by J. Castrillo Santos, *Las rutas de la libertad* (1928), F. Villanueva, *Obstáculos tradicionales* (1928), Marcelino Domingo, *¿A dónde va España?* (1929), and J. Sánchez Guerra, *El pan de la emigración* (1930), Marañón expresses his political engagement as a necessary act "por su patria" (for his homeland).[9] And then, with José Ortega y Gasset and Ramón Pérez de Ayala, he founded the political movement Agrupación al servicio de la República in 1930. Both reflected his growing belief that Spain's intellectuals needed to play a more direct role in the nation's political future. Later, when Republicans, allied with Lerroux's radical socialists, won widespread support in the April 12, 1931 elections, Marañón coordinated Alfonso XIII's exile and the installation of the Second Republic's provisional government. Approached by party leaders and offered the presidency, the ambassadorship to France, or a ministerial position, Marañón opted to run for election as a *diputado* (member of parliament) to the Cortes Constituyentes.[10] In that office, he helped create the 1931 Constitution and served in the Cortes until his resignation in 1933.

Moreover, Marañón maintained a clinical practice and research agenda throughout the 1920s and 1930s. In addition to *Gordos y flacos* (1926), a monograph on diet and nutrition, he wrote sixteen other book-length texts, and had four-hundred articles published in medical journals. He authored 220 prologues in his lifetime, converting what was once understood as "texto de complacencia" (a promotional or courtesy text) to an essay that served as vehicle for political and social thought.[11] Cooking and gastronomy were frequent topics, including a prologue to Eduardo García del Real's *Cocina Española y cocina dietética* (1929), titled "Breve ensayo sobre la cocina española"; a number of book-length works, among them *La regulación hormonal del hambre* (1937), *Cátedra de vino*, and *Sobre la composición química de los alimentos* (1932); a series of essays about cuisine, "Cuatro meditaciones sobre la cocina española," in *Meditaciones* (1933); "Ensayo apologético sobre la cocina española," published in *El alma de España* (1951); and *Elogio médico de la naranja* (1932/1961).[12] In 1933 alone, the year in which he wrote the prologue to Nicolasa Pradera's cookbook, Marañón was active as a politician, doctor, researcher, member of the *Real Academia Española*, and writer.

Given the intensity of Marañón's activity during the early 1930s and the sum of his professional responsibilities, one may ask why Marañón would author the prologue to a book of recipes by this female chef. Certainly, his history as prologuist gives some indication that his contribution to Pradera's cookbook served as more than a gesture of goodwill or marketing. This chapter will argue that Marañón discursively creates Pradera, reinscribing her into traditional class and gender roles and erasing her as an empowered entrepreneur in order to further his political/cultural aims. His culinary writing facilitates what I will show to be a modern Spanish authenticity consistent with the logic of the Second Republic's embrace of tourism as a mechanism of economic modernization. However, it also downplays the political instability that comes with modernization and that had provoked his own withdrawal from politics in the early years of the Republic.[13] Arguably, such a vision betrays the Second Republic's commitment to mass democratization and sanitizes the unrest, tension, and instability that came with those changes.

Marañón and Pradera were working, living, and responding to a set of political, social, and economic circumstances that were accelerating change in Spain in the 1930s. These changes both inspired the optimism seen among left-leaning citizens in their articulation of Second Republic values and also elicited criticism, resistance, and fear among those who felt that Spain was ceasing to be Spain, that things were changing too quickly, or not quickly enough. We see this fundamental tension across a number of contexts, from what historians have framed as the uneven modernization of Spain during the nineteenth and early twentieth centuries, to scientific responses to social instability and fears of degeneration, to debates about the roles of women, to the government-led development of a tourism industry. Marañón's writing and Pradera's work elucidate how culinary discourses convey a series of tensions in relation to this raft of modernizing changes.

First, the association of Spain with a "leyenda negra" or black legend encapsulates a number of the challenges the country faced in implementing modern political and social changes. Spanish journalist Julián Juderías may have formulated the phrase in 1912, but it referred to a perception of Spain extending back to the sixteenth century as a country characterized by ignorance, intransigent Catholicism, superstition, and general backwardness.[14] Juderías's writing about it attests to its lingering influence and the degree to which Spain's inability to modernize had long troubled intellectuals. For example, Mesonero Romanos, Larra, Cadalso, Valera, and Unamuno all believed that Spain's authenticity belonged to the Siglo de Oro while the modernity of the nineteenth and early twentieth centuries belonged to France.[15] A modern Spain would involve imitating modernity from elsewhere and would unavoidably dilute or taint Spain's authenticity. Conversely, painters Ignacio Zuloaga and Ramón and Valentín de Zubiaurre represented "España arcaica" (archaic Spain) in their work, while writers Darío de Regoyos, J. López Pinillos, Eugenio Noel, and Ramón del Valle-Inclán aestheticized the "decrepitud del país" (decrepitude of the country).[16]

Despite its exaggerated and negative representation, the *leyenda negra* encapsulates the *casticista* elements considered to be authentic and essential to Spanish identity.[17] At the same time, similar concerns about Spain's inability to modernize influenced the biologic and organic slant of debates about Spain's degeneration after 1898. Fears that backwardness indicated an inborn deficiency of the Spanish people led to the development of a eugenics discourse that overlapped with politics. Writers like radical republican Martínez Vargas, in *En defensa de la Raza* (1918), attributed Spain's degeneration to the fact that the Spanish race had lost its "national vitality."[18] Scientists like Marañón had inherited the work of nineteenth-century reformers whose focus on poverty allowed them to frame social problems and slow modernization in terms of physical illness.[19] These discourses informed perspectives on the poor and converged in a practice/theory of social hygiene in which Spanish intellectuals from across the political spectrum framed poverty in biological terms and proposed its eradication through state policy.[20] For example, reports on Alfonso XIII's visit to Las Hurdes and representations like Buñuel's 1933 film *Las Hurdes, tierra sin pan* focused on the spectacle of diseased bodies supposedly genetically predisposed to poverty. Rather than attribute the poverty in Las Hurdes to the complete absence of a transportation and communication infrastructure and insufficient agricultural production to feed the population, these reports framed the poor as biologically inferior organisms.[21] Marañón and others like him, then, were following an established scientific tradition in attempting to diagnose the illnesses of society in order to cure them. He applied a scientific mindset to social issues, the human body, literature, and the arts, in order to promote modernization, an approach that José Ortega y Gasset believed essential to liberating Spanish culture from its pre-scientific and pre-theoretical backwardness in order to cultivate a genuinely modern society.[22]

While one vein of historiography has largely understood Spain as the country that missed its opportunity for the modernization, higher living standards, and the liberal democracy that took root elsewhere in Europe during the nineteenth century, others including David Ringrose, Jesús Cruz, Adrian Shubert, and their followers have demonstrated that Spanish modernization was an uneven process. This better accounts for the changes in technology, economy, and politics characteristic of urban life and the urban networks that transmitted material goods, new ideas, and social change even if Spain's middle class did not develop in economic terms until well into the twentieth century.[23] That said, as mentioned also in previous chapters, existing pockets of middle-class culture gave rise to middle-class practices in Spain, even if the financial wherewithal to support those practices was insubstantial. A country could partake in cultural modernity even if its capitalist modernization was incomplete or uneven.[24]

By the 1920s and '30s, urban metropolises like Madrid, Barcelona, and Bilbao had developed consumer cultures similar to those of other European cities. Popular media showcased new ideas about decorating, fashion, hygiene, and cooking to an affluent urban public. Articles, photographs, and radio broadcasts, however, depicted a lifestyle available only to the few. By contrast, rural Spain remained distant from the processes that created these consumer cultures and, further, was dissociated from "the new liberal-national identity, one of 'citizens' and 'Spaniards.'" Second Republic politicians may have sought to implement widespread reforms, in education via the Misiones Pedagógicas, for example, but attempts to promote democratic practices and culture among the rural populace resulted only in protests and violence.[25]

Clearly, democracy under the Second Republic was not a magical solution to Spain's uneven development. The social instability of this period deeply troubled Marañón and eventually contributed to his decision to leave politics. In his three years as a *diputado* to the Cortes Constituyentes Marañón renounced the violence of the Círculo Monárquico church burnings in May 1931. He had distanced himself from Republican repression and appropriation of Jesuit assets in 1932, citing that the religious order carried out the public services that the state could not provide. Marañón was also troubled by attempts to prosecute individuals for collaboration with Primo's dictatorship.[26] In 1932, he and the other members decided to dissolve the Agrupación al servicio de la República. Members stated publicly that the group's mandate had been fulfilled with the establishment of the Second Republic, but its dissolution presaged what Carr describes as the Summer 1933 exodus of intellectuals from direct involvement with Republican politics due to its upheavals.[27] In November of 1933 Marañón resigned from politics himself.

During the Second Republic several decades of debate over the social roles of women in a modern society culminated in significant changes; among them, the 1931 Constitution awarded women the rights to vote and divorce. Nonetheless, significant parts of society including intellectuals from across the political spectrum continued to support a traditional gender ideology for women with roots in the sixteenth century.[28] The social and economic factors that constructed the private sphere as a feminine domain stem from Spain's transition from an agricultural society, in which women's work was included as part of the productive labor of a household, to an industrialized society. As productive work moved from the home to factories or businesses, women, by and large, were restricted from participating. Fray Luís de León's sixteenth-century *La perfecta casada* was a precursor of the ideology of domesticity that flourished throughout Western Europe in the nineteenth century. Embodied in the traditional model of the "angel of the house," women belonged in the private, domestic life of the home and homemaking; men functioned in the public and political sphere. Women were idealized in their roles as mothers (biological production) and as nurturers (future citizen production), and the home otherwise became a place of consumption.[29] Although this ideology functioned best in bourgeois families, it was adopted by working-class families, too. The resulting double subordination, due to gender and class, helped weaken class consciousness among women, ensuring that these values and compliance passed to the next generation.[30]

Even still, the first decade of the twentieth century marked the beginning of a slow emergence of women as a visible part of the public labor force. Declining birth rates, later marriage, and increasing levels of illness among female workers at home drove an increasing need for women to work in the productive sphere to support themselves and their families. Rising levels of female employment created anxiety among male workers who feared that women's participation in the labor market would reduce salaries. Women's work in the public sphere was acceptable in situations of absolute necessity, but preferably in jobs aligned with their supposedly natural abilities.[31] Further, Conservatives and the Church saw women's public labor as threatening to the "sublime misión de madre y 'angel del Hogar'" (sublime mission as mother and 'angel of the House') and as demeaning of the authority and dignity of husbands. Among leftists, some viewed women's remunerative work as a human right (José Francos Rodríguez), while others theorized that it would cause home life to deteriorate.[32] By the 1930s, this model was being challenged by that of the "new" woman. She was independent and resistant to restrictions that kept women from universities, professions, business, and public space.[33] Viewed by scholars as a "symbolic device for adapting women to new social, political, economic, and demographic contexts," the model functioned to show women that they were allowed access to "education, culture, social welfare, and new sectors of the labor market."[34]

Notwithstanding the dominant traditional gender model and the more subversive new woman model, Pradera likely occupied some intermediary space. Montserrat Miller's research on public market halls and the women vendors who ran them illustrates the contradictions that existed between these models, prevalent gender iconographies, and the lived experiences of women who had long worked in the public sphere. Popular representations had associated women vendors with both independence and a bawdiness that echoes other representations of working-class women from the nineteenth century and before. Urban theorists considered vendors as clearly working class during the mid-nineteenth century, but by the early twentieth century many either aspired to or had achieved upward social mobility and a middle-class social and economic status.[35] Like the vendors Miller studies, Pradera was an entrepreneur whose work and livelihood deviated from the gendered segregation of other economic sectors. As this analysis will show, her connections with food provisioning, like that of market vendors, obscured her upward class mobility.

The development of a tourism industry also contextualizes the impact of Pradera's and Marañón's culinary writing. Throughout the early twentieth century, the state actively pursued the development of a tourist infrastructure as part of national regenerationist plans, beginning with the creation of the Comisión Nacional de Turismo in 1905 led by the Conde de Romanones. Elites imagined tourism as an instrument of modernization that would invigorate economically and socially stagnant areas.[36] Further, organized travel was a nation-building exercise that helped generate a sense of belonging to both the nation and its native lands.[37] An active tourist culture, economy, and offerings would also allow Spain to "claim its rightful place among the CULTURED PEOPLES."[38] The 1905 Comisión Nacional focused on promoting "sunny Spain" to foreigners and foregrounding local heritage. Municipalities were required to provide tourist services; an incentive system encouraged the modernization of hotels. And tourism interests were used as a justification for improvements in rail- and roadways during Primo de Rivera's dictatorship.[39] This emphasis intensified during the Second Republic as the tourism board was folded into the Interior Ministry in 1931 and Spain joined the League of Nations Tourism Committee.[40]

San Sebastián, the location of Pradera's first and second restaurants, had been identified with Spain's nascent tourism industry since Isabel II's first visit in 1845. It served as a thruway for the rail line that connected Madrid to France, and city officials promoted its architecture and urbanity as representative of an "agradable, rico y sano" (pleasant, wealthy and healthy) version of Spain without the class conflict or urban unrest that rocked other cities in the country.[41] In addition to its beaches, the city offered the ludic pleasures of a casino (opened in 1887), an aerial tram, an amusement park ("de tono aristocrático" [in synch with aristocratic tastes]), and then in 1912 the Igueldo funicular. By 1924 the efforts of city officials to promote the city as a tourist destination had been so successful that its marketing focus shifted from domestic visitors to international ones. San Sebastián was one of the healthiest cities in the world and contributed to its image as the "imagen de una ciudad moderna" (the image of a modern city). The city developed a strong service sector to cater to well-to-do travelers, both bourgeois and aristocratic.[42] Visitors and the city's bureaucrats, lawyers, physicians, architects, and engineers became clients of restaurants like Pradera's.[43]

MARAÑÓN'S CREATION OF NICOLASA

Secondary sources give little information about Nicolasa Pradera herself. Casa Nicolasa was described as a "sencillo comedor" (simple dining room) and as the site of meals eaten by "prácticamente todo el mundo político, financiero y cultural de Donostia-San Sebastián" (practically all of Donostia-San Sebrián's political, financial and cultural figures).[44] Her cookbook *La cocina de Nicolasa* was published first in 1933 with Rivadeneyra and since then, has been reprinted at least twenty times. Each edition includes Marañón's twelve-page prologue, which introduces 328 pages of recipes organized by course and type of preparation.[45]

Historians Mardones Alonso and Luis Haranburu Altuna praise Pradera's work and cuisine. The latter credits the book, alongside *El Amparo: sus platos clásicos* (1930) by sisters Ursula and Sira Azcaray, with codifying a Basque and Vizcayan cuisine that resulted from the application of French techniques to both autochthonous and newly arrived ingredients to the region.[46] Pradera's cookbook was successful due to her cuisine and her reputation as the "feliz cocinera" (happy cook) who "consiguió justa fama entre los donostiarras y los cortesanos que veraneaban en la capital guipuzcoana en compañía de los reyes de España" (achieved justifiable fame among city dwellers and court members who summered in the Guipuzkoan capital in the company of the monarchs of Spain).[47] Yet, Marañón's fame and "authorship" make Pradera nearly invisible to historians and culinary critics. For example, Néstor Luján omits any mention of Pradera at all and Manuel Martínez Llopis only reproduces elements of Marañón's prologue. The journal *Cuadernos de Gastronomía y de cultura alimentaria* (1995, numbers 11 and 12), for example, devotes three articles to Marañón's gastronomical writing and lists Pradera's cookbook among *his* culinary texts.

Unlike many other writers of cookbooks, Pradera herself offers little in her own writing to give readers a sense of who she is. Recall Leonardi's work on how cookbook paratexts—forewords, introductions, or epilogues—construct an "embedded discourse" that tells readers how to use the recipes and offers some personal connection to the author.[48] She further demonstrates how a writer develops a relationship with a community of readers through narrative. For example, in *The Joy of Cooking*, Irma Rombauer uses a story about a handyman with a wooden leg to emphasize to readers that "correct preparation, cooking and time of food" should concern them more than a dish's appearance.[49]

The prologues studied in other chapters of this monograph by Pardo Bazán and Carmen de Burgos make similar connections with readers, as does Picadillo, who includes anecdotes and witty sketches of the people whose recipes he includes in *La cocina práctica* (1905). And chef Teodoro Bardají, working in the same period as Pradera, writes extensively about himself in his cookbooks. Comparing Pradera to Bardají illuminates the full extent of her authorial modesty. Author of *Índice Culinario* (1915, 1925) and *La cocina de ellas* (1935), Bardají worked as the chef to the Duques del Infantado, among the "brigada de cocineros" (brigade of cooks) that prepared Alfonso XIII's wedding feast, in the Zaragoza Hotel Europa, and several aristocratic households.[50]

In his cookbook prologues, Bardají emphasizes his status as chef and creator of culinary culture. He instructs his "queridas lectoras" (dear [female] readers) that his recipes "están hechas con verdadero lujo de pormenores" (are made with a veritable luxury of details), attributing potentially tiresome repetition to the fact that he offers cooking formulas rather than literary articles. His less-competent women readers may be challenged by "tecnicismos oscuros" (obscure technicalities), but Bardají is the expert who will guide and instruct them.[51] Critics give his writing at least as much praise as they accord his cooking and his recipes. For example, Dionisio Pérez raves:

> Teodoro Bardají, uno de los mejores cocineros que tiene España, es fácil escritor además y singular autoridad en materia coquinaria [. . .] Es uno de los iniciadores del renacimiento y glorificación de la cocina nacional. No se puede tratar de cocina sin citarle y enaltecerle."[52]

> Teodoro Barjadí, one of the best cooks that Spain has, is a skilled writer in addition to being a singular authority in all related to the culinary [. . .] He is one of the founders of the renaissance and glorification of the national cuisine. It is impossible to discuss cooking without citing and exalting him.

With these brief examples, it is clear that Bardají creates an authorial persona in his culinary writing. Additionally, as a professional chef with high-status appointments in households and hotels, he authors an authoritative discourse about food and cooking in Spain that transcends the merit of any one recipe or even collection of recipes. More than a mere practitioner of cooking, Bardají authors an image of himself as a creative professional.

Middle-class women cookbook authors like Adriana de Juaristi and María Mestayer de Echagüe (the Marquesa de Parabere) also create discourses about themselves, their training, and their ideas about the intended readership of their books. For example, Juaristi in *Cocina* (1928) addresses the "Mujercita" (Little woman) in the prologue and invites the reader along with her on a trip to the market as the starting point for their cooking instruction.[53] Parabere begins the preamble of *La cocina completa* (1940) by stating "Certifico que cuantas recetas que integran esta obra han sido experimentadas por mí" (I certify that all the recipes that comprise this work have been tested by me).[54] New editions of their texts include critics' assessments of their culinary and literary work, in part because their recipes and authorial personae are embedded in a socio-cultural discourse that involves their readers.

Searching Pradera's cookbook for such a narrative or embedded discourse reveals little that would draw readers into a relationship with the author. Indeed, it's just the opposite: only rarely does Pradera write an authorial persona directly into her recipes. Her contributions, hints for easing preparation or suggestions about ingredients, are frequently enclosed in parentheses, making them seem an aside rather than an integral part of the recipe or gesture that would build a relationship with the reader. These parenthetical comments most often take the form of a suggested variation for the recipe; in her recipe for "Cola de merluza rellena" (stuffed tail of hake), Pradera advises "Cuando esté hecha se saca a una fuente y se adorna con las almejas que se han quitado la media cáscara, las ronchas de patata que se han asado con el pescado y unos champignones (si se quiere)" (When done it is moved to a serving platter and adorned with the fish and some mushrooms [if desired]). Or they acknowledge the flexibility of that recipe: "En el jugo de la tartera se le añaden dos cucharadas de tomate y un par de cucharadas de nata (si hay) [...]" (In the liquid from the plate add two tablespoons of tomato and two more of cream [if there is any]). On other occasions, she shares a minor detail of her own preparation. For example, the parenthetical note in the recipe for "Lengua rebozada" (Battered tongue), "(Naturalmente, se sirve en salsera)" ([Naturally it is served in a sauce bowl]), tells readers how to present the dish while serving it, and in the recipe for "Lengua en salsa de tomate" (Tongue in tomato sauce), where she specifies one set of instructions for Calasparra rice and another for other types of rice, she also notes "(Yo empleo el Calasparra)" ([I use Calasparra]).[55]

By placing her comments in parentheses, Pradera both makes the text of the recipe and the dish itself central and her commentary peripheral. This further communicates to readers that the recipes are not inventions that Pradera accepts credit for creating. Just the opposite: her book and writing style within the recipes indicate that the preparations themselves are her practice. But the dishes themselves belong more broadly or widely to a shared cooking tradition. Nonetheless, these insertions reflect her expertise as a chef and the knowledge she has gained in the experience of preparing these dishes. Without these comments, the recipes would be a list of steps that take readers through a dish's preparation, reflecting little relationship with an imagined readership. Pradera's spare writing style may seem to reduce her contribution to the text, since there is no "Al que leyere" (To the one who will read) dedication or extended description of her professional training or her imagined purpose for the cookbook. Yet, one must keep in mind Pradera's gender and social class as contributors to the relationship she establishes with readers via her writing. The cookbook itself compounds this gender- and class-based status since the only information about her career and her cuisine is provided by Gregorio Marañón in his prologue.

Marañón provides the context that frames Pradera's recipes, and the image of Pradera herself; he controls the meaning of her project for the cookbook's readers. Essentially, Marañón creates the persona of Nicolasa Pradera. He shapes Pradera's persona to fit his own political and ideological agenda. While he may acknowledge her as an artist, he uses the facts of her gender and her social class to essentialize her as a maternal figure and as a representative of the Basque *pueblo*. He fosters this impression with a number of strategies.

First, he identifies Pradera by her first name throughout the prologue, which immediately indicates to readers that her social status is inferior to his: "Con mucho gusto escribo estas líneas de introducción al libro de Nicolasa, gran artista de la cocina vasca" (With great pleasure I write these lines of introduction to Nicolasa's book, the great artist of Basque cuisine).[56] This level of familiarity would not be employed with a woman of Marañón's intellectual or social class; Emilia Pardo Bazán, for example, is never "Emilia" when mentioned by critics; she is "Doña Emilia" or "la Condesa" (the Countess). Furthermore, in the same prologue, Marañón refers more formally to other women writers and their cookbooks. The nineteenth-century author of *Libro de Cocina apropósito para la Mesa Vizcaína* (1890) is "la señora viuda de Uhagón" (the widow of Uhagón); the Azcaray sisters of the Bilbao restaurant El Amparo and their mother are "doña Felipa Eguileor" (Mrs. Felipa Eguileor) and the "señoritas Ursula y Sira de Azcaray y Eguilor" (misses Ursula and Sira de Azcaray y Eguilor).[57] Marañón uses the title "señorita" (Miss) to denote their middle-classness.[58] By identifying Pradera only as "Nicolasa," Marañón obscures the fact that Pradera clearly belonged to the middle class in 1933. She owned a restaurant and had married butcher shop owner Narciso Dolhagaray Picabea.

Marañón compounds this impression by suggesting a contrast with the Azcaray sisters and their cookbook, which was created and sold as an act of charity. Marañón explains, the cookbook was

> legado por voluntad testamentaria a la Santa Casa de Misericordia; y cito este dato porque es también representativo de la dignidad social que alcanza en una gran ciudad un libro de cocina cuando se considera como fuente de ingresos para la caridad oficial.[59]

> bequeathed by the stipulations of her will to the Santa Casa de Misericordia; and I cite this fact because it also represents the social dignity that exists in a great city when a cookbook can become a source of income for official charity.

Developed from two manuscripts that the sisters' brother Eduardo presented to the Casa de Misericordia of Bilbao, the cookbook was published to benefit patients. It contains emblematic Basque recipes, for example "bacalao a la vizcaína y en salsa verde" (Vizcayan cod in green sauce) and "pisto a la bilbaína" (stir-fried vegetables Bilbao style).[60] And, like Pradera's cookbook, the recipes point to the purchasing power of San Sebastián's middle class. Although the restaurant Amparo had closed, this solidly bourgeois family could donate their culinary wealth to charity. This marks an implicit contrast with Pradera: he praises the Azcaray sisters' beneficence but ignores Pradera's role in creating a financially successful restaurant. Marañón states that only in a modern city would a cookbook generate enough income to make a notable charitable donation. He writes nothing, however, about how a modern city would enable a female chef to create a successful career for herself.

Pradera clearly does not fit the model of the middle-class woman that Marañón has as a frame of reference. Instead, he expresses the commonly held set of standards about women that neither acknowledged the rapid changes in women's roles taking place in Spain nor the debates that engendered those changes. As a restaurant owner and cookbook writer, Pradera is outside of the purely domestic sphere represented by traditional notions of women's place and their obedience to the ideology of domesticity. The Azcaray sisters fit into that ideology because Marañón frames their work as done for charity, a type of public presence seen as appropriate for middle-class women going back to the work of reformers like Concepción Arenal in the nineteenth century. Marañón praises the Azcaray sisters for their charity work but makes no comment about their participation in creating the reputation of their restaurant. This selective mention endorses public roles for women as long as they conform to models that do not contradict domestic ideology; in other words, working in public is fine for women as long as it is done to benefit charitable causes. Marañón's description of middle-class women and their cookbooks, together with the dominant ideology that limited women's work outside the home to circumstances of dire economic necessity, places Pradera outside of the traditionally defined middle class.

Marañón's familiar treatment of Pradera, especially in contrast with his way of referring to other women, reveals a discomfort with a woman who breaks with both traditional gender and class roles. Pradera is not an example of a middle-class woman who, as Margarita Nelken describes in *La condición social de la mujer en España* (1919), attempts to present her work "no parezca un medio *completo* de vivir" (so that it doesn't appear as the *sole* income). Nor is she a "trabajadora que no quiere que se sepa" (worker who doesn't want anybody to know).[61] The model of the *nueva mujer moderna* (new modern woman) also seems an unlikely fit for Pradera even if it exemplified broader changes that made new careers like Pradera's possible, and despite that her association with a task linked to the domestic sphere for women—cooking—obscured her entrepreneurship. Yet, Marañón makes no effort to link her success as a restaurateur and cookbook writer to the greater opportunities available to women.

Instead, Marañón constructs her as a figure outside the middle class. This association is revealed in a number of passages, all of which emphasize how her culinary skills sustain a privileged link to the tastes and culture of the popular classes. In one example, he connects Pradera's book "que ahora aparece para delicia de la Humanidad" (that now appears to the delight of Humanity) to how the author herself embodies "la tradición popular con la propia creación y por la extensión y eclecticismo con que se trata la delicada materia" (popular tradition with her own creation and by the expanse and eclecticism with which she treats this delicate subject).[62] She is a manifestation of popular tradition whose cooking practice elevates her cuisine.

In another passage, readers see how he essentializes Pradera's racial characteristics as a Basque woman.

> Claro es que la cocina cuidada y sapiente tiene, no hay duda, tradición centenaria en estas provincias; porque no se improvisa en pocas generaciones la profunda disposición (casi específica de esta raza) que para el arte gastronómico tienen las mujeres vizcaínas, guipuzcoanas y navarras; mujeres hechas de elementos nobles y antiguos, entre los que coloco esta admirable actitud cocineril.[63]

It is clear that the careful and wise cooking, without a doubt, has centenary tradition in these provinces; because one does not improvise in just a few generations the deep disposition (almost specific to this race) for the gastronomic arts that Vizcayan, Guipuzkoan, and Navarran women have; women made of noble and old elements, among which I categorize this admirable culinary disposition.

For Marañón, Basque women, Pradera included, are the *sacerdotisas* (priestesses) of a cuisine. His use of the terms *sacerdotisa* and *numen* (deity) classifies them and their culinary skills as belonging to an ancient wellspring of noble knowledge.[64] In an additional passage, we see how "noble" becomes a type of shorthand for a "Basque pueblo," to which he refers when he attempts to create a parallel between Pradera and his childhood nursemaid, a peasant from the Basque town of Munguía.

> Yo, que tuve a mi lado, desde que nací hasta que ella murió de vieja, a una *noble* mujer, campesina de Munguía, llevo unidos a mis recuerdos primeros—ya hace años de ello—el sabor de las angulas, del pimiento en sus formas más variadas, del bacalao con sus diversas salsas, del agrio chacolí y de casi todo el repertorio de la eminente escuela culinaria que comento.[65]

> I, who had at my side, from the time I was born until she died an old woman, a *noble* woman, a peasant from Munguía, [and] I carry as part of my first memories—many years now since—the flavor of the baby eels, of peppers in their most varied forms, cod with its diverse sauces, of the bitter *chacolí* [a Basque wine] and of almost all the repertoire of the eminent culinary school that I am commenting upon.

Marañón's reference in these two passages to essentialized "mujeres hechas de elementos nobles y antiguos" (women made of noble and old elements) and to his nursemaid, the "noble mujer, campesina de Munguía" (a noble woman, a peaseant from Munguía), invokes the definition of *pueblo* that Derek Flitter describes in *Spanish Romanticism and the Uses of History* (2006). Marañón casts these women into the "reassuring role of historical guarantor for Volksgeist."[66]

Furthermore, the cuisine they produce because of their race and class inspires Marañón's nostalgia. For example, he alludes to a sensory memory that links ingredients specific to the Basque region to nurturing from his nursemaid: "llevo unidos a mis recuerdos primeros—ya hace años de ello—el sabor de las angulas, [del] pimiento en sus formas más variadas [. . .]" (I carry as part of my first memories—many years now since—the flavor of the baby eels, of peppers in their most varied forms).[67] The flavors he recalls create a visceral link between his contemporary self and his nostalgia for the care he received in childhood. His *campesina* nursemaid, Pradera, and women like them preserve those flavors through time, passing them from mother (or mother figure) to child.

Marañón's association of specific ingredients with the childhood nurturing from his nursemaid conceals the labor of household food production by framing it as part of the practice of mothering. Nancy Chodorow frames women's mothering as instinctual "emotion work"; social scientists like Marañón tended to view it as indistinct from the biological fact of maternity and, thus, a "natural product" rather than a social construct.[68] Since Pradera is indisputably female, she must conform to an essentializing understanding of women as mothers. Marañón's parallel between Pradera and his nursemaid reframes her professional work in the language of nurturing and motherhood. It also underscores the class dynamics at play; the nursemaid he remembers in the same breath with Nicolasa Pradera was a servant. The effect is to re-package her artistry and career in terms that are coherent with tradition.

Although Marañón advocated for Spain's modernization, his misrepresentation of Pradera's social class and profession indicates that his thinking on women was less progressive than other positions he held. Intellectuals from across the political spectrum grappled with how motherhood complicated any greater involvement of women in the public sphere during the Restoration period. And Marañón certainly considered women biologically different from men. Their primary function was that of mother and wife; other activities or roles were limited by this condition; responsibilities belonging to men should only be undertaken during circumstances of need or duress.[69] On the one hand, feminists criticized his ideas for being antifeminist since he worked to secularize traditional ideas about women's roles by glossing with scientific authority existing opinions about women's social functions, specifically their biological functions as mothers.[70] On the other, feminists like Carmen de Burgos defended Marañón's work since he "con gran espíritu de justicia, no habla de superioridad de un sexo sobre otro, sino de necesidad de diferenciación" (with a great spirit of justice, does not discuss the superiority of one sex over another, but of the necessity of differentiation).[71] Most feminists in Spain during the 1920s and 1930s favored a definition of feminism that recognized women's unique strengths rather than one centered on equality.[72] Maternity was one aspect of that radical difference, and thus coherent with Marañón's theory of sexual difference.⁷³

The maternal relationship Marañón describes between the middle-class *viuda de Uhagón* and her daughters, for whom she writes her cookbook, reinforces Marañón's construction of a maternal bond centered on food. Their cookbook, *Libro de Cocina apropósito para la Mesa Vizcaína,* contains recipes for dishes that Marañón lists—"angulas, chipirones, bacalao, etc" (baby eels, cuttlefish, cod, etc.)—and which he describes as "guisos excelentes que hoy son honor de esta cocina y regalo de buenos comedores" (excellent preparations that today are a virtue of this cuisine and the gift of good eating places). Furthermore, he extols the Uhagón cookbook:

> En este catecismo sin desperdicio, que ha sido durante muchos años depósito y oráculo de la ciencia gastronómica del país, hay un prologuillo, que la autora dedica a su propia hija, en el que, en palabras sencillas y tiernas, está encerrada toda la filosofía y toda la moral del arte culinario: 'una buena ama de casa—escribe la autora—debe entender el arte del cocinero para preparar a su esposo y familiar el bienestar confortable que le haga preferir la comida sencilla de su casa a los mayores festines fuera de ella.'⁷⁴

> In this culinary catechism, that has been over many years the archive and oracle of gastronomic sciences of the country, there is a little prologue, that the author dedicates to her own daughter, in which, in simple and tender words, she communicates all the philosophy and morality of the culinary arts: 'a good housewife—the author writes—should understand the arts of the [male] chef to prepare for her husband and family the comfortable well-being that causes him to prefer the simple preparations of his home rather than the noteworthy feasts from outside of it.'

By invoking religious (*catecismo*) and mythological (*oráculo*) terminology to describe the significance of cuisine to Spain, Marañón makes Uhagón's *catecismo*, the cookbook that reflects the affective bonds between mother and children, the model for all culinary arts in Spain. His use of *prologuillo*, instead of the more straightforward *prólogo*, denotes the tenderness of Uhagón's act of writing recipes for her daughters. He extends this notion to the nation as a whole by making women's domestic roles central to Spain's culinary excellence; women who work in the private sphere as *amas de casa*, whose work encompasses the "emotion work" of nurturing, sustain the philosophy and morality of the culinary arts. ⁷⁵ Marañón makes it clear not only that cuisine in Spain is feminine but that it is structured upon the maternal relationships that women have with their children (Uhagón) or with the children they are paid to nurture (the nursemaid).⁷⁶

Marañón also measures Spain's progress according to this dynamic. He continues,

> Pocas cosas dan idea del grado de progreso de un pueblo como el que las señoras encopetadas piensen y hablen así; y además que califiquen de "sencillas comidas" a las suculentas descripciones que siguen al prefacio que comentamos.⁷⁷

> Few things give an idea of the degree of progress of a people as the fact that its posh ladies think and speak in this way; and, moreover, that they name as "simple meals" the succulent descriptions that follow the preface under discussion.

By making domesticity and the culinary arts borne of housewives' nurturing the sign of a *pueblo*'s progress, Marañón erases the social changes happening for women in Spain during the 1930s. Instead, he expresses a preference that Spain measure its progress in terms of the strength of its middle class and the adherence of women in particular to traditional gender ideology.⁷⁸

Marañón's focus on the home and cooking during a period of dramatic changes in women's social roles was not unique to Spain. Samantha Barbas traces a parallel phenomenon in the United States as restaurants embraced "home cooking" as a culinary style in response to increased production of industrialized food and increases in numbers of women who sought jobs outside the home. Restaurants shifted in response, evolving from "greasy spoons" serving primarily male workers to mixed-sex, middle-class eating establishments. Although the "home cooking campaign" reached its peak in the 1920s, "restaurants would continue to woo customers by promising to retrieve middle-class domesticity." Restaurant "home cooking" retained a personal connection to the woman who made it. It maintained "distinctive flavors," in contrast to the artificial flavors of factory-produced food and reflected the regional traditions of the woman who made and served it with "loving care."⁷⁹ Recreating home-like domesticity in the public restaurant was one response to changing social roles of women and the modernization that made them possible.

Similarly, by identifying Spain's progress with women who nurture in their kitchens, Marañón responds to fears that women might abandon domesticity. Instead, his representation of Pradera erases the social conditions that made possible her professional training as a chef, focusing instead on the author as a maternal and still domestic guarantor of culinary traditions.

FOUNDATIONAL CONTRADICTIONS: MODERNITY AND AUTHENTICITY

To construct Pradera within this traditional paradigm based on her gender and social class, and to frame the effects her cuisine has on consumers, Marañón tells readers that he suspends his scientific mind when writing about her. He adopts instead the perspective of a Spanish everyman. Yet, in his prologue to her cookbook and in "Breve ensayo sobre la cocina española" (1929), Marañón only rhetorically abandons the scientific position that he applied to his analyses of everything from social issues to literature and the literary figure of Don Juan. He actually uses the authority his reputation grants him to promote Pradera contradictorily, not just as a representative of tradition, but as a representative of tradition that proves Spain's capacity to modernize.

To understand this contradiction, it is helpful to examine Marañón's work on nutrition and the body's well-being in his study *Gordos y flacos* (1926) as one of the numerous scientific discourses from this period that attempted to diagnose, understand, and correct Spain's social problems. Organic inheritance, psychic inheritance (dependent on the interaction between social and organic), and social inheritance (wealth, science, trade, communication, and cooperation) are the elements that form and shape individuals, their body types, and their propensity to be slim or fat, Marañón argues. Thus, diet and nutritional hygiene are part of the biological determinism that informs Spanish eugenics and social hygiene. The genetic makeup of individuals determines difference in ways that religion and race do not. In the "Prólogo" to the study, Marañón asserts:

> Hombres de raza diversa, de distintas religiones, de edades diferentes, pueden ser casi idénticos en su moral, en su psicología y en sus hábitos. Pero un gordo y un flaco, coetáneos y feligreses de la misma parroquia, se diferenciarán por caracteres esenciales inconfundibles.[80]

> Men of diverse races, of different religions, and distinct ages, can be almost identical in their morality, in their psychology and in their habits. But a fat man and a skinny one, contemporaries and parishioners of the same church, will distinguish themselves through unmistakable essences.

Furthermore, "[. . .] la palabra 'gordo' resume multitud de conceptos de herencia, de costumbres, de carácter, de modalidades de la sensibilidad y de la inteligencia; que son exactamente el inverso en el 'flaco'" (the word "fat" encompasses a multitude of concepts of inheritance, of customs, character, manners, sensitivity, and intelligence; these are the exact inverse in the "skinny one").[81] Any number of organic characteristics or social circumstances (social class, for example) can account for an individual's weight, diet, and nutrition. Yet, Marañón reduces the entire range of human potential to a biological predisposition to be fat or slim.[82]

Marañón does not extend the same perspective to his work on cuisine. In "Breve ensayo sobre la cocina española," he states that cuisine and nutritional hygiene require fundamentally different measures and vocabularies. Hygiene and *cocina* are "palabras irreconciliables" (irreconcilable words).[83] On the one hand, "El higienista calcula, con sus tablas en la mano, la ración conveniente; fija las calorías necesarias para que la máquina humana dé su rendimiento máximo y no se deteriore por las escorias del exceso de combustible [. . .]" (the hygienist calculates, with his tables at hand, the advisable serving; he sets the necessary calories so that the human body gives its maximal performance without breaking down from waste from excessive fuel). By contrast,

> El cocinero—la cocinera, sobre todo—atiende a la satisfacción de los sentidos. No posee otra ciencia que ese empirismo milenario que ha ido depurando, de generación en generación, las combinaciones más sutiles de las especias, el grano preciso de la sal o de la pimienta; el tiempo justo de la cochura. [. . .] Y, en fin, ese trance de dar el 'punto' al alimento, en el que toda ciencia desaparece para dar un paso a un arte de los más delicados y subjetivos.[84]

> The [male] cook—the [female] cook above all—attends to the satisfaction of the senses. She does not possess any other science than that of the millenary empiricism, that which has refined, from generation to generation, the most subtle combinations of spices, the precise grain of salt or pepper; the exact cooking time. [. . .] And, ultimately, the fixation with cooking a food just right, in which all science disappears to make way for the most delicate and subjective artform.

The *cocinera*—note his emphasis on gender—uses her senses while the hygienist—unquestionably male—rationally measures. Similarities in the languages of hygiene and of cooking exist: a chef monitors the "grano preciso" (precise grain) of an ingredient as the scientist calculates (*calcula*). However, a *cocinera* knows when a dish is "al punto" ([at its] perfect point) because of an "empirismo milenario" (millenary empiricism), a type of knowledge passed from one individual to another and rooted in the experiences and practices of individuals. The hygienist who creates the "cocina dietética" (healthy diet)—marked by "frialdad en las sensaciones, sobriedad, reglamentación, higiene" (frigidity of the senses, sobriety, regulation, hygiene)—has no place in the world of cuisine.[85]

Marañón demonstrates in these examples that he clearly marks a difference between the science of nutrition and the sensuality of the culinary arts. Yet, he abandons his usual scientific focus in his argument for the importance of Pradera's cuisine. Where he uses the logic of biological determinism to predict a tendency to be slim or fat in *Gordos y flacos*, he defends cuisine as a "pre-theoretical" and "sensual" practice that is a requirement for Spain's modernization. Marañón accomplishes this move in two steps. First, he draws a comparison between Pradera's work as a chef and his work as a physician to illustrate that they both work to better the reputation of Spain:

> Quien ha hecho, como ella, gratas tantas horas de la vida de muchos seres humanos; quien, como ella, ha contribuído a que centenares y centenares de extranjeros contemplen a España, a través del vaho transcendente de sus guisos, con admiración y con optimismo, bien merecido este homenaje, de quien no tiene otra misión que la de aliviar, cuando puede y con métodos menos agradables que los de la autora de este volumen, el dolor de sus semejantes.[86]

> Who has made pleasant, like her, so many hours of so many humans; who, like her, has contributed to the fact that many hundreds of foreigners contemplate Spain, through the transcendent steam of her dishes, with admiration and optimism, well-deserved this homage, from he who has no other mission than that of alleviating, with methods less pleasant than the author of this volume, the pain of his fellow men.

He presents his public work and Pradera's as two sides of the same coin; Marañón deals with the ugly parts (starvation in Las Hurdes, for example) and Pradera offers a sensual experience, the pleasure of a tasty meal. Marañón attempts to alleviate through his dual practice of medicine and politics the underdevelopment of the country's inhabitants, while the "vaho transcendente de [Pradera's] guisos" (transcendent steam of her dishes) communicates optimism to foreigners about Spain's possibilities. Both roles are a kind of caretaking.

Secondly, Marañón rhetorically abandons his scientific authority to show readers how he falls under the influence of Pradera's cooking. He acknowledges the position his career would seem to require:

> Y ahora tal vez estaría en su lugar que me acordase de mi sacerdocio de médico y abordarse el estudio de estas comidas suculentas desde el punto de vista de la higiene. Ahora sí sería ocasión de repetir mis críticas austeras contra el abuso de las salsas.

> And now may be the place for me to be reminded of my priesthood as a physician and treat the study of these succulent meals from the perspective of hygiene. Now it would be the time to repeat my austere critiques against the abuse of sauces.

He echoes his description of Pradera as a *sacerdotisa*: "mi sacerdocio de medico" (my priesthood as a physician).[87] The repetition places his career in parallel to Pradera's; both are similarly engaged in the drive for modernization. Rhetorically, they are priest and priestess of their respective undertakings.

Yet, Marañón only seems to abandon his position as a medical expert. He emphasizes this role in choosing not to criticize Pradera's cuisine: "sería hacer traición a la autora de este libro" (it would be a betrayal of the author of this book). Marañón writes that he prefers the humble role of "simple pecador y como español amante de las glorias nacionales" (simple sinner and Spanish man who loves [the country's] national treasures). Nonetheless, this attempt to distance his cookbook prologue from his status as a public health expert actually draws attention to him as a powerful adjudicator of health and taste in Spain. Marañón's roles as an actual *técnico* (expert) and not just rhetorical *sacerdote* (priest) of Spain's modernization give authority to his final assertion that "hoy la cocina de España—hay que repetirlo—es una de las mejores del mundo y uno de los blasones más auténticos de su progreso" (today Spanish cuisine—it must be repeated—is one of the best in the world and one of the most authentic displays of her progress).[88]

Most importantly, this assessment goes to the heart of the contradiction in Marañón's construction of Pradera: Not only is Pradera's cuisine one of Spain's "glorias nacionales" (national treasures), but that cuisine, one of the most authentic representations of Spain's progress, is the work of a woman whom Marañón identifies as the incarnation of Basque tradition.

Contemporary readers may want to understand Marañón's identification of Pradera's cooking with Basque tradition within a nationalist paradigm. This was certainly the case; but Marañón and other intellectuals understood regional diversity like that which Pradera expresses as representative of Spanish nationalism rather than a Basque one. Lara Anderson and Eugenia Afinoguénova have demonstrated that Spanish cuisine of this period, in addition to Spanish national identity, was defined by the unity in its regional diversity. Anderson explores this through the state's commissioning of Dionisio Pérez's *Guía del buen comer español* (1929) to promote tourism as part of a "top down" model of creating national cuisines.[89] Afinoguénova's work details how Spanish officials experimented with tourism to engage regional patriotisms to unify the Spanish nation.[90] Even if there is no contradiction between Pradera's Basqueness and how it represents a Spanish national identity, the contradiction that still exists is between tradition and progress.

Thus, the idea that Marañón advances is that Basque traditions are both preferable and more modern than *castiza* ones. Pradera's Basque cuisine maintains its ties to tradition even as it embodies Spain's progress: "Quien ha hecho, como ella, gratas tantas horas de la vida de muchos seres humanos; [. . .] y hacer resaltar, en cuantas ocasiones se le presentan, los progresos y excelencias de su patria" (Who has made pleasant, like her, so many hours of so many humans' lives; [. . . and who] distinguishes, on so many occasions, the progresses and excellences of her homeland). And it is part of the "primera línea, el auge de las cocinas regionales, que han dado gracia, modernidad y suculencia a la vieja y tradicional cocina castellana, también excelente, pero más propicia para paladares rigurosas e indígenas que para ser gustada por las gentes extranjeras" (first line, the boom of regional cuisines, that have bestowed grace, modernity, and succulence to the old and traditional Castilian cuisine, also excellent, but more suited to severe native palates than to those of foreigners). Basque cuisine contributes its modernity and grace to a traditional "cocina castellana" (Castilian cuisine) better suited for native palates.[91] Unpacking these assertions reveals two sides to Marañón's culinary thinking.

First, this perspective, like those studied by Afinogúenova, ignored the growing political activity of Basque nationalists, a reactionary traditional identity that rejected industrialization in the region and the accompanying industrial bourgeoisie. By contrast, Marañón acknowledges how cuisines like Pradera's are of a "relativamente" (relatively) modern boom; it is part of a "tradición centenaria" (centenary tradition), not an ancient one. And it was made possible by the industrial development of the area and San Sebastián's tourism industry (la moda del veraneo), to which he credits the refinement of Pradera's cooking and diffusion of her renown. With these connections, Marañón distances Pradera from association with Basque nationalism; the industrialization he credits was bitterly opposed by nationalists. What he links instead is a taste for cuisine like Pradera's cultivated by tourists, foreign and domestic alike, who arrived to the city via railroads.[92]

Marañón identifies Pradera as an unequivocally modern phenomenon. Her cooking would not be possible in the absence of the economic and infrastructural changes brought about by the Basque Country's development, nor would her restaurant, which depended on the service and tourist economy that developed as a result of industrialization. For example, Marañón makes a case for connecting cuisine, modernization, and modern culinary attitudes in the example of fish. Previous to improvements to the transportation infrastructure that occurred under Primo in the 1920s, in the interior, fish was reserved for days of "mortificación y vigilia" (self-denial and fasting); it was a "castigo del cuerpo en los días de cuaresma, pero no regalo de los sentidos" (a punishment to the body during Lent, but not a gift to the senses). With the modernization of the roads system, fish and the Basque "arte ligero en su preparación" (light art of their preparations) could disperse throughout the country and thus became a symbol of "el buen comer español" (Spanish good eating).[93] Regional preparations, ingredients, and specialties could become part of a national culinary tradition due to domestic tourism.

Further, in his description of Pradera's cooking and the industrialization that made her cuisine and culinary success possible, Marañón extrapolates the development that gave rise to Pradera's cuisine and supported her restaurant to the modernization occurring throughout Spain. This perspective hides the fact that development like what was happening in San Sebastián did not happen all across Spain. The sweeping economic changes that converted a supposedly traditional way of eating into something appreciated by a monied and powerful bourgeoisie masks how these same dynamics were making the lives of peasants and workers more precarious. Recipes for Basque fish dishes may represent "el buen comer español" (Spanish good eating) in Marañón's vision, but outside of coastal areas, the significant expense of the ingredients makes them a symbol of bourgeois acquisitive power.

Secondly, a modern Spanish cuisine reflecting regional tastes is necessary because the traditional Spanish cuisine—a *castiza* one—is off-putting for modern palates. Regional cooking styles enhance and give variety to Spanish national cuisine.[94] Recall that they are graceful, modern, and succulent in contrast to the old and traditional Castilian cuisine appreciated by natives if not foreigners. Moreover, "son las que elaboran la reputación buena o mala de las cosas en el mercado de la opinión internacional" (they are those that create the good or poor reputation about things in the market of international public opinion).[95] The tradition represented by the "mesa castiza" (the *castiza* table), according to Marañón, is not appealing to "gentes extranjeras" (foreigners).[96] In referring to ideations of Spanish tradition based on medieval and early modern *casticismo* and how regional cuisines like Pradera's give "gracia, modernidad y suculencia" (grace, modernity, and succulence) to *castiza* ones, Marañón reveals the stakes of his promotion of Pradera.[97] Pradera is both an essentialized, popular figure of Basque tradition and the author of a cuisine that trumpets the "excelencias y progresos" (excellences and progresses) of Spain. Representing Spain's modernity through Pradera's cuisine allows Marañón to adjust what constitutes Spanish "authenticity" to promote a modern vision of Spain to foreigners—"el mercado de la opinión internacional" (the market of international public opinion).[98]

In this way, Marañón attempts to shift the paradigm framing Spain's modernity. Pradera's cuisine is modern and represents progress at the same time that she is traditional and "authentic" due to her deep ties to the popular (national) practices of Spain. This construction is essentially and necessarily contradictory. Spain's "traditions" are fundamentally anti-modern; they are rooted in an imagined medieval heritage and become the central issue in the early twentieth-century debates about the persistence of the *leyenda negra* and Spain's regeneration. The primary image circulating in the international market—primarily Europe, but elsewhere, too—was one of backwardness, not progress.

In both his prologue to Pradera's cookbook and in his "Breve ensayo," Marañón writes about how tourists to Spain—the international market for Spain's reputation—function as a mechanism of Spain's development. Eugenia Afinoguénova and Jaume Martí-Olivella articulate how tourism circulates identity as a commodity to a marketplace of consumers, and state support of the circulation of Spain's identity, history, and landscape would promote Spain's development.[99] As Marañón alludes, for tourism to work as a development project, the tourist's experience of Spain must be a good one, not one that continues to reinforce the *leyenda negra*.

In the prologue to Pradera's cookbook, Marañón laments the *leyenda negra*'s persistence:

[E]n el caso de España la famosa leyenda negra, que pesó durante siglos sobre nosotros, como una nube sofocante, estaba en gran parte formada con la humareda densa del mal aceite frito; humareda, en parte, real; pero sobre esta realidad, amplificada y ensombrecida por la ligereza de unos, la mala voluntad de otros y la indiferencia de los más.[100]

The case of Spain [and its] famous black legend, which weighed over us for centuries, like a suffocating cloud, was mostly formed by the dense cloud of smoke from bad frying oil, a dense cloud that, in part, is real; but in addition to this reality, is amplified and has cast a shadow due to the superficiality of some, and the poor will of others and the indifference of everyone else.

His description of the suffocating cloud from bad frying oil echoes criticism of Spain's gastronomical offerings by nineteenth-century travel writers like Washington Irving (1832), Théophile Gautier (1843), Richard Ford (1846), Alexander Dumas (1851), and Hugh Rose (1875, 1877). Their Romantic interest in "wild and romantic scenery" made Spain's remoteness, its mixture of Moorish and medieval heritage, and popular culture a favored destination.[101] These same elements (*casticismo*, the "medieval revival," for example, in addition to Mérimée's novel and Bizet's opera *Carmen* and the development of the *españolada*) comprised Spain's national identity, one promoted by adventure tourists abroad and embraced domestically.

Furthermore, in his "Breve ensayo," Marañón attributes the persistence of the "leyenda negra de la cocina española" (black legend of Spanish cuisine) to travel writers' and tourists' scathing descriptions of Spanish cuisine: "No hay un viajero inglés, francés o de otro país que, al referir en sus conversaciones o en el papel impreso sus impresiones personales, haya dejado de pintar con tintas sombrías la parvedad, la insipidez o el condimento agresivo de los manjares españoles" (There is no English, French, or traveler from anywhere else who, in their personal impressions in conversations and publications, hasn't represented the scant quantity, insipidity, or aggressive seasoning of Spanish delicacies with their dark ink). He blames Mme D'Aulnoy for writing about the "penalidades gastronómicas" (gastronomic hardships) she suffered, and Ford merits censure in an otherwise "penetrating" representation for overlooking the importance of food.[102] Even more "modern" writers misrepresent Spanish cooking and unfairly perpetuate Spain's deficiencies as a tourist destination. Marañón finds Ali-Bab's 1928 assessment to be the most unjust: "España es un hermoso país; pero su cocina es bastante mediocre. [. . .] Realmente, en España sólo es bueno el cerdo" (Spain is a beautiful country; but her cuisine is quite medicore. [. . .] Really the only good thing in Spain is the pork).[103] Ali-Bab's mistake, he insists, was to be guided by "malas compañías" (poor companies) that led him through Spain's "fondas con pretensiones cosmopolitas, y casas con la cocina gobernada por jefes que hicieron su aprendizaje en los transatlánticos o en los trenes" (taverns with cosmopolitan pretensions, and establishments with kitchens overseen by chefs who completed their training on ocean liners or trains).[104]

It appears that Ali-Bab merely took advantage of the tourist infrastructure that guided foreigners to those *fondas* (taverns).[105] By 1928 more than twenty years of state-initiated tourism planning had succeeded in making the country more accessible, in contrast with the inhospitable accommodations and slow transport of previous centuries. Elites saw tourism as a way to integrate Spain into Europe via travel systems and as a method of economic development. That said, how would tourists encounter a version of Spain that was "authentically" Spanish and yet not representative of the backwardness of the *leyenda negra*?

Marañón himself details some obstacles. Spain's emerging tourist infrastructure should have made possible a more satisfying visit for Ali-Bab if not for a lack of information: "Es cierto, sin embargo, que la visión extranjera, al llegar a nuestras tierras, frecuentamente se deforma por insuficiencia de información [...] (It's true, however, that the foreigner's view, upon arriving to our lands, is frequently distorted by a lack of information [...]). Another challenge: "[l]a auténtica y maravillosa cocina española queda reducida a las casas particulares y a ciertos lugares semipúblicos, al margen de las guías oficiales [...]" (the authentic and marvelous Spanish cuisine is only available in the homes of individuals and in semi-public locales that don't show up in official guides). And Spaniards themselves, Marañón writes, persist with "la necia manía de muchos españoles de excitar la atención de los extraños hacia el elemento de casticismo agresivo e inhabitable de nuestra vida, y no hacia el otro: el hospitalario y cordial [...]" (the foolish habit of many Spaniards of drawing the attention of outsiders to the aggressive and uninhabitable *casticismo* of our lives, and not to the cordial and hospitable ones).[106]

Even still, the "authentic" Spain that well-informed travelers might encounter, if they are lucky, may well be the same version that fueled the *leyenda negra*. Marañón suggests that *casticista* Spain is incompatible with Spain's modernity. Its aggressive and uninhabitable *casticismo* authenticates the poor reputation of Spain abroad. To change this requires presenting a version of Spanishness that represents a softer side, the hospitable and cordial element.[107] It must undo the paradox that Spain's modernity precluded authenticity, and vice versa, that Spanish authenticity obstructed modernity.

This is what Nicolasa Pradera represents for Marañón. Marañón's writing about Pradera, then, needs to construct a representation of Spain that is both authentic and modern.

MARAÑÓN'S IDEAL CULTURE

By proposing Pradera as one of Spain's "glorias nacionales" (national treasures), as a representation of Spain's progress, and as an embodiment of the "hospitalario y cordial" (hospitable and cordial) side of Spain that is attractive to tourists, Marañón attempts to redefine "Spanishness" as something that is no longer *casticista*. Through Pradera Marañón suggests a shift in the "components" that comprise Spain's "ideal culture."[108] Spain can be modern and authentic by substituting the traditions at the center of constructions of Spanish nationhood (*casticismo*) for other, equally authentic traditions—like the "popular" cuisine that Pradera cooks. This new representation may remain distant from what tourists can experience just as its excellent cuisine is often "al margen de las guías oficiales, tan sólo conocidos del comedor experto" (outside of official guidebooks, and only known by restaurant experts). Or, presaging what happens later in the twentieth century, Marañón expresses some anxiety about its culinary/cultural commodification: "Es la cocina más propensa a prostituirse por el industrialismo" (It is the cooking most likely to be exploited by industrialization).[109] Nonetheless, Marañón's project has less to do with justifying the existence of Spanish national culture or cuisine, as it was during late-nineteenth century discussions about a national novel or a national cuisine. Instead, the stakes of Marañón's discussion are rooted in the "authored nature" of the national characteristics that he wants to restructure.[110] That is, in his dissection of the *leyenda negra*, the experiences of tourists in Spain, and how Spaniards perpetuate the representation of dark Spain, he makes explicit the act of authoring to which Bendix refers; he proposes that Spain reshape its authentic self.

As a vehicle for Marañón's re-packaging of Spain and his representation of Spain's modernity, Pradera stands up to the tests of both authenticity and modernity. Her cuisine dismantles the *leyenda negra*: "Esta leyenda, digámoslo con júbilo, se ha desvanecido" (This legend, and let's say it with joy, has faded).[111] Marañón celebrates her as as one of "los artistas consumados del fogón que hoy poseemos" (one of the consummate artists of the stove that we have) and makes her an example of Spain's ability to create something modern that incorporates foreign elements without crassly imitating them.[112] In describing how her "descrubrimientos culinarios" (culinary discoveries) quickly become "clásicos" (classics), Marañón praises Pradera for her skill in incorporating elements "extraños" (outside) into her own dishes:

> Y esta es la señal más expresiva de su mérito; que aquí, como siempre, la personalidad se mide, más que por ninguna otra cosa, por la capacidad de captación e incorporación de los valores extraños a la propia sustancia.[113]
>
> And this is the most expressive signal of her merit; that here, as always, renown is measured, more than anything else, by the capacity of one to acquire and incorporate outside/foreign values to one's own essence.

While Marañón never explicitly acknowledges the training Pradera most likely received in French culinary techniques, he refers to it indirectly when he characterizes her success as a consequence of her own merit and adaptability. In this way, he acknowledges France's influence in the production of something in Spain that represents Spain's modernity, but shows that the contact Pradera has had with France and French cooking does not dilute the originality and essential Spanishness of her work: "Es tan recia la fuerza del estilo y de la manera vasca, que aun esos elementos adevnizos o recientes se incorporan con rapidez [. . .]" (The strength and manner of the Basque style is so robust, that even these new or recent elements are incorporated quickly).[114]

Moreover, Marañón places Pradera's cuisine in competition with French cuisine: "como la famosa Nicolasa, que a su paso por la frontera francesa, en San Sebastián, desafía a los mejores maestros de allende del Pirineo" (like the famous Nicolasa, who alongside the French border, in San Sebastián, challenges the best masters from the other side of the Pyrenees). Even in San Sebastián, in a city at France's border that attracts other Europeans who know French cuisine, Marañón asserts that Pradera's skills are outstanding enough to compete for attention with the supposed *maestros* of French cuisine from across the border. She and the other *sacerdotisas* of Spanish cuisine "han hecho, de un modo silencioso, más por el buen nombre de España que casi todos nuestros ministros de Estado" (have created, in their silent way, more for the good name of Spain than almost all the new legislators of the State).[115] Not only does Pradera contribute to the national reputation of Spain, but she is a culinary ambassador who can promote Spain's interests abroad.

RE-PACKAGED AUTHENTICITY AT HOME

Marañón's suggestion that Spain shift the components of its ideal culture—its national identity—in order to create a tourist experience that is both authentic and coherent with modernity has domestic implications in addition to international ones. The circulation of a commodified representation of Spain was as important for citizens as for international tourists, as the following examples demonstrate.

Domestic tourists had been a market for this type of representation since the railroads first arrived to San Sebastián in 1864, soon followed by Isabel II and her coterie of courtiers. Since 1870, media acknowledged the importance of attracting foreign tourists; there were also economic benefits to "keeping wealthy Spaniards 'at home' rather than taking their *reales* to Biarritz or Deauville."[116] A domestic tourism industry focused around seaside resorts and spas like those in San Sebastián attracted increasing numbers of visitors and catalyzed what Walton has described as a "globalization of Spanish social practices and consumption patterns."[117]

This version of Spanishness played a role in masking domestic unrest. Celebrations of local and regional identities served to attract and entertain tourists; it also erased conflicts and strife within Spain. Further, Pack relates that tourism authorities "sought most of all [. . .] to present foreign tourists with a Cosmopolitan and in some ways *dissociated* leisure experience—and to present the same to Spaniards."[118] And writing about San Sebastián, Castells describes how city officials deliberately cultivated an image of a community without conflicts or tensions, in contrast to the class tensions rocking the rest of Spain during the period of San Sebastián's growth as a tourist destination.[119]

Another clear example of this intentional image cultivation comes from Francisco Javier Sánchez Cantón's tourist guide, *Spain*, published in 1930 by the Patronato Nacional del Turismo. Published in English, the book describes Spain's art, architecture, and history to reassure readers that the image of Spain created by nineteenth-century travel writers is no longer accurate. Instead, a modernized, industrialized Spain can cater to tourist comforts. Sánchez Cantón references "outlets for [business] enterprise," "metallurgical industries [which] are worked in accordance with the most efficient technical methods [. . .]," and agricultural progress made possible by "modern machinery and by the introduction of new crops, such as sugar-beet."[120]

Contemporaneous with the development of a tourism industry that crafted an easily consumable experience of Spain were the International Exhibitions staged in 1929 and 1930. Like Marañón's re-packaging of the modernity of Pradera's cuisine, these exhibitions sought to present a version of Spain that could be easily consumed by tourists. Robert Davidson describes these kinds of world's fairs as events in which commerce and nationhood come into contact, and in which participant spectators compare the constructed images of nations to one another.[121] Visitors see representations of progress, or technological advances, and they participate in an experience designed by elites that reaffirms collective national identity.[122] And, as Brad Epps has written, the Poble español from Barcelona's 1929 Exhibition offered "el elevadísimo grado de civilización a que ha llegado la floreciente, sana, laboriosa, honrada y siempre hidalga nación española" (the significantly elevated degree of civilization that has arrived to the flourishing, healthy, laboring, honorable and always noble Spanish nation).[123]

Home, the image of a united nation, and the absence of insecurity, domestic or otherwise, constructed a modern representation of Spain. Marañón's re-packaging of Pradera serves a parallel purpose. She and her cuisine can distract readers or consumers from the specter of national breakdown. Marañón may configure Pradera as an authentic and modern representation of Spain's progress, but his presentation, like a world's fair exhibition, applies a veneer of stability and civility over the unrest incited by the processes of Spain's modernization.

CONCLUSION

As a number of scholars have argued, modern cultural practices can and do exist even in the absence of the economic underpinnings that accompany capitalist modernization (Labanyi, Valis, Cruz). Pradera's and Marañón's roles within modernizing Spanish society contribute to a foundational tension between her culinary practice and the discourses he creates around her, not to mention the meanings he ascribes to her cooking, persona, and career. Marañón distills an image of Spain's modernity in Pradera that elides the upheavals of modernization. He reinscribes a very modern woman, Nicolasa Pradera, into traditional gender and class models, invoking a nostalgia for the sensual links between the foods he consumed as a child and the mother-servant figure who prepared them. Marañón's mythology of Spanish modernity ignores the fact that Pradera is a modern subject whose access to education and training in French culinary techniques along with her upward class mobility ground her culinary project just as much as her peasant Basque origins do.

Using his status as a scientist and statesman, Marañón urges readers to see Pradera and her cooking as the best of *cocina española*. She and her art represent the best of Spain's progress to both an international and domestic market. The public and consumers of this mythology eat according to choice, and Pradera's food in Marañón's framing is seasoned with essentialized ideas about its connection to tradition. This perspective ignores the fact that peasants who created a particular cooking style did so out of necessity and reframes subsistence foodways as meaningful for the state and a national economy focused on tourist experiences. By crafting an experience of Spain that shifts attention from the elements associated with Spain's violence and uneven development, its *casticismo*, to an experience of Spain characterized by the "hospitalario" (hospitable) Nicolasa Pradera, and by converting Pradera into a culinary ambassador for Spain, Marañón promotes a version of Spain not encumbered by the legacy of a *casticista* identity.[124] He repackages Spain's "authenticity" so that it can be compatible with modernity and promotes instead a version of what Spain's modernity could look like if only the processes of modernization—the unrest and threat of breakdown that overshadowed Spain's Republican democracy in 1933—could be safely represented in the figure of a "feliz cocinera" (happy cook) like Nicolasa.

CHAPTER 4

COOKING AND CIVIC VIRTUE
Women, Work, and Barcelona

Maria Badia was one of the thousands of Barcelona women who took cooking classes at the Institut de Cultura i Biblioteca Popular de la Dona (Women's Cultural Institute and Popular Library). Born in the countryside of L'Espluga de Fancolí in 1911, she began her working career as a nanny at ten years old. Seven years later, as a waitress and cook's apprentice, she moved to Barcelona to serve in the home of a German family and began to attend classes at the Institut, specifically those of Josep Rondissoni, one of Spain's earliest celebrity chefs and a long-term cooking professor. Badia labored as a cook for her entire working life. Even after her marriage, and during the years of hunger following the Spanish Civil War, she supported her family through her profession, continuing to work until her seventieth year.[1]

The practices of individuals like Badia are challenging to capture in cultural texts from the early twentieth century. This is especially true for foodwork due to its ephemerality, the characteristics of the women who performed it, and the political and social circumstances that meant such labor was infrequently and incompletely documented. Fortunately, the archival materials of the Institut can elucidate the dynamics and ideas that structured and informed foodwork like Badia's in the context of modernizing Barcelona.

The Institut was founded in 1909 to offer education and vocational training to thousands of Barcelona women. As a destination for a massive migration of peasants, Barcelona became home to a newly mobilizing, urban working class. The Institut sought to engage working-class women as well as those at the margins of the middle class. Its cooking lessons reached thousands of women every year, from those like Badia to the *señoritas* (young ladies) of Barcelona's best families.

Even as the concept of a distinctive cuisine failed to engage all Spaniards in imagining a singular national culinary identity, cooking education that involved "modern" diets and nutritional ideas shaped how women understood their work and their role in modernizing society.[2] This study builds on Charlotte Biltekoff's analysis of modern nutritional science and the discourses of diet and health that were circulating in the late nineteenth- and early twentieth-century United States as part of a movement that sought to teach people how to "eat right." Such a parallel critical lens can help us understand how transnational discourses of home economics and nutrition shaped the training that women received from an institution that legitimized their public-sphere work and acquisition of "culture." If "eating right" is linked to creating a responsible moral citizenry and maintaining social order, as Biltekoff argues, then it is worth examining how "cooking right" was taught in institutions like the Institut and how it promoted values related to women's foodwork and their status as nascent citizens in the rapidly modernizing context of Barcelona.[3]

Both scholarly and lay audiences know something about how Catalan gastronomy has moved into the global public eye through high-profile projects of haute cuisine, Michelin-starred chefs. The antecedents of such projects—visible in the texts and contexts that inform this study of the Institut—have long been ignored, but food studies scholars have begun to forge connections between the processes of modernization, nation-building, social and economic development, and the food cultures of Barcelona and Catalonia. H. Rosi Song and Anna Riera, in *A Taste of Barcelona: The History of Catalan Cooking and Eating* (2019), trace the city's distinct history and culture through its cuisines, demonstrating how food traditions create identities. They argue that pedagogical initiatives encapsulated in culinary texts authored by women contributed to codifying a popular body of Catalan dishes in both the domestic sphere and the developing hospitality industry.[4] Moreover, Montserrat Miller in *Feeding Barcelona* (2015) studies the city's culinary cultures through its market-hall system to understand it as an incubator of female entrepreneurship, flourishing consumer culture, and upward social mobility.

Modern nutrition and modern ideas about the domestic economy also inform the activities of the Institut, consistent with how preoccupations with eating and cooking right characterize Spanish domestic economy handbooks published between 1847 and 1950, according to Enrique Perdiguero-Gil and Ramón Castejón-Bolea.[5] They emphasize how lower-class illiteracy limited the reception of ideas about nutrition and cooking even when the information was designed precisely for that social class. Furthermore, they attribute to Rosa Sensat, the pedagogue whose ideas inform Institut curricula, the framing of domestic economy as another scientific discourse.[6] In a parallel vein, Montserrat Duch Plana and Montserrat Palau Vergés connect the Institut to an understudied version of the *mujer moderna* (modern woman), one that had conservative, nationalist, and Catholic ideals at its heart. They argue that because the space of the Institut was centric and visible in the city, not part of the urban periphery, it created a site of sociability. Courses, education, and social contacts helped women across a spectrum of social classes find a life in common based on courtesy and rational links.[7]

One may ask why a book oriented to feminist-identified and progressive intellectuals also engages the work of the Institut. This is especially the case since common knowledge focuses on its Catholic and conservative identity and associates its cooking classes primarily with the privileged daughters and tastes of the Barcelona bourgeoisie and the imagined readers of the magazines it published, *La Dona Catalana* (1925–1938) and *Claror* (1935–1936). Yet, these perspectives mask the emancipatory ethos that grounded the Institut, especially in its early days: the dignity of women in their working lives and their need for education in order to acquire "culture." It also participated in forging a new, modern culinary identity for the city through the foodwork it engendered and the ways it educated women about nutrition and the domestic economy. A close analysis of the Institut *Actas*, in addition to cookbooks recording the classes taught there, and the testimony of key players, like founder Francesca Bonnemaison, reveal complex and evolving circumstances between its founding in 1909 and the outbreak of the Civil War in 1936.[8] Institut activity and discourses were consistent with first-wave feminist thought from this period even as they revitalized practices associated with traditional domesticity. Institut discourses also framed women's foodwork and home management as legitimate labor and as part of how women contributed to Barcelona's and Spain's modernization in all of its social and political complexity. That cooking and the roles of food had such a prominent place in Institut curricula is hardly surprising given the degree to which both cooking and eating right were theorized as essential ways to strengthen the citizen bodies within the shifting dynamics of modernizing Barcelona.

This chapter will first offer an analysis of the Institut as a progressive if also Catalan nationalist and Catholic organization. With information gleaned from its *Actas* (annual reports) from years 1912 to 1935 (formerly held at the Biblioteca Francesca Bonnemaison), in addition to the records of cooking classes published in the series of *recetarios* (recipe books) by head professor Josep Rondissoni, I will show how the Institut defined itself, its programs, outreach, and students in relation to the changes taking place in the city.[9] This analysis aligns the Institut and its offerings with several currents of first-wave feminist thought from within Spain in addition to transnational ideas about modernizing women's education that were circulating during this period. A close study of the writing of Rosa Sensat reveals the politics and concerns to which the Institut's educational and cultural initiatives responded: specifically fears about nutritional degeneracy, which education and "socialization" would ameliorate. Ultimately, the Institut's classes re-framed women's activity to give it broader social relevance and provided them with the cultural, moral, and practical education that would enable their economic independence, facilitating what historian Julie Reuben describes as community-based citizenship. And yet this education also inoculated women with ideas and values that undermined their identification with the working class, whose political and social unrest was associated with degeneracy and a lack of preparation for modern liberal citizenship.

MODERNIZING BARCELONA AND WOMEN WORKERS

Barcelona, and Catalonia more broadly, was a locus of modernization and industrialization. Known throughout the nineteenth century for its textile manufacturing, its population doubled between 1860 and 1910 from 244,401 to 587,284.[10] Although industrial opportunities brought people to the city, it also meant that the poverty characteristic of rural life was transferred and concentrated there. Tensions emerged between the growing working classes and an increasingly powerful haute bourgeoisie eager to spend. Robert Davidson characterizes Barcelona during the most raucous years of this period as a boom town. The streets were marred by bombings and political assassinations. Protests and strikes precipitated a suspension of civil rights.[11] At the same time, the prosperous built new monuments to their increasing wealth.

Barcelona's well-known *Eixample* or enlargement/expansion was imagined by Utopianist Idelfons Cerdà in 1860 to respond to the demographic shifts brought on by modernization. Decades later, material improvements to the city's infrastructure, including sewers, gas lines, transport, phone lines, and new buildings were all things Barcelona sought to show off during the 1929 Exposition. This modernization also involved food. According to Miller, the city's market halls supplied food to the growing popular classes in all the city's neighborhoods.[12] At the same time, they indicated how the women whose labor provisioned it and who moved through the city's public spaces acquired new social roles as actors in Spanish modernization.

Women comprised significant numbers of Barcelona's increasing population and its workforce: of the more than half a million inhabitants in 1910 52.62 percent were women; they were 81,000 of the 156,000 textile workers with regular work in the city. An early adopter of the capitalist rationale that industry could pay women less—in textiles particularly between 30 and 50% less—Joan Güell, the industrialist whose name you recognize due to the Gaudí-designed Parc Güell, hired more women than men at his Vapor Vell factory beginning in 1846.[13]

According to Álvaro Soto Carmona's study of the working class, women's activity in the labor market was one marker of the transition between the household as the primary site of family labor and public space. Male worker salaries were woefully insufficient to cover the basic needs of proletariat families, so women's work outside the home was commonplace, even if considered as an "ayuda" (help or aid) by the state, rather than the primary financial support of a family.[14] Data about the numbers of women working outside the home throughout Spain is difficult to generate since it was common to falsify this information or simply not report it, especially in the spheres of domestic service or agriculture. That said, Juan José Morato's study, "La vida de la mujer," published in the *Heraldo de Madrid* in 1906, indicates that 52 percent of women were employed in the agricultural sector, 24 percent labored in domestic service, while 5 percent had jobs in the liberal professions or commerce.[15] State legislation regarding women's work, rather than establish protections or ease women's participation in the labor market, functioned to create more obstacles based on ideology and "la necesaria protección de los más débiles" (the necessary protection of the weakest), a circumstance that persisted even under the Constitution of 1931. The result was the state's institutionalization of women as a "mano de obra barata, con limitada oferta de empleo, pero, a la vez, con gran movilidad y escasa cualificación, a la cual lo único que se le garantiza es el poder reproducir la clase a la que pertenece" (an inexpensive workforce, for whom limited employment existed, with significant mobility and few qualifications, meaning that the only guarantees were the ability to reproduce the social class to which they belonged).[16] Even with working-class women comprising 15 percent of the female population in Barcelona, according to the 1905 census, this data leaves invisible the numbers of women who worked from within their homes or the homes of others.[17]

For factory workers and the increasing number of women who began to seek paid employment in stores and restaurants, as telegraph operators, and as secretaries, the nineteenth-century separate spheres ideology in which women influenced public life as mothers and wives from within the home became less relevant to their daily lived experiences. At the same time, women also began to seek training for new work opportunities from a number of civic institutions, ranging from worker unions to organizations like the Institut.[18]

WOMEN'S CULTURE IN A MODERNIZING CITY

The Institut was directly engaged in bringing "culture" to women and preparing them for public employment. Founded in 1909 following Barcelona's Semana Trágica, it was the first women's lending library in all of Europe and America.[19] From the beginning, its founders planned to offer courses in subjects ranging from stenography and typing to languages, bookkeeping, and applied arts. Its mission: to offer scientific, artistic, and manual knowledge to foment the moral and material well-being of working-class women.[20] Over the next decade it would expand its offerings to include basic and secondary instruction, advanced courses in domestic economy and business, and even a specialized *Escuela de camareras y cocineras* to train women for restaurant work.[21]

Its politics were Catholic and linked through its founders and high-profile patrons to the Catalan Lliga Regionalista, a conservative political party that represented the interests of industrialists and middle-class Catalan nationalists. Its leader Francesc Cambó was a close ally of Institut founder Francesca Bonnemaison and her husband Narcís Verdaguer Callís, who was also a member of the Lliga.

The Institut prepared women to take on the demands of modern life without losing their "bienestar moral y material" (moral and material well-being). With employment as a central pillar of its early activity, it aligned with early twentieth-century feminist thinkers and activists who championed women's economic independence. The shortages and economic crises of the First World War (during which Spain remained neutral) gave employment for women a new acceptability. This contrasted with the hegemonic ideology of domesticity that made women the economic responsibilities of fathers, husbands, or other male relatives, as Nelken frames it.

First-wave feminists in Spain held a diversity of ideas about civil and legal rights or suffrage for women (conventionally seen as the heart of liberal citizenship).[22] The vote and a number of additional rights would come in 1932. Left-leaning thinkers and activists used sexual difference as a paradoxical strategy in arguing for equality with men and recognition of rights specific to women.[23] Conversely, conservative Catholic feminists linked Catholicism to national-liberal patriotism and gave Catholic women public roles in establishing this link. Leaving the domestic sphere of the home would allow women to use their maternal natures to combat threats to the nation, society, and church. Women's progress was framed as a sign of much-desired modernity for Spain, even if its most radical and left-leaning proponents were those who thought women unprepared for and unsuited for suffrage.[24]

In addition to outside employment, household work and motherhood were primary concerns of feminist writers of the period. Women's roles within the domestic space were part of the "revolution" that began in the nineteenth century and that required "el cambio de la condición política, doméstica, económica, educativa y moral de la mujer" (the change of the political, domestic, economic, educational, and moral condition of women).[25] Essays in the Barcelona magazine *Ilustración de la mujer* addressed domestic work "and the need to uncouple it from woman's culturally assigned roles"; for example, the assignment of domestic work should fall to women or men based on logical aptitude rather than whim.[26] In other examples like the Spiritist and anticlerical magazine *La luz del porvenir*, published also in Barcelona between 1879 and 1894, Cándida Sanz de Castellví establishes a "paralelo entre el claustro y el hogar" (a parallel between the cloister and the home) based on the idea that sensibility and ideas are interdependent. She uses socialist language to describe the home as the "gran taller de su progreso" (great workshop of progress), and the mother is "una de las principales obreras de la civilización" (one of the principal workers of civilization). Domestic work and reproduction have value like public-sphere work. As Arkinstall argues, "female-authored essays in *La Luz* did not reject the figure of the Angel in the House, but insistently reworked this conservative symbol to give her a greatly extended sphere of influence and underscore the inseparability of home from nation."[27] Carmen de Burgos, as studied in Chapter 2, and María Martínez Sierra also voiced feminist perspectives that engaged a woman's femininity, that is, her "domesticity, maternity, and care-giving."[28]

The First World War became "un momento clave" (a key moment) for Spanish feminist thought, during which working-class and lower-middle-class women entered the labor market in numbers that exceeded those of previous periods and spurred the creation of feminist reform.[29] The involvement of women outside of the aristocracy and haute bourgeoisie meant that Spain's spectrum of feminist thought—radical, conservative, and Catholic—became more complex, divided, in Scanlon's assessment, or even antagonistic, according to Nelken.[30] Further, these divisions also reflected women's frequent "double militancy" as both political and feminist activists.[31]

The two roles—women as domestic angels whose labor was essential to progress and modernization and also as social and political subjects who increasingly sought greater roles in the public sphere through their work—were present in how the Institut was structured by founder Francesca Bonnemaison. She was most well known for her militancy within the Lliga Regionalista and as an advisor to her adoptive son Francesc Cambó during Primo de Rivera's dictatorship. This profile, along with the association of the Institut with the Francoist Sección Femenina after the Civil War, have obscured her broader contributions to the city and its women. She could have followed the traditional path of women of her class (the monied, conservative, and Catalan bourgeosie). In opting for public service, she founded what biographer Dolors Marín Silvestre describes as an "escola de ciutadania per a totes les dones de Barcelona" (a citizenship school for all of Barcelona women).[32] She left no body of formal writing for scholars to consider today; yet, her political activities and her work with the Institut must be considered alongside that of other Barcelona-based feminist thinkers of her time, among them Carme Karr d'Alaforetto i Alfonsetti and Catarina Albert i Paradis, in addition to Josefa Massanés Dalmau and Dolors Mondserdà who directed their efforts toward the church, beneficent organizations, and educational activities.[33]

The initial idea for the Institut was first suggested to Bonnemaison by Josep Ildefons Gatell (1834–1918), the priest who ran the Casa de Caritat of Barcelona in addition to l'Acadèmia de la Verge de Montserrat i de Sant Lluís Gonzaga. Gatell theorized new roles for women that could "contenir els marits en moments de revoltes urbanes, o de militància radical" (restrain husbands in moments of urban unrest or radical militancy). He was among the most progressive in the Church at the time, notwithstanding his writing against freethinking and concern about the appeal of socialism and anarchism to the working class. He sought to keep the working classes connected with the Church and away from the "reivinicacions laborals" (demands for just worker rights) of labor unions and worker associations. Part of his strategy was to educate workers. By creating a library for women within the Santa Anna parish, Bonnemaison could work within this vision to introduce "una petita modernització" (a small modernization) of women's social roles from within the Church. Bonnemaison ran with the idea, initially within the established parameters to "donar cultura" (give culture) to girls within the parish, only to convert it into her own more progressive project that aligned with the need to provide women with a technical education, in addition to a moral one. She understood that women needed training in order to earn their own way in the labor market.[34]

These aspects of Bonnemaison's political identity and work place her activities and those of the institution she founded squarely within a Catholic feminist framework. According to Inmaculada Blasco Herranz, Catholic feminism was relational in nature and considered women as liberal subjects in the classical sense, while emphasizing the family, motherhood, and complementarity between men and women, in contrast with equality feminism or individualist oriented feminisms associated with Anglo-Saxon models. Catholic feminist activists developed a framework for their departure from the home: their maternal qualities could be deployed to combat the threats facing the nation, society, and the Church.[35] Women's projection of feminine qualities through social action was the key to social reform. Ultimately, Blasco Herranz argues that this common discourse based on patriotism "permitted [women] to claim political citizenship."[36] Marín Silvestre also locates Bonnemaison's activism within this context: her feminism was linked to the "reformisme catòlic, que reivindica el dret a la pertinença dins la societat de la dona, però segueix subordinant-la a un paper secundari d'auxiliar de l'home" (Catholic reformism, that reclaims the rights of women and their belonging to society, but continues to subordinate them to a secondary role of helper).[37]

Bonnemaison's creation of the Institut was decidedly progressive: it acknowledged the realities of working and working-class women in Barcelona and created programs and installations to support them. For example, its primary offerings, the "Clases generales," were imagined for working women—"las clases trabajadoras"—to provide education and support so they could "ganarse mejor la vida" (better earn their living).[38] To that purpose, evening course schedules were reserved for working women to accommodate a day's labor, while *obreras* between the ages of 12 and 14, along with women who were not employed, were encouraged to attend daytime classes.[39] Sunday programming offered workers both entertainment and time to relax, in addition to expanding their professional and domestic knowledge.[40]

In addition, members were allowed to pay tuition and dues on a sliding scale: "protectoras" (protectors or patrons) from the middle class paid 1 peseta a month in 1918, while "numerarias" (numerary members), workers age 12 and above, paid 2 pesetas per year or 2 cents a month.[41] When the Institut moved from its Carrer Elisabets location in 1922 to its new installations in the Carrer de Sant Pere Més Baix, it installed a space with baths and showers so members could practice good hygiene, in addition to an affordable restaurant where women from peripheral neighborhoods could take their midday meal. Furthermore, the Institut maintained a Bolsa de Trabajo (Jobs Board) that facilitated employment for women educated there. According to an interview with Vincenta Carreras, Secretary of the Institut in 1927, the Bolsa de Trabajo was so well known that women from "lejanos países" (distant countries) wrote to the Institut for support in finding a position in Spain, "una gloria" (a treasure) that demonstrated its far-reaching reputation.[42]

Throughout the 1910s and 1920s the Institut emphasized its focus on working-class women. In 1923, *Actas* state:

> El movimiento de socias del Instituto de Cultura y Biblioteca Popular de la Mujer ha sido notablemente progresivo durante el año 1923. Las socias activas, que lo són todas las de la Institución, se dividen en Socias Protectoras y Socias Numerarias, con igual derecho unas y otras a las ventajas que les ofrece la Institución. [. . .] Las clases [. . .] constituyen la base y fundamento de nuestra Institución, se fundaron en el año 1910, con vistas a que las muchachas pudiesen beneficiar de la introducción del servicio femenino en despachos, casas de comercio, bancos, etc. que entonces se iniciaba. Esta circunstancia, aprovechada a tiempo, y el no haber escaseado nunca los medios a fin de que nuestras alumnas encontrasen en las enseñanzas del Instituto de Cultura todo lo que las preparase para darles superioridad sobre las demás empleadas en general, ha sido sin duda alguna la causa de que, con la bendición de Dio, las clases hayan adquirido un desarrollo siempre progresivo bien manifiesto.[43]

> The activities of members of [the Institut] have been notably progressive during the year 1923. Active members, which include all members of the Institution, are divided into Protectors and Numeraries, each with rights to the advantages that the Institution offers. [. . .] Classes [. . .] constitute the base and foundation of our Institution, they were founded in 1910, with the idea that young women could benefit from the introduction of women's service in offices, retail spaces, banks, etc., that was just beginning. This circumstance, taken advantage of in time, and given that resources have never lacked so that our students find in the Institution's teachings all that prepares them and makes them superior to other employees in general, has been without any

doubt the reason that, with God's blessing, the classes have acquired a well-established progressive growth.

This extended quotation emphasizes that both working-class and middle-class members enjoy the same opportunities within the Institut and that the education of women is tied directly to their potential as superiorly prepared candidates for positions outside the home. The Institut frames its mission and work in progressive terms. This quotation also stresses that the Institut was *interclassista* (crossed class barriers) and engaged in fomenting a model of the emancipated and educated *mujer moderna* (modern woman) within a space of "sociabilidad femenina" (feminine sociability) undergirded by Catholic and Catalan nationalist ideals, as Montserrat Duch Plana and Montserrat Palau Vergés have argued.[44] Somewhat paradoxically, especially for those who tend to see women's kitchen work through the paradigm of domesticity, this progressive ethos extended to how the Institut taught cooking—the most successful and in-demand of all the classes offered between 1911 when they first began and the outbreak of the Civil War.

COOKING RIGHT

"Cooking right" as taught at the Institut was a pathway toward culture, education, and stability for women of both the working and the middle class. The curriculum presented a model of culinary taste tied to Barcelona and its modernity, a taste that women had key roles in developing. Examining the focus, content, and ingredients of Institut classes gives insight into how women embodied a new political subjectivity and how cooking intersected with social class. The evolution of "cooking right" also illuminates the history of the Institut itself, from its *interclassista* founding ethos to its gradual loss of progressive values through the 1920s and '30s.

Despite dominant associations with middle-classness or a cosmopolitan and transnational cooking style, Institut classes were transformative for working-class women. The earliest were taught under the direction of Monsieur J. Pince (or Mr. Pince) in 1912. As segments of mini courses lasting approximately eight days, "Culinaria" (Of cooking) classes took place between 6 and 7 or 8 p.m. Subsequent years saw the development of "Cocina práctica" (Practical cuisine) classes taught by Mr. Pince (1914–1915) and a weekly course on "Confitería y repostería" (Sweets and baking) taught by Don José Jansá. The intended audience for these classes were women who cooked in their own homes but whose knowledge was deemed inadequate to the nutritional needs of their families. We see this in the example of classes in "Cuina casolana" (Home cooking) from 1915 that combined cooking lessons with rewards for punctuality and attentiveness: students were quizzed on class topics and could earn money for correct answers; attendees who arrived on time shared the prepared dishes; and the scheduled times enabled women to attend after work.[45]

Additionally, classes in "Cuina popular" (popular cooking) taught a specific set of dishes, but also provided an opportunity for instruction about students' "deberes morales, de la higiene, de la dietética y de todo lo que pudiere ser de utilidad para ellas y para el cumplimiento de su obligación" (moral obligations, about hygiene, nutrition, and all that could be useful for [women] to fulfill their responsibility). Most compellingly, *Actas* indicate that a number of women attending this particular class in 1923 requested additional instruction in reading and writing: "se abrió exclusivamente para ellas unas clases de lectura y escritura [...]." Their skills progressed so much that by the end of the term they could take their own class notes: "algunas que al ingresar en las clases no sabían escribir, antes de terminar el curso tomaban por si mismas las notas de la clase de cocina."[46]

These classes in "Cuina popular" (popular cooking) were the most sought after among working women. Segura Soriano describes them as a success without precedent that, in 1922 alone, drew in more than 40,000 women. Those who attended regularly earned certificates of accomplishment to help with employment as *cocineras* (cooks) in private homes, restaurants, or hotels. The Institut also taught limited classes in "Cuina de règim" (Cooking for special diets), classes on cooking for diabetics or those suffering from other gastrointestinal illnesses, nutrition for children and infants, and *rebostería* classes that were never quite as successful as other courses.[47] Another example of how an Institut education offered paths toward professionalization: it opened a specialized Escuela de Camareras y Cocineras in the early 1920s. Advertisements for the course were published via weekly menus in Barcelona newspapers.[48]

Information about the working women in the "Cuina popular" classes exists mostly as anecdotes with few exceptions. Among them, Maria Badia, whose career is referenced in the introduction, has had her life and those of "àvies treballadores" (worker grandmothers) like her fictionalized in *El camí de les Aigües* (2017) by Carme Martí i Cantí.[49] Additionally, Segura Soriano references others who went on to work at and direct some of the most well-known restaurants in the city—for example, Can Borrel de Meranges—or who later published well-known cookbooks like *La cuina de l'àvia*.[50] Their careers are difficult to trace in official discourses, but these are the women

FIGURE 4.1. *Classe de cuina pràctica.* Report documentat / Crònica documentada. (AGDB_ICBPD_Report1922_01). Institut de Cultura i Biblioteca Popular de la Dona, 1922. (CAT AGDB UI183). Image provided by and printed with permission of the Secció d'Arxiu i Gestió Documental, Diputació Barcelona.

whose training at the Institut made possible their professionalization and allowed them to support themselves via cooking outside the home.

And yet, Josep Rondissoni is the culinary figure most closely associated with the Institut's cooking classes, rather than the women who actually took them. His story begins in 1918, when he was listed as the professor of "Cocina práctica," in addition to Don Maneul Muñoz and Don José Torras who worked as professors of "Repostería" and Srta. Adela Medrano who oversaw courses in domestic economy.[51] Supposedly of Italian origin and Swiss family, his biographical details are difficult to confirm.[52] He was born in Turin in 1890 and perhaps spent part of his childhood in Switzerland. He came to Barcelona from France in 1914, possibly to avoid conscription, and worked as a chef in a variety of restaurants and hotels, including the Casino de l'Arrabassada. His identity and European connections, especially with the French culinary giant Escoffier, added to his allure, as the Casino attracted a mostly foreign clientele with a taste for French cuisine.[53] He stayed with the Institut after it passed into the hands of the Sección Femenina until 1953.[54]

Actas do not specify which cooking classes Rondissoni taught directly or merely supervised; they do indicate, however, that he taught "Cocina práctica" courses regularly from the day of his arrival. This course was designed for middle-class women who did not work outside the home and were thus

FIGURE 4.2. *Laboratori de cuina.* Report documentat / Crònica documentada. (AGDB_ICBPD_Report1922_02), Institut de Cultura i Biblioteca Popular de la Dona, 1922. (CAT AGDB UI183). Image provided by and printed with permission of the Secció d'Arxiu i Gestió Documental, Diputació Barcelona.

able to attend in the late morning. *Actas* from 1924 indicate "Se matricularon a la misma buen número de señoras y señoritas de la alta sociedad de Barcelona que asiduamente asistieron a ella" (The same good number of ladies and misses from Barcelona's high society matriculated [in the courses] and attended regularly).[55] This division between the "Cocina popular" classes imagined for working-class women and the "Cocina práctica" classes for women from "l'alta societat de Barcelona" (the high society of Barcelona) continued into later years as well, despite the fact that both classes featured many of the same dishes and menus.

The styles of cooking taught at the Institut under Rondissoni's supervision were no longer based on practices of necessity nor transmitted through traditional networks of women. Even in courses like "Cuina casolana," teaching home cooking in a professionalized instructional space indicated that the knowledge and skills of women about how to feed their families no longer cohered with how cooking and eating were understood in the modern city. The Institut's teaching kitchens reinforced a gendered culinary authority and also framed cooking as a scientific practice: one was a theater-like space in which women were seated in a semi-circular formation on elevated platforms, which enabled them to observe Rondissoni at work. The other, located on the fourth floor, was a "Laboratori de cuina" (Cooking laboratory) reserved for students completing supervised hands-on activities.[56]

While Segura Soriano connects the male supervision of women's cooking to its growing "cientifisme" (scientific thinking) in the 20th century, what we actually see in the Institut is a manifestation of gendered culinary authority that has existed for much longer. In Spain, the model of a male culinary professional has antecedents in early modern court chefs like Montiño. Jennifer Davis identifies this as the dominant patriarchal narrative, one that obscured in France a more flexible system with both male and female cooks.[57] Following these models, it is no surprise that culinary authority at the Institut resided with male professors. Even though female leaders at the Institut were actively disrupting limitations on women's professionalization, the culinary hierarchy persisted and is still visible in professional kitchens to this day.

Through its in-person classes and the cookbooks it published beginning in 1924 the Institut communicated a transnational style of cooking accessible to "todas las inteligencias los más sútiles refinamientos de la cocina más adelantada" (all levels of intelligence [and] the most subtle refinements of the most advanced cuisine).[58] Menus were sophisticated and complete, including references to culinary practices outside of Spain interspersed with practices that were clearly linked to Catalan cooking. For example, the menu for the week of November 10, 1924 features Nyoquis a la Romana (Roman gnocchis), Tonyina a la Bordelesa (Bordeaux-style tuna), Perdiu a la Catalana (Catalan-style partridge), Mousseline d'espinacs Francfort (Frankfurt-style spinach mousse), Delícies a la Loreta, Pastissos Princesa Lluïsa (Princess Louise Cakes).[59] This sample menu includes recipes that are meant to feed between two and six people. One striking characteristic involves Rondissoni's use of manufactured ingredients, including canned goods, Maggi seasoning drops, and the Bensdorp brand of cocoa.[60] Otherwise, all other ingredients are whole foods that could be procured in a city marketplace, with recipes calling for between 7 and 12 ingredients each.[61] Quantities are indicated with precision—in grams, *cullerades* (tablespoons) or *copetas* (small cups)—as is the time required to prepare a dish. For example, about the recipe "Perdiu a la Catalana": "Ho deixarem coure tot plegat destapat, a foc viu el 15 minuts primers, i a foc més lent y tapat, el restant de la cocció, que ha de durar aproximadament 45 minuts" (Let it cook all together, uncovered and at high heat the first 15 minutes, and then at lower heat and covered during the rest of the cooking time, which should last around 45 minutes). Each recipe also indicates instructions for the presentation of the dish; for "Tonyina Bodelesa," instructions specify that the plate used must be heat resistant and also appropriate for the table. Most recipes also include a final paragraph with precise instructions about the style of dish for service, the arrangement of the food on the plate with any garnishes, instructions for sauces, and how to ensure it is served at the appropriate temperature.[62] Characteristics of any authorial voice that could be attributed to Rondissoni are limited. That said, the written form of these recipes uses first person commands (prepararem, tallarem, deixarem), which reflects the format of the book as a representation of in-person cooking classes in which Rondissoni, observed by students, followed the steps to create the dish. Further evidence of this dynamic comes from the notes at the end of many of the recipes that specify who the scribe was for the day's class: for example, "Nota presa en el dia d'avui per la senyoreta Dolors Coris" (Note taken on this day by Miss Dolors Coris).[63]

What do all these details about Rondissoni's cooking style actually mean, for Barcelona and for his students? Contemporary thinkers attribute to Rondissoni and his courses a shift from a "modest" and "monotonous" cuisine shared by middle-class *señoras* and working *cocineras* alike to one that was decidedly modern.[64] That shift involved attention to details: time, quantities of ingredients, presentation, the formation of an "appropriate" menu, all of which communicated the modernity of the family eating this food in addition to the professionalization of the *cocinera* who prepared it. Attention to the cost of a recipe or meal's preparation is another consideration that has been attributed to Rondissoni, even though this detail is not indicated in the cookbooks the Institut published or the *Actas*.

Curators of the exhibition *Menús de Guerra* identify Rondissoni as one of a generation of chefs from Spain's Second Republic whose innovations established a special culinary tradition in Barcelona/Catalonia that has been continued by contemporary celebrity chefs such as Ferran Adrià, Carme Ruscalleda, Joan Roca, Carles Gaig, and Nando Jubany (Montañés). Manuel Vázquez Montalbán, one of Spain's most famous contemporary gastronomical writers, attributes the creation of the "mejor paladar barcelones" (best Barcelona palate) to Rondissoni, who "no solo enseñaba a cocinar desde un gusto sintético de cocina francesa y Española, sino que además enseñaba a armonizar menús desde el punto de vista del paladar, la dietética y el presupuesto" (not only taught cooking from a syncretic taste involving French and Spanish cuisines, but also taught how to harmonize menus from the perspective of taste, nutrition, and budget). He links Rondissoni's "syncretic" style to the apex of the Barcelona bourgeoisie's development of taste, which also produced its well-known Modernist art and architecture.[65]

This notion of bourgeois taste encapsulates new criteria related to how folks thought about cooking and food beyond their association with modernity. The *señoras* and *señoritas* demonstrated their status through joining the Institut and attending Rondissoni's classes. For the working-class women who sought to improve their employment prospects, Rondissoni facilitated "modern" ways to think about and practice foodwork while offering opportunities to improve their reading, writing, and general nutritional knowledge. Davis has discussed the role of the cookbook as an educational resource that performs "social work" in order to facilitate "communication between classes."[66] Institut classes and cookbooks participated in this dynamic. They consolidated a new and modern version of elite/bourgeois taste in Barcelona in addition to re-educating non-elite cooks. Davis writes, "taste both distinguished one class from another and operated as a social currency, binding members of each class to one another in relationships of service and obligation."[67] As a site of encounter for these dynamics the Institut created representations of cooking—through classes, cookbooks, meals served at the *comedor*, or that showed up in popular media—that "socialized food," a "modern," transnational style, that became associated with the city's culinary identity. [68]

Cooking classes were easily the most prominent and visible parts of the Institut's culture and its version of women's education. They incentivized working-class women's professionalization as cooks and in other domains and also communicated modern ideas of nutrition to improve the health and well-being of women and their families. However, they also maintained class divisions, divisions that ultimately had consequences for the Institut and its evolving identity. Cooking right within the Institut meant one thing for its middle-class members and something quite different for the working-class women that it was founded to serve.

FROM CULTURE TO CONSUMPTION

Despite its *interclassista* ethos, Institut archives demonstrate how its progressive agenda lost traction even as it legitimized women's entry into the public sphere through its vision of community-based citizenship. [69] We see this in several areas ranging from its increased reliance on middle-class students and patrons to make up for diminishing financial resources from the government, to closer associations with home-related manufacturers that sponsored its activities.

Archives show that from early on, curricula evolved to cater to the interests of bourgeois families. Requests from "distinguidas familias de nuestra sociedad barcelonina" (distinguished families of our Barcelona society) prompted the Institut to expand daytime "clases especiales" (special classes) that offered the same instruction by the same professors with a side of class stratification.[70] Other offerings underscored that the educational needs of women differed according to class as well. Workers needed courses focused on "enseñanzas comercial, profesional y doméstica" (commercial, professional, and domestic teachings) so that "se les procuran colocaciones en las que puedan ganarse mejor la vida" (they can find positions that enable them to better earn a living). By contrast, "Clases Especiales," along with "cursillos, conferencias, audiciones musicales, visitas instructivas" (short courses, conferences, musical auditions, instructive visits) are for and "soclicitadas por socias que pertenecen a las clases media y alta para ampliar su cultural general" (requested by members that belong to the middle and upper classes to expand their general culture).[71]

Alongside the stratifications in the cooking classes it offered—popular cooking for workers and practical classes for middle-class women—the Institut also embraced a *dona forta* (strong woman) model of Catalan femininity for bourgeois members. Exemplified by founder Francesca Bonnemaison, this woman represented "una petita modernització de l'estat de coses" (a small modernization in the status of things). She was "burgesa i moderna, cultivada i lectora, amatent de la llar i de la tradició" (bourgeois and modern, cultured and a reader, attentive to the hearth/home and to tradition); she was also the partner of her husband, concerned for the most vulnerable, and dedicated to social action all within the boundaries of the patriarchy.[72] The Institut modeled how middle-class women could move into the professions in ways that took advantage of their education and abilities. With the exception of Rondissoni and the chef-professors he supervised, instructional staff, directors, and administrators were all women, many of them among the first to complete university studies in Spain; they included accomplished writers, artists, musicians, researchers, and pedagogues.[73]

Bourgeois women were also essential to the financial functioning of the Institut. It solicited sponsorships from among *protectoras* and other monied affiliates to finance the San Pere installations. Funds were raised via subscription, and different classrooms were sponsored for fees ranging between 5,000 pesetas for a regular *aula* (classroom), 25,000 for the "Clase de cocina," and 50,000 pesetas for the *comedores* (dining rooms).[74] *Actas* reference budget shortfalls regularly after the move to San Pere, especially in relation to expenses for running the kitchens and providing services (cafeteria, baths, showers, etc.) to working-class women.[75] When Primo de Rivera's dictatorship (1923–1931) brought the cessation of subsidies the Institut received from the Catalan Mancomunitat, two Institut administrators, Dolors Baladia Sala and Clotilde Coll, stepped in as patrons of the extraordinarily popular *comedor* (dining room), turning it into a "menjador economic" (economic cafeteria) open to Institut women and other members of women's Catholic organizations.⁷⁶

While outreach to Barcelona businesses had characterized some activities of the Institut since early days—for example, the development of a course of studies for workers at Almacenes El Siglo—the Institut consolidated this type of relationship in 1925 by accepting the sponsorship of the Catalana Gas i Electricitat. The Catalana installed "cuinas de gas" (gas cooktops) in exchange for sponsored classes beginning in April 1926. Initially offered for free, the classes began to charge a small sum (.25 pesetas) after the first year. With two weekly meetings, Wednesday classes were designated for *obreras* (workers) and Saturdays for "las señoritas que ya están colocadas, ya que la mayoría de las casas donde trabajan tienen establecida la semana inglesa y les facilita la asistencia" (the misses who already have placements, given that most of the houses where they work follow the English week and this makes possible their attendance).⁷⁷ In 1927, la Catalana further consolidated its sponsorship by funding a "càtedra de cuina" (professorship of cooking) with a salary of 2,500 pesetas per trimester.⁷⁸

This sponsorship marks a significant shift in terms of the Institut's mission and the women it purported to serve. In media produced by the Institut and its affiliates we begin to see the Institut as a site that cultivates women in the "cooking right" activities, that not only require technical skill but also involve them as consumers. For example, Miller's analysis of the Institut's publication *La Dona Catalana* (1925–1938) charts a presentation of politics, ideologies, and values that present an aspirational model of women as "tasteful consumers" of products ranging from Maggi drops (also present in many of Rondissoni's recipes) to depilatory creams and Kotex sanitary napkins.⁷⁹ In *Ménage: Revista del arte de la cocina y pastelería moderns* (1931–1956), the magazine supervised by Rondissoni and closely linked to the Institut, advertisements feature items and brands that, if purchased, will connote the purchaser's modernity: for example, toilet paper is advertised for "las personas prácticas, modernas y recabidas" (practical, modern, and cautious people) while a recipe for SOS-branded rice gives detailed instructions for how to identify a "saquito acreditado arroz SOS" (authorized packet of SOS rice) from one that is "falsificado" (falsified).⁸⁰

Most significant is also how the Institut itself was marketed to a reading/consuming public. From the second issue onward, Rondissoni's cooking courses were advertised in a correspondence course format with sample recipes to give prospective students an idea of what they would learn. Advertisements for the Institut indicate the range of course offerings and benefits but give special emphasis and a complete paragraph of copy to the cooking classes.[81] By 1934, the success of Rondissoni-branded classes taught in different formats through the magazine and in person had grown significantly with courses held in other capital cities. Furthermore, *Ménage*-affiliated classes at the Institut distributed 25 "obsequios" (gifts) to *Ménage* subscribers in attendance, including everything from the three dishes prepared in the class to olives from the company Aceitunera Española, Dentsana toothpaste, a certificate for the creation of a dress from modiste Fanny, and, notably, a gas cookstove from the latest 1934 Prometheus line.

Historian Megan Elias identifies corporations' interpellation of women as consumers of household goods as the competing discourse that weakened the progressive foundations of institutions that sought to professionalize their activities in the domestic sphere.[82] The previous examples demonstrate how Rondissoni's links to the Institut enabled him to foster the development of branded presence in media circulating in Barcelona during this time. The Institut gained from these connections, undoubtedly as one way to remediate the financial losses of the 1920s. What is also clear is that middle-class women, or women aspiring to that class, were the imagined consumers of the products featured in these media, and less so the working women that the Institut was founded to support.

Compounding this dynamic, the relevance of the Institut's brand of feminism and support was waning in the early 1930s due to the political wakening of other feminist voices and their double militancy, or activism, within left-wing labor movements. In contrast to the goals of these movements, the Institut's brand of "progressive" education was seen as out of step.[83] Evidence for this comes indirectly from descriptions of the activities of its jobs board. *Actas* feature the Bolsa de Trabajo in early years for its success in placing women in a range of positions in Barcelona's growing commercial sector.[84] In the 1920s, however, *Actas* become more critical: women apparently want jobs that they are not qualified for. The Institut blames applicants rather than any deficiencies in their curricula or offerings.[85]

This evolution of Institut values is also visible in perspectives offered by founder Francesca Bonnemaison herself. The Institut had a large role in shifting the prejudices associated with women, making it possible for women to find employment in modern offices and industry. This was so much the case that founder Bonnemaison thought the whole thing might have gone too far in that women had "desatendido 'los gozos de la vida familiar'" (neglected "the pleasures of family life").[86] Segura Soriano recounts interviews with Bonnemaison and Institut secretary Vicenta Carreras in the late 1920s. In a first example, interviewer María Teresa Gilbert begins the interview with a description of the Institut as a "prueba evidente" (obvious proof) that "el feminismo avanza sabiamente encauzado" (feminism is advancing with wise guidance).[87] Segura Soriano notes the diverse connotations communicated by the term *encauzado*, from a sense of control to that of not deviating too much from cultural norms. The interview ends with a statement about the Institut's distance from those of other feminist positions that sought radical changes in the civil rights awarded to women.[88] Bonnemaison herself was even more circumspect in the magazine *Mujeres* in March 1928. When asked if women should occupy positions that previously were destined only for men, she responds, "en algunos casos sí" (in some cases yes) but emphasizes in the closing clauses of her statement that "la mujer pudiera ayudar a su familia sin la necesidad de moverse de su casa" (a woman could help her family without needing to leave her home). She further opines that she does not like the idea of women in politics and prefers instead the model of woman who "con preferencia dedica al hogar todo su tiempo y sus actividades" (with preference dedicates to the home all of her time and activities).[89]

Finally, in the late '20s and early '30s, reiterations of the Institut's mission to support working women all but disappear. Instead, *Actas* from 1932, for example, describe the Institut and the services it offers as "el complemento del hogar de cada una [. . .] no son otra cosa que servicios domésticos puestos al alcance de todas, cuando temporalmente les precisa alejarse del techo familiar" (the complement to the home of each [woman] [. . .] they are nothing other than domestic services made available to all, when for a short time they must leave the family house).[90] In contrast to the progressive vision communicated in earlier *Actas* when working women were the Institut's focus, the tone in 1932 communicates a vision of women as happy homemakers. The sense of the Institut's progressive social purpose has waned.

The cooking right taught in Institut classes must be understood both as part of women's culture and also as an emancipatory intervention. The overwhelming success of these courses shows that the institutionalization of women's cooking labor had an impact on Barcelona's modernizing society. "Cooking right" allowed working-class women to earn their way and enter into the public sphere, and Rondissoni's classes trained generations of them in the cultivation of a specifically Catalan and Barcelona cuisine, according to Manuel Vázquez Montalbán.[91] In this way, the Institut facilitated what Julie Reuben describes as community-based citizenship, distinct from a citizenship based solely on individual political rights.[92] It fomented "community welfare" among members and other women who took classes there, in addition to teaching healthy habits of behavior, hygiene, and morality.

Biltekoff frames "eating right" as a cultural politics that "communicates emerging cultural notions of good citizenship and prepares people for new social and political realities."[93] The civic virtues of eating right and cooking right are linked to citizenship, whether through caring for the social body by educating and bringing culture to women in their home and work lives or through women's practices in public space that indicate identities as political, social, and economic actors. The "cooking right" taught at the Institut was also prescriptive: following Rondissoni's recipes would create healthy, modern, citizen bodies. As Biltekoff has studied in the US context, cooking right, or "eating right," was thought to ameliorate social ills like alcoholism and participation in labor unions with their "demagogues and partisans."[94] These same dynamics—the politicization of women's domestic and culinary work and the use of domestic reform to combat degeneracy—were also at work in Barcelona and influenced the principles upon which the Institut was founded.

DOMESTIC EDUCATION AND DEGENERACY

If we look at the Institut with the broader perspective indicated in Biltekoff's study in mind, one that seeks to understand progressive institutions focused on educating women as similar to others existing elsewhere in Spain, Western Europe, and the United States, it's no surprise that the Institut evolved toward abandoning its progressive roots. Home economics was doubly faceted: as a transnational intellectual movement it offered women employment, emancipation, and a way to use their skills in "that larger household in the city."[95] At the same time, it was also rooted in fears of degeneracy, a concern that became more pressing as the Second Republic ushered in increased political polarization.

Could Spain's underclasses be productive liberal citizens? Preoccupation with Barcelona's "mala vida" indicates that this was a key area of anxiety, one that criminologist Rafael Salillas linked to nutrition.[96] Meanwhile, Rosa Sensat, the foremost theoretician of modern and reformed domestic education in Spain, led the 1918 curricular revisions at the Institut, articulated the scope of a new and "scientific" home economics, and justified its relevance to women across the class spectrum. Institut cooking classes, courses on domestic economy, and Catholic religious instruction transmitted "culture" to women. They also re-defined middle-class practices as scientific and modern. Song and Riera and Miller have studied how cooking education politicized women's foodwork, linking it to Catalan nationalist identities.[97] Understood as part of home economics, it also politicized women's household work as one attempt to mitigate civic degeneracy.

Degeneration, according to Richard Cleminson and Teresa Fuentes Peris, was "seen as a product and a cause of social evils" and manifested through "political subversion" in the form of striking workers. The degenerate exemplified the dark side of progress and modernization. Deviance could be produced as a by-product of poor housing, inadequate working conditions, or the lack of sanitary education.[98] German social theorist Max Nordau identifies it as a side effect of industrial capitalism, while criminologist Rafael Salillas saw it as the potential for a return to a past savagery.[99] The degenerate required discipline and curtailment either through isolation and segregation or through public hygiene campaigns.[100] Anthropology (and its corollary criminal anthropology or criminology) developed in the late nineteenth and early twentieth centuries and used racial ideas to delegitimize workers' movements, separatist initiatives, and other perceived threats to social order.[101] The degenerate were framed both in terms of race—as the result of "missteps, breaks, or derailments in the process of the proper racial fusion that characterized the noncriminal Spanish population"—and in terms of environmental factors ranging from poor hygiene to malnutrition.[102] In other words, degeneration was feared due to its public-sphere manifestation as criminality and political subversion. It could also be prevented through changes in the environment in which children were raised. Nutrition was key to this environmental improvement and also the responsibility of women.

Rafael Salillas y Panzano was a prominent Spanish criminologist who sought a scientific explanation for degenerate behavior in order to reform Spanish penal codes and the treatment of prisoners.[103] He argued that degeneration took place when events interrupted evolutionary development, causing a "stagnation of the character." Goode writes,

> Environmental conditions, not just racial heritage, affected this evolutionary progression. The environment, the levels of nourishment and care one received at the liminal moments of development, as one passed between various stages, were the most important in ensuring proper, healthy, racial formation. Deficiencies in these moments helped create human beings who were degenerate, or delayed, in their physical development.[104]

We can trace this focus on the environment, and specifically the role played by nutrition, or its lack, in Salillas's text *El Delincuente español (Hampa)* (1898).

Salillas writes that the development of deviant figures is linked to "la propia evolución de la nutrición" (the own evolution of nutrition). An accumulation of nutritive elements determines personality type. For example, the "acúmulo más o menos intensivo de los elementos nutritivos" (the more or less intensive accumulation of nutritive elements) produces the social state of *sedenterismo* (sedentariness) "y este estado implica un modo de constitución social que se manifiesta con especiales carácteres sociológicos, psícologicos, y hasta anátomo-fisiológicos" (and this state implies a type of social constitution that displays special sociological, psychological, and even physiological personalities). By contrast, those distinguished by the *nomadismo* (nomadic) type—representatives of the *hampa* (underworld) like gypsies, for example—have in common an ultimately insufficient, disseminated nutritional base.[105] In this way, Salillas links malnutrition to social degeneracy: malnutrition, especially during infancy or childhood, gives rise to delinquency.[106] The home, however, serves as the fundamental "cellular unit" of society and space from which development toward delinquency or toward appropriate civic behavior occurs.[107]

What I've highlighted here displays the common thinking associated with the social and political unrest that were part of modernization, thinking that spanned a range of political ideologies. The connections that Salillas identifies between food, the bodily health of races, and the home also show up in culinary texts. For example, in *La Cuina Catalana* (1928), Josep Cunill de Bosch writes:

> Good female cooks make good foods;
> Good foods are eaten with pleasure;
> Food eaten with pleasure is that which is most beneficial;
> Food that is most beneficial is the fittest for maintaining the individual in a healthy state.
> Maintaining the individual in a healthy state means that its functions are regular;
> Regular functions make the strong races;
> The strong races lead all the others and over the long term become masters of the world.[108]

These ideas underscore the importance of both cooking right and eating right to modern politics, the modern state, and a Catalan nationalist identity.[109] Following Cunill de Bosch's (or Rondissoni's) recipes for cooking and eating right will create healthy, modern, citizen bodies. Failing to do so threatens degeneracy. This is essentially an argument for euthenics, the corollary philosophy to eugenics.

Where theories of eugenics propose that a "race" could reverse degeneracy and improve its future by "encouraging better breeding" and "eliminating the unfit" through sexual selection, euthenics focuses on improved living environments. Euthenics could create better citizens in the present, rather than wait on subsequent generations. Dietary reform was understood as a central way for a society to protect itself from the threats signaled by degeneracy and a way to encourage improved living conditions in the home.[110] Euthenics, and its central idea that social problems ranging from malnutrition, criminal behavior, and also housewifely drudgery, could be solved through scientific research endured under the label of home economics.[111]

In Spain domestic education, including cooking, was a standard component for those girls who had access to it since the nineteenth century.[112] However, early twentieth-century activists saw reforms in its teaching as essential for Spanish modernization. Reformers called for improvements at the First Congress on School Hygiene in Barcelona in 1912 and at the Fourth International Conference on Popular Education in Madrid in 1913. Like their contemporaries in North America and elsewhere in Europe, they proposed to make its teaching "scientific" and to re-frame the kitchen as a laboratory. As outlined in the Introduction, Emilia Pardo Bazán also connected home cooking to the health of the nation and the Spanish race.

In the US context, the transnational home economics movement has been studied at length. Dismissed initially by women's historians as a "conspiracy" to limit women to domestic roles, historians have since focused on the field as an organized social movement that sought to professionalize and rationalize women's domestic work through the application of physical and social sciences to the domestic space.[113] Movement leaders sought to discover the best ways to perform housework and also imagined new professions for the women who would be drawn to remunerated work connected to the home. From the outset the field encompassed "interconnected and sometimes contradictory agendas."[114] And yet, it articulated how the home and its dangers—from malnutrition to poison and disease—could be managed by women via the sciences of nutrition, bacteriology, and interior design.[115]

The Institut also exemplifies the contradictory facets of the home economics movement. It was led by women and, with the exception of cooking classes, women formed the ranks of its faculty. It professionalized women's knowledge and the areas of education most often associated with

FIGURE 4.3. *Cuina del restaurant. Pràctiques de les alumnes de l'Ensenyament Domèstic.* Report documentat / Crònica documentada. (AGDB_ICBPD_Report1922_03). Institut de Cultura i Biblioteca Popular de la Dona, 1923. (CAT AGDB UI183). Image provided by and printed with permission of the Secció d'Arxiu i Gestió Documental, Diputació Barcelona.

domesticity, and it taught domestic economy as a scientific field. Cooking education made up a significant part of its home economics courses.[116] For example, class plans and notes from Magdalena Cambrera's "Curset d' Economía Doméstica," taught in 1916 through 1918, links women's education to public society emphasizing that "totes les nacions avençades se preocupen per la creació d'escoles menagére" (all advanced nations are concerned with the creation of schools that teach domestic science).[117] Of the 22 lessons offered, more than half dealt with "scientific" nutrition.

Rosa Sensat was a key proponent of understanding domestic economy as a scientific subject alongside Dolores Villan Gil and Dolores Nogués Sardá. This group of thinkers framed the kitchen as a focal point of a household, as a home laboratory.[118] A first-wave feminist with ties to Carmen Karr, Leonor Serrano, and Dolors Mondserà, among others, Sensat connected the world of feminist thinkers of her generation to that of the new teachers she was training to modernize education for girls. Author of *Les ciències en la vida de la llar* (1923) in addition to *Cómo se enseña la economía doméstica* (1927) among other books, book chapters, and reports, Sensat also re-designed Institut curricula in 1918 as its pedagogical director.[119]

Recall that the early twentieth century saw women and girls arriving in Barcelona for factory work or employment as domestic servants in private homes, hotels, or restaurants. At the same time, women who in previous decades might have hidden their paid labor inside the home to maintain the appearance of middleclassness now entered the public labor force in increased numbers with the new acceptability that employment acquired after World War I. Even as the Institut served both groups of women, theories of home economics that were grounded in science and, at the same time, oriented toward improving the social environments of women and their families were part of the education on offer. We see all this in Sensat's writing.

Her manuscript "Per a l'escola secundària en projecte de l'Institut de Cultura i Biblioteca Popular per la Dona" (1922-1923), indicates the school should be a center for technical and professional education in service to women's economic independence. Language from Institut *Actas* and its mission appears in Sensat's text, relating to how the women preparing for paid employment would be enriched by "una base de cultura científica i artística" (a foundation of scientific and artistic culture) that would ensure their success and superior performance in their professions.[120] More generally, women would acquire a "cultura general intensa, per a guiar-se en la vida, 'qualsevulga que sia la direcció que hagi d'emprendre i ésser dona de sa casa capaça de vetllar per l'educació dels seus fills i conduir la seva llar amb ordre i precisió'" (strong general culture, to guide them in life, 'in whatever direction she sets out for and to be a woman of her home, capable of providing an education for her children and managing her home with order and precision').[121] Education within the framework that Sensat outlines would strengthen the environments in which all women lead their lives, organize their homes, and raise their children. Order and precision would structure these efforts.

In her later work, *Cómo se enseña la economía doméstica* (1927), Sensat acknowledges an entire spectrum of women: those who take advantage of new educational opportunities and like men achieve economic stability; urban wage earners; and those who may only aspire to marriage and homemaking. For all, she prescribes a new, practical way of learning about domestic economy. By focusing on the critical thinking behind household practices, "el cómo y el por qué" (the how and why), domestic drudgery is transformed from the domain of the "vulgar" housewife to an "intelligent activity."[122] In kitchen laboratories, like the one that formed part of the Institut's installations, women carry out cooking experiments in chemistry, physics, and mathematics. Classes and classrooms are adaptable to the "medio en que la joven ha de vivir" (circumstances in which a young woman has to live), meaning that teachers' homes can be converted to laboratory-classrooms in rural areas or instruction can be offered through "cursos ambulantes . . . que pasan de un pueblo a otro" (mobile courses . . . that move from one town to another).[123]

Most importantly, a "progressive," "scientific" education about domestic economy inoculates the groups of women most worrisome for the reform-minded against the socially created conditions that foment degeneracy: the liberally educated "new woman" whose modern ideas and possible disdain for the domestic that sociologists link to possible "desquiciamiento y ruina" (madness and ruin), according to Sensat; and working-class women who earn wages through their labor but who lack knowledge about the best way to spend those wages in support of themselves and their families.[124] Traditional venues of domestic education are no longer sufficient: "La economía doméstica como conjunto de recetas de prácticas caseras, transmitidas de madres a hijas [. . .] ha desaparecido" (Domestic economy as a collection of recipes and household practices, transmitted from mothers to daughters [. . .] has disappeared).[125] And really, it was always suspect, according to Sensat, because unenlightened women would ignore the "deberes más elementales" (most basic tasks) which had deleterious consequences for the health and hygiene of the entire family, and, by extension, Spanish society and the nation.[126]

When women prepare dishes like the "cocido del país," "Arroz a la milanesa," and "Macarrones a la italiana," calculate "los tantos por ciento de alimentos simples que contienen las sustancias" (the percentages of basic nutrients that foods contain), and monitor dishes, quantities, and prices, they practice modern, scientific cooking. They also practice setting the table correctly, serving and being served in the Institut *comedor* (dining room), ensuring that dishes look appealing, and that they exhibit "buen gusto" (good taste).[127] These practices of cooking and eating right are not "una cadena opresora" (an oppressive shackle) in Rosa Sensat's words, but a "guía amable y una orientación que preserve a la mujer de caer en las equivocaciones y errores" (friendly guide and orientation that keeps women from making mistakes and errors) of problematic nutrition.

And yet, these calculated quantities, precise times, and exact budgets also attempt to impose discipline over home kitchens, environments, and domestic practices. They communicate middle-class values cloaked in scientific language. If bourgeois stability is what the degenerate threatened with strikes, alcoholism, and malnutrition, lessons in cooking right serve to introduce women to ideas and ideals that inhibit their identification and that of their families with the working class. The ideal and imagined publics for domestic education were working-class women. Their increasing identification with members of the same social class could only lead to degeneracy even in the thinking of Spain's most progressive.

CONCLUSION

The culinary discourses disseminated through the Institut sought to reach women across the class spectrum as economic and political subjects with roles in Barcelona's modernization and that of Spain. As political/economic subjects, women participated in ways of cooking, doing, and thinking about their foodwork and other domestic tasks that signaled their modernity, a modernity shared across nation-states in Europe and the United States. This study of the Institut reveals that its legacy was rooted in progressive feminist values even if they shifted for ideological and economic reasons over the three decades toward increasing conservatism.

The Institut's culinary legacy has persisted in the form of Josep Rondissoni's work, which is credited with informing a transnational and cosmopolitan culinary style for the city. But credit must be given as well to the many thousands of women who took classes with him, learned about modern cooking and nutrition at the Institut, and took that knowledge into their homes and their paying jobs. What these women also took with them was a cooking style newly dependent upon the branded and manufactured items that Rondissoni included in his recipes and that Institut-aligned publications raffled off to students and advertised as essential to modern life. As in other contexts, this interpellation of women as consumers of the household goods produced by corporations contributed to diluting the progressive identity of the Institut just as it shadowed the intellectual movement of home economics elsewhere.[128]

Examining women, the institutions that supported them, and their foodwork critically produces contradictions and juxtapositions.[129] The Institut's food politics were complex, ingrained in first-wave feminist thought that sought to value women's contributions and their potential as political, social, and economic subjects. At the same time, its version of feminism seems discordant with those that sought to liberate women from the responsibilities of the home. In this sense, Montserrat Miller's assessment that the Institut "rejected and ridiculed feminist discourses that might encourage women to overlook their essential domestic responsibilities" is accurate.[130] But it's also accurate to say that the Institut promoted feminist discourses that redefined domestic work as a professional and professionalized domain that would shape the environments that produced modern citizens. It legitimized and institutionalized that working women were community citizens and part of Barcelona's modernity, despite ideological values that would seem to support the persistence of the angel of the house paradigm. Criminologist Rafael Salillas identified nutrition and the home as elements that produced degeneracy; modern, scientific cooking and domestic work could improve the environments producing Spain's future, liberal citizens.

The dominant paradigm through which we tend to understand home economics and domestic economy is certainly not a feminist one. Roberta Johnson communicates this clearly in her outline of the chronology of Spanish feminist thought in her book *Major Concepts in Spanish Feminist Theory* (2019). About the dictatorship of Francisco Franco, when "gains made under the Second Republic were rescinded and earlier legal codes reinstated," she writes, "[e]ven worse, some aspects of women's roles that were formerly a matter of social convention (e.g., domesticity) became institutionalized through the Sección Femenina de Falange that required women to attend courses in cooking, housekeeping, and child-rearing."[131] What I discern in this framing is that women's work was only aligned with the social convention of domesticity previous to the Francoist institutionalization. But my investigation of the Institut shows that this is not the case. The Institut institutionalized women's labor associated with the home—particularly their foodwork—as part of Barcelona's modernization. What we don't see is a version of what Lara Anderson describes as women's culinary subjectivities under Francoism: that women became subjects who followed [culinary] instruction and showed an absolute respect for male authority.[132]

It does a disservice to understanding early twentieth-century women and culinary discourses when we conflate institutions like the Institut with what we understand about the Sección Femenina and nineteenth-century ideas of domesticity. Studying the cultural and food texts produced by the Institut and its affiliates through a feminist food studies lens reveals the range of meanings produced by women's foodwork as part of a larger cultural politics. And it also calls on scholars to re-examine how foodwork intersected with both feminism and class politics during early twentieth-century Spain.

CONCLUSION
FEMINIST FOOD STUDIES AND SPAIN

This exploration of women's foodwork and its representation in culinary discourses from early twentieth-century Spain has allowed us to answer these questions as posed in the introduction: What are the roles of culinary writing in the oeuvres of key twentieth-century intellectuals like Pardo Bazán, Burgos, and Marañón? Why did they produce in these genres and what do those works indicate in relation to their other writing on modern Spain and its future? Given that culinary discourses, cookbooks especially, were conventionally aligned with women and domesticity, how do these writers engage and dispute that framework? Are women interpellated in new ways? Does the genre elicit new behavior or thinking? Finally, how does the study of the culinary discourses, feminist concerns, and political activities of these writers and of the Institut enrich our understanding of first-wave feminism in Spain as it developed toward democracy?

We have seen that Pardo Bazán's culinary writing makes home cooking part of a national discourse, where Spanish women both safeguard a national patrimony and through elegant and modern cooking help bring about Spanish modernization. At the same time, Pardo Bazán appears to give in to cynicism about the capacity of middle-class women to adopt the ideas of feminism that she sought to impart. What she ignores—as a consequence of her social status and class conservatism—are precisely the ideas that working-class women might adopt. Her writing about this population is anything but progressive. It's all too consistent with perspectives of other elites whose fears about workers becoming liberal citizens led them to suppress and resist their organizing efforts. In Pardo Bazán's culinary writing, rather than being recognized as proto-citizens, working-class women are depicted as incapable of modern cooking. In this sense, it's worth asking whether her cookbooks were intended to elicit new ways of thinking, or whether she wrote them for herself with an imagined audience of her male peers in mind. For Pardo Bazán, the working class is only meaningful as an idealization: women contain the traditions of the past in their culinary practice. In the present, in order to "count" as modern, they must adopt middle-class attitudes and mindsets in order to fulfill the pre-requisites of modern, liberal citizenship.

By contrast, the paratextual materials that Carmen de Burgos included in her cookbooks indicate clearly that she considered her culinary writing a valuable aspect of her strategy to reach Spanish women through genres and formats aligned with their interests and means. She was an *escritora-ama de casa* because that role, despite its pejorative connotations, gave her special insights into how to engage her *ama de casa* readers. She demonstrates clearly how cooking and its discourses have public-sphere and political consequences. Her sociology of Spanish cuisine indicates that cooking and eating have long been discourses engaged by the erudite and the intellectual, and she proposes a modern definition of Spanish taste with women at its center.

Gregorio Marañón's construction of chef Nicolasa Pradera offers additional insights into how Spanish elites understood the importance of culinary discourse even as they mythologized food and foodwork. Through Pradera, Marañón offers a version of Spanish modernity and cuisine that remain authentic even as they appeal to outsiders. However, he also erases how Pradera moved from being a member of the working class as a household servant, through culinary education, to the status of an established restaurateur. This erasure serves as a metaphor for how his culinary writing also ignores the challenging social and political events of the 1930s in its efforts to promote a mythology of Spanish modernity coherent with the ideals of tourism rather than those of a developing democracy.

Finally, what does a culinary education similar to the one Pradera acquired from Ignacio Doménech make possible for working-class women in Spain? To answer this question, I looked to the Barcelona Institut de Cultura i Biblioteca Popular de la Dona, one of a number of institutions in Spain (and across Western Europe and the United States) that taught cooking classes in addition to home economics and professional skills. Each year the Institut reached thousands of Barcelona women across the class spectrum, institutionalizing their cooking and other nutritional practices as part of Barcelona's modernization and also engaging them as political and economic subjects. Josep Rondissoni's connection with the Institut and the culinary activities that took place there has certainly cemented its reputation and style of cooking as part of Barcelona's identity. And yet, despite a progressive founding ethos—to support women in their working lives and bring them culture—the Institut must be understood in a context where cooking and other domestic practices were taught to stave off degeneration and prevent these women from identifying with the working class.

Reflecting on these ideas, we can see that the print cultures of cuisine also played a key role in modernization by circulating new thinking about food and domestic spaces. Representations of cooking as a legitimate discourse with consequences for the nation, citizenship, and modernization influenced women. But some degree of literacy, even if it was just developing as was likely the case for some Institut students, was a requirement in order to engage cuisine as a meaningful cultural code.

Our first three chapters contextualized the work of three women who challenged hegemonic thinking about the roles they could occupy. What makes their culinary discourse fascinating is how they operated within a genre that superficially communicated no challenge at all. This demonstrates the complexities and juxtapositions of women's foodwork, especially when those who represented that work in print also needed to negotiate the power dynamics that shaped their lives, influenced what and how they could write, and determined how their successes would be represented in the press or literary history. All this adds nuance and dimension to how we understand feminist thought and women's activity in the first decades of the twentieth century. Foodwork deserves consideration as an area of feminist study despite its long-term association with domesticity. This approach is all the more pressing given how the Franco regime institutionalized a regressive domesticity and rolled back so many of the political and social gains women had made under the Second Republic and before. That this indoctrination persisted throughout the long years of Franco's regime is another reason for serious scholarly attention.

This study makes clear that the culinary discourses of these writers and the Institut were important to Spain's modernization and also compelled new thinking about the roles of women and new behavior among them. Pardo Bazán's writing shows this in relation to the roles of idealized popular women and Spain's national cuisine, in addition to revealing how women can practice modernity by caring for aesthetics of their cooking and their tables. Burgos makes feminist ideals approachable and compatible with mainstream understandings of women's work in the period. Moreover, her framing shows women how they are already doing feminist work with the tasks that comprise their daily lives; her historicization of that work demonstrates its broader social and political impacts. As a site of education in modern cooking and modern civic ideals, the Institut is perhaps the most powerful example of how women's practices shifted. The cooking taught at the Institut prescribed new processes, ingredients, and values (in contrast to the "modest" cooking transmitted through traditional networks of practice). It framed women's foodwork as a professional domain and also taught scientific home economics in order to stave off degeneracy among those at most risk, working and working-class women. These analyses together show the cultural, political, and literary significance of women's work, both as significant for understanding Spain's modernization process and demonstrating the centrality of a feminist perspective.

In looking toward future areas of study about women, their foodwork, and culinary discourses more broadly, we must begin to ask why critical studies of food and food cultures have been slow to develop within Iberian cultural studies. In their field-defining collection, Helen Graham and Jo Labanyi identify the elitism of twentieth-century Spanish thinkers who focused on national identities (or a singular national identity) rather than construct a body of cultural theory that would later on serve as the foundation for the development of Spanish cultural studies as a field.[1] They also note how Republican intellectuals and other progressive thinkers were polarized between several positions that also show up in this study. Some posited culture as a way to achieve civilization, a version of the position we see articulated within the Institut. Others sought to preserve expressions of popular culture even as they "were difficult to reconcile with modernity"; Pardo Bazán exemplifies this position in how she romanticizes popular food practices, while Marañón attempts to mythologize them in ways that are coherent with modernity. A third position was that of elitists who reacted to these circumstances by turning against the cultural expressions of the masses in the vein of Ortega y Gasset. Then Franco's regime, as Labanyi and Graham note, used culture as a tool of national unification and political pacification.[2] In relation to food culture, this third point is key.

The strength of food identities is reinforced through the daily necessity of eating. National cuisines also exert strong pulls, even when the conditions to create and sustain them across the regions of a nation-state and its social classes, as in the case of Spain, are uneven. The Franco regime's creation of food ideologies made this identity even more powerful, as we are just beginning to understand. Work by Suzanne Dunai and Lara Anderson shows that food is a site of control for authoritarian regimes more generally and that Franco's regime introduced and enforced hegemonic notions of participation in national life.³ Food discourses showed up everywhere in the 1940s in medical texts, media outlets, and cookbooks.⁴ Spaniards "consumed" them even as they also went hungry.⁵ That food rationing continued in Spain into the 1950s, in addition to how the regime exerted control over what could be published about food, undoubtedly left a lasting legacy that has continued to influence which texts and ideas merit scholarly attention, and which do not. Moreover, food's association with women and domesticity has long discouraged serious consideration, even among feminist scholars who continue to frame the kitchen and food practices as spaces of oppression rather than creativity.⁶ Given this it's no wonder that it's taken so long for critical attention to engage food and for food to become a compelling cultural text within cultural studies more broadly. Additional attention to the intersections between Francoist control, women's foodwork, and the construction of a food studies field will continue to be an area of research.

The study of the Institut in Chapter 4 offered an opportunity to dive more deeply into women's work and how it was debated among first-wave feminist writers from a diversity of ideological positions, ultimately focusing on that located within a Conservative-leaning, Catalan nationalist institution, which also identified as progressive and feminist. During this period, both organizations like the Institut and worker unions taught cooking to their affiliates while *cocinas ambulantes* (mobile kitchens) brought cooking education to rural women. These circumstances point to the need for a deeper understanding of Spain's working-class culinary cultures in this period—how did workers navigate food discourses, ideas, and/or regulation—as does the degree of anxiety caused by workers that shows up in Pardo Bazán's writing and in discourses about nutritional degeneracy. Some would argue that "cuisine" is only relevant to those who have the privileges of choice in cooking and eating. Yet, all groups have an identifiable "cuisine," or a set of "protocols," usages, communications, and behaviors in common.⁷ This is more so the case due to the degree that workers navigated the loss of old patterns of life and alienation related to migration and capitalist production.⁸ This issue is also a feminist one: to what degree did Spain's first-wave feminists understand working-class women and domestic servants as engaged in the feminist ideals of modern, emancipated womanhood? ⁹

Future work on projects like those outlined earlier depends heavily on the availability and conservation of archival materials. Even in the case of the Institut, whose legacy still thrives in the Biblioteca Francesca Bonnemaison located at the Institut's San Pere installations, this study owes a great debt to Isabel Segura Soriano's history of the space and its people, in addition to her longstanding relationships with Barcelona archivists and librarians.

The introduction to her book acknowledges the multiple challenges she encountered: archives were housed in a number of different institutions. For access to the boxes of those archives she relied on the goodwill of librarians and archivists, in many cases, working side-by-side with her to identify interesting bits and pieces, and encountering difficulties and challenges, including mold infestations. This example of long-term engagement, persistence, and access to remaining records of early twentieth-century cultural institutions will be necessary to continue work on food and its discursive representations.

In this sense, the publication of *A Taste of Barcelona* by H. Rosi Song and Anna Riera gives an interesting model for future food cultural studies work and collaboration. Song is an established literary and cultural studies scholar of Spain formerly located in the United States and now in Great Britain. Riera, in Barcelona, has a background in communications and marketing, with a particular focus on gastronomy. Experts like Riera and other Spanish scholars of communications and journalism, nutrition, and marketing have formed exciting interdisciplinary institutes that bridge academic works with those oriented toward a more general public. For example, Ana Vega Pérez de Arlucea's writings on several of the authors in this study are another example of this turn as is the research and educational institution she is affiliated with, The Foodie Studies.[10] The dominant fields represented in these interdisciplinary programs tend to be communications and marketing, the social sciences (sociology and anthropology), and the odd nutrition sciences or chemistry faculty member. What is often absent, however, and what cultural studies scholars like Song offer in the model of collaboration represented by *A Taste of Barcelona*, is an analytical toolbox aligned with cultural theory.

In relation to future work, a food cultural studies methodology brings attention to how power circulates in society. It guides scholars toward thinking about how and why certain food practices acquire institutional legitimacy and to inquire how the promotion and representation of food discourses respond to the interests of governments and states, hegemonic groups within those states, and transnational capital. These topics are not neutral. All too often the dominant, highly visible paradigms that frame food and food identities in Spain are accepted and circulate uncritically.

Examples of this dynamic point to an additional area of future study on how food and food cultures are adopted into neoliberal cultural marketing schemes. In 1995 Graham and Labanyi wrote about the "cultural jamboree" produced and reproduced by the concentration of economic power. Multinational capital alongside "plural cultures 'at play'" mask how hierarchal relationships still exist and how power operates.[11] In relationship to food, powerful food paradigms constructed by collaborations between industry, state actors, and non-governmental organizations frame what it means to cook and eat in Spain today in ways that conceal the deeper and more complex narratives of Spanish foodways and those who do foodwork in Spain today. One example is the initiative titled Gastro Marca España, a project of the Real Academia de Gastronomía supported by the Ministerio de Asuntos Exteriores y Cooperación, el Ministerio de Agricultura, Alimentación y Medio Ambiente, ICEX España Exportación e Inversiones (a state entity promoting business and internationalization), and the Cámara de Comercio de España. This site aims to market culture, tradition, and quality of life as elements of gastronomy that have been "siempre vinculada a los atributos más fuertes de la imagen de España" (always connected to the strongest attributes of Spain's image) without mentioning specific details about those elements or indicating which parts of Spanish society, for reasons of social class, education, or insider status, have enjoyed access to them. Its representation is neither scholarly nor particularly nuanced, but it tells a neatly packaged story of food identity without apparent conflicts or tensions.[12]

While this website is a relatively obvious target for criticism since it clearly designates its marketing purpose, the uncritical ways it represents food cultures extends to other culture institutions in Spain. Another example is visible as a part of a feature sponsored by the Biblioteca Nacional de España. Titled ChefBNE, the project brings together a diverse array of scholars (historians and archeologists primarily) with chefs, leaders of various gastronomy academies, and food media specialists. The project is a "recorrido por nuestra gastronomía" (tour through our gastronomy) through twelve historic cookbooks held at the BN with chefs and researchers who contextualize the history of "una cocina, el mestizaje de sus ingredients y su evolución" (a cuisine, the fusion of its ingredients, and its evolution). The marketing tagline is "Aprender del pasado para cocinar el futuro" (Learn from the past to cook the future). Of note, the project is sponsored by the Biblioteca, el Ministerio de Turismo y Agenda Digital, and red.es, a public entity working to improve public services and develop the digital economy. It is thrilling to see Carmen de Burgos's culinary writing featured alongside preparations for the *olla podrida* (hodgepodge stew), *Berenjenas a la morisca* (Morisco-style eggplant), and *Letuario de mebrillo* (quince paste), among others. The latter preparations acknowledge the Muslim and Jewish foodways of the peninsula that scholars like Gómez Bravo and Nadeau are treating in food studies criticism. Yet, the decision to juxtapose chef Javi Estévez's preparation of *casquería* (offal), a recipe that appears in Burgos's

La cocina moderna, with commentary about the time it took to prepare traditional recipes for offal and that neither women nor men have time for such preparations today, overlooks two key points. As a woman who worked outside of the domestic space to support herself through her writing, it is unlikely that Burgos as an early twentieth-century working woman had time to prepare the kind of recipe featured. Second, Burgos as a writer and feminist is treated critically (noted biographer Concepción Nuñez Rey makes an appearance), but the food video and the recipe itself completely decontextualize her. Instead, the video markets a male professional chef who seeks to recover traditional recipes for contemporary Spanish consumers with Burgos as an "inspiration from the past" garnish.

The fascinating foodscapes that characterize modern and contemporary Spain involve haute cuisine chefs whose projects since Spain's transition to democracy have converted them into key stakeholders in discussions and debates of Spanish food cultures. They also involve understanding Spain as a compelling site for culinary tourism and studies of such phenomena. I wrote in 2009 about a group of cultural studies scholars from the University of Calgary who traveled with food studies students to explore sites in the country and examine theories of food culture. Rather than study the sociopolitical circumstances that gave rise to a restaurant like Casa Nicolasa, as analyzed in Chapter 3, or the Basque Country's "sociedades gastronómicas" (gastronomic societies), this group focused on Spain as one of any number of sites where twenty-first-century food culture phenomena could be observed. At that point, it offered "the highest number of Michelin stars per capita in Europe," and was "one of the hottest foodie destinations in the world."[13] To understand the foodscapes of Spain and future work should involve a critique of these hegemonic cultural stakeholders' representations of food, in addition to the commonalities between cultivating markets and practices for gastronomical tourism and the "Spain is Different" tourism development of the past.

The questions *Women's Work* raises about culinary discourses and the politicization of women's practices aligned with the home are no less pressing today than they were a hundred years ago. In *Home Away from Home* (2018) N. Michelle Murray brings our attention to the new contours of domestic labor in Spain: that it is largely undertaken by immigrant women. Migration reveals the colonial histories that continue to structure Spanish national cultures. Moreover, domestic labor continues as a site that elicits marginalization, now based on race, nationality, and gender. Spanish law—Royal Decree 1620/2011—frames domestic work as a different class of labor.[14] It legally encodes difference on the basis that domestic work features a special relationship between employee and employer guided by care and an affective relationship. This twenty-first-century labor law encodes disparity based on familiar tropes about women's "natural" proclivities to nurture, which degrades that labor.[15]

As we head into the second decade of the twenty-first century, it is clearer than ever that "food politics is a feminist issue."[16] Women are those most involved in the paid and unpaid labor of producing food, the emotional and caring work to support families, communities, and countries. And yet, all of this work is still tied up in structures of dominance and hierarchies.[17] Women's foodwork connects them explicitly to politics, economic and social changes, and shifting ideas of citizenship. Analysis of this foodwork does reveal tensions and contradictions. And yet, exploring them through culinary discourses allows us to learn more about how women navigated early twentieth-century modernization and new ideas about what it meant to be part of a modern Spanish society. Continued critical attention to women and their foodwork promises to reveal new ideas and new approaches to understanding how women have navigated the complicated cultural shifts of Spain over the last centuries.

NOTES

INTRODUCTION

1. Pardo Bazán, "Condesa de Pardo Bazán (Día 3 de diciembre de 1916)," in *Conferencias dadas en la Escuela del hogar y profesional de la mujer: Curso de 1916–1918* (Madrid: Imprenta de Cleto Vallinas, 1919), 85–103.
2. Pardo Bazán, "Condesa de Pardo Bazán," 90.
3. Pardo Bazán, "Condesa de Pardo Bazán," 93, 96.
4. Roberta Johnson, *Major Concepts in Spanish Feminist Theory* (Albany: SUNY Press, 2019), 115, 118. See also Ubaldo Martínez Veiga, *Mujer, trabajo y domicilio: Los orígenes de la discriminación* (Barcelona: Icaria, 1995), on how women's domestic labor is considered "no-trabajo" (non-work), in Marxist terms.
5. Eric Storm, "When Did Nationalism Become Banal? The Nationalization of the Domestic Sphere in Spain," *European History Quarterly* 15, no. 2 (2020): 205.
6. María Paz Moreno, *De la página al plato: El libro de cocina en España* (Gijón, Asturias: Trea, 2012), 13.
7. Priscilla Parkhurst Ferguson, *Accounting for Taste: The Triumph of French Cuisine* (Chicago: University of Chicago Press, 2006), 8.
8. Susan Leonardi, "Recipes for Reading: Pasta Salad, Lobster à La Riseholme, Key Lime Pie," in *Cooking By the Book: Food in Literature and Culture*, ed. Mary Anne Schofield (Toledo, OH: Bowling Green State University Popular Press, 1989), 126–37.
9. Arlene Voski Avakian and Barbara Haber, *From Betty Crocker to Feminist Food Studies: Critical Perspectives on Women and Food* (Amherst: University of Massachusetts Press, 2005), 2.
10. McFeely explores cooking as a tool of repression in that it designates women's space as the kitchen and as an activity that grants women control over a specific space and work. Inness identifies cooking and cookbooks as practices and texts that offer a path toward power and influence for women in their communities. Theophano identifies the genre as one that allows women to probe

social and cultural identities and transgress them. Mary Drake McFeely, *Can She Bake a Cherry Pie? American Women and the Kitchen in the Twentieth Century* (Amherst: University of Massachusetts Press, 2000), 1; Sherrie Inness, *Secret Ingredients: Race, Gender and Class at the Dinner Table* (New York: Palgrave, 2006), xi; Janet Theophano, *Eat My Words: Reading Women's Lives through the Cookbooks They Wrote* (New York: Palgrave, 2002), 227.

11. Psyche Williams-Forson, foreword to *Feminist Food Studies: Intersectional Perspectives*, eds. Barbara Parker, Jennifer Brady, Elaine Power, and Susan Belyea (Toronto: Women's Press, 2019), x.
12. Barbara Parker, Jennifer Brady, Elaine Power, and Susan Belyea, introduction to *Feminist Food Studies*, 1.
13. Luce Giard, "Doing-Cooking," in *The Practice of Everyday Life, Volume 2: Living & Cooking* (Minneapolis: University of Minnesota Press, 1998), 157, 275.
14. Jack Goody, "The Recipe, the Prescription and the Experiment," in *The Domestication of the Savage Mind* (Cambridge: Cambridge University Press, 1977), 136.
15. Pierre Bourdieu, *The Logic of Practice*, trans. Richard Nice (Stanford, CA: Stanford University Press, 1980), 140–41.
16. Lara Anderson and Rebecca Ingram, "Introduction. Transhispanic Food Cultural Studies: Defining the Subfield," *Bulletin of Spanish Studies* 97, no. 4 (2020): 471–83.
17. Helen Graham and Jo Labanyi, "Introduction. Culture and Modernity: The Case of Spain," in *Spanish Cultural Studies: An Introduction. The Struggle for Modernity* (Oxford: Oxford University Press, 1995), 5; Abril Trigo, "General Introduction," in *The Latin American Cultural Studies Reader*, eds. Ana Del Sarto, Alicia Riós, and Abril Trigo (Durham, NC: Duke University Press, 2004), 3–4. Also see Anderson and Ingram "Introduction" and Parasecoli, "Food, Cultural Studies and Popular Culture," in *Routledge International Handbook of Food Studies*, ed. Ken Albala (London: Taylor and Francis Group, 2012), 274–81.
18. Angela Meah, "Gender," in *Food Words: Essays in Culinary Culture*, ed. Peter Jackson (London: Bloomsbury, 2013), 88; Krishnendu Ray, *The Ethnic Restaurateur* (London: Bloomsbury, 2015), xv.
19. Jacob Wenzer, "Foodscapes," in *Food Words: Essays in Culinary Culture*, eds Peter Jackson and CONANX Group (London: Bloomsbury, 2013), 83–84. See also Appadurai, "Disjuncture and Difference in the Global Cultural Economy" *Theory, Culture & Society* 7 (1990): 296.
20. Rachel Laudan, "Foodways and Ways of Talking about Food," *Rachel Laudan: A Historian's Take on Food and Food Politics* (blog), February 16, 2017, https://www.rachellaudan.com/2017/02/19542.html.
21. Carol Counihan, *The Anthropology of Food and Body: Gender, Meaning, and Power* (New York: Routledge, 1999), 2.
22. Meredith Abarca, *Voices in the Kitchen: Views of Food and the World from*

Working-Class Mexican and Mexican American Women (College Station: Texas A&M University Press, 2006), 5–6.
23. Raymond Carr, "Liberalism and Reaction," in *Spain: A History*, ed. Raymond Carr (Oxford: Oxford University Press, 2001), 224.
24. Carr, "Liberalism and Reaction," 229, 233.
25. José Álvarez Junco, "Rural and Urban Popular Cultures," in *Spanish Cultural Studies: An Introduction*, eds. Helen Graham and Jo Labanyi (Oxford: Oxford University Press, 1995), 82.
26. Carr, "Liberalism and Reaction," 23–34.
27. Raymond Carr, *Spain: 1808–1939*, eds. Alan Bullock and F. W. D. Deakin (Oxford: Clarendon Press, 1966), 521.
28. Carr, *Spain: 1808–1939*, 521–23.
29. Carr, *Spain: 1808–1939*, 241.
30. Álvarez Junco, "Rural and Urban Popular Cultures," 83.
31. Brigitte Mangien, "Cultura cotidiana: Ciudad y campo," in *Los felices años veinte: España, crisis y modernidad*, eds Carlos Serrano and Serge Salaün (Madrid: Marcial Pons Ediciones de Historia, 2006), 136.
32. Jo Labanyi, *Gender and Modernization in the Spanish Realist Novel* (Oxford: Oxford University Press, 2000), 90; Adrian Shubert, *A Social History of Modern Spain* (New York: Routledge, 1990); Jesus Cruz, *Gentlemen, Bourgeois, and Revolutionaries: Political Change and Cultural Persistence among the Spanish Dominant Groups, 1750–1850* (Cambridge: Cambridge University Press, 1996).
33. Roberta Johnson, *Gender and Nation in the Spanish Modernist Novel* (Nashville, TN: Vanderbilt University Press, 2003), 15.
34. María Jesús Matilla and Esperanza Frax, "La doble opresión. Las mujeres de las clases populares entre el XIX y el XX," in *Las mujeres y el 98. Dirección General de la Mujer* (Madrid: Comunidad de Madrid, 1999), 90–94
35. Mary Nash, "Estudio preliminar," *Mujer, familia y trabajo en España 1875–1936* (Barcelona: Grupo A, Anthropos, 1983), 16–18.
36. Mary Nash, "Un/Contested Identities: Motherhood, Sex Reform and the Modernization of Gender Identity in Early Twentieth-Century Spain," in *Constructing Spanish Womanhood: Female Identity in Modern Spain*, eds. Victoria Lorée Enders and Pamela Beth Radcliff (Albany: State University of New York Press, 1999), 31–32.
37. Jean-Francois Botrel, *Libros, prensa y lectura en la España del siglo XIX* (Madrid: Pirámide, 1993), 309.
38. Marco Antonio García, "Propósitos filológicos de la colección 'Clásicos Castellanos' de la editorial La Lectura," in *X Congreso de la Asociación Internacional de Hispanistas* (Centro Virtual Cervantes, n.d), 91.
39. Roger Chartier, "La sociedad liberal: Rupturas y herencias," in *Orígenes culturales de la sociedad liberal (España siglo XIX)*, ed. Jesús A. Martínez (Madrid: Biblioteca Nueva, 2003), 273–74.

40. Carolyn Nadeau, *Food Matters: Alonso Quijano's Diet and the Discourse of Food in Early Modern Spain* (Toronto: University of Toronto Press, 2016), 4–5.
41. Nadeau, *Food Matters*, 22–23. See also the works of Ana Gómez Bravo on Jewish foodways and culinary treatises from the medieval period.
42. Nestor Luján, *Historia de la gastronomía* (Barcelona: Folio, 1997), 193.
43. Maria de los Ángeles Pérez Samper, "Los recetarios de las mujeres y para mujeres. Sobre la conservación y transmisión de los saberes domésticos en la época moderna," *Cuadernos de Historia Moderna* 19 (1997): 138.
44. Luján, *Historia de la gastronomía*, 194.
45. See also Iñigo Sánchez Llama and Catherine Jagoe about how these texts both uphold and subvert domestic ideals.
46. Luján, *Historia de la gastronomía*, 194.
47. Muro was a friend of Emilia Pardo Bazán, Juan Valera, and literary gastronomist Mariano Pardo de Figueroa (Thebussem). In addition to *El Practicón*, he also authored *Diccionario de la cocina* (1892) and a number of articles under the title *Conferencias culinarias* between 1890 and 1897. The *Conferencias* were published in numerous editions in the period. Editions of five thousand volumes would sell out; a single volume would sell for 1 peseta. He was among the first in a group of male chefs and gastronomes that also includes newspaper writer and editor Manuel Puga y Parga (Picadillo), Teodoro Bardají, Ignacio Doménech, among others, whose writing about cooking in the media attracted a wide readership.
48. Ángel Muro, *El Practicón* (Barcelona: Tusquets Editores, S.A, 1894), 13.
49. Muro, *El Practicón*, 13.
50. See Néstor Luján's *Historia de la gastronomía* (first published in 1988) and Manuel Martínez Llopis's *Historia de la gastronomia española* (1981).
51. María del Carmen Simón Palmer, *Bibliografía de la gastronomía española: Notas para su realización* (Madrid: Ediciones Velazquez, 1977).
52. Rafael Climent-Espino and Ana Gómez Bravo, eds. *Food, Texts, and Cultures in Latin America and Spain* (Nashville: Vanderbilt University Press, 2020,), 2.
53. Food studies as an interdisciplinary field is anchored by scholars associated with the Anglo-dominant Association for the Study of Food and Society, in addition to the France-based European Institute for the History and Cultures of Food. The framework of this study reflects this author's engagement with food studies, peninsular cultural studies, and positionality within US academia. As an emerging interdisciplinary field, food cultural studies builds upon scholarship produced across geographic contexts and from distinct disciplines to analyze Spain and its food texts. This approach is one that seeks to dialogue and generate understanding rather than imply that other secondary sources are arbiters of authority. See also Anderson and Ingram, "Introduction."
54. Christine Arkinstall, *Spanish Female Writers and the Freethinking Press* (Toronto: University of Toronto Press, 2014), 4.

CHAPTER 1

1. Nelly Clèmessy, *Emilia Pardo Bazán como novelista: De la teoría a la práctica*, trans. Irene Gambra (Madrid: Fundación universitaria española, 1981), 258.
2. María Paz Moreno, "La cocina española antigua de Emilia Pardo Bazán: Dulce venganza en intencionalidad múltiple en un recetario ilustrado," *La Tribuna: Cuaderno de estudios de la Casa-Museo Emilia Pardo Bazán*, no. 4 (2006): 243–51.
3. Moreno, "La cocina española antigua de Emilia Pardo Bazán," 243–44.
4. Lara Anderson, *Cooking Up the Nation: Spanish Culinary Texts and Culinary Nationalization in the Late Nineteenth and Early Twentieth Century* (Woodbridge, UK: Tamesis, 2013), 110–11.
5. Kate Good, "Women and Huevos: Matters of Food, Religion, and Gender in Emilia Pardo Bazán's 'Los huevos arrefalfados,'" *Decimonónica* 14, no. 1 (2017): 1–15.
6. Hazel Gold, "Del foro al fogón: Narrativas culturales en el discurso culinario de Emilia Pardo Bazán," in *La literatura de Emilia Pardo Bazán* (A Coruña: Casa Museo Emilia Pardo Bazán, Fundación Caixa, 2009).
7. Gold, "Del foro al fogón," 315.
8. Joyce Tolliver, *Cigar Smoke and Violet Water: Gendered Discourse in the Stories of Emilia Pardo Bazán* (Lewisburg, PA: Bucknell University Press, 1998), 36.
9. Raymond Carr, *Modern Spain 1875–1980* (Oxford: Oxford University Press, 2001), 60.
10. Álvarez Junco, "Rural and Urban Popular Cultures," 82.
11. Álvarez Junco, "Rural and Urban Popular Cultures," 82, 85.
12. Labanyi, *Gender and Modernization*, 26.
13. José María López Sánchez, *Heterodoxos españoles: El Centro de Estudios Históricos, 1910–1936* (Madrid: CSIC, 2006), 294; Sebastian Balfour, "The Loss of Empire, Regenerationism, and the Forging of a Myth of National Identity," in *Spanish Cultural Studies: An Introduction*, eds. Helen Graham and Jo Labanyi (Oxford: Oxford University Press, 1995), 30.
14. López Sánchez, *Heterodoxos Españoles*, 296. The ILE was the principal source of liberal nationalism and responsible for its intellectual underpinnings, according to José Carlos Mainer, "De historiografía literaria española: El fundamento liberal," *Estudios de historia de España. Homenaje a Manuel Tuñón de Lara* (Madrid: Universidad Internacional Menéndez y Pelayo, 1981), 471. Additional examples of these canons include Manuel Rivadeneyra's *Biblioteca de autores españoles* (1846); Menéndez Pelayo's continuation of the series under the name *Nueva Biblioteca de Autores Españoles*; additionally, his *Historia de los heterodoxos españoles* (five volumes, 1880–1882), *Historia de las ideas estéticas en España* (five volumes, 1883–1891), and *La ciencia española* (three volumes, 1887–1889); and Padre Blanco García's *La literatura española en el siglo XIX* (1891–1894). Labanyi, *Gender and Modernization*, 14.
15. Botrel, "La novela por entregas," 309.

16. Álvarez Junco, "Rural and Urban Popular Cultures," 83.
17. Jean François Revel in Anderson, *Cooking Up the Nation*, 24–25.
18. Parkhurst Ferguson, *Accounting for Taste*, 19.
19. Anderson, *Cooking Up the Nation*, 25. Labanyi notes that the laws, literature, and history that succeeded in writing the nation into existence formed the representation of a modern Spain that largely existed on paper rather than in measures of modern infrastructure or economic development. Labanyi, *Gender and Modernization*, 26.
20. Anderson acknowledges that Pardo Bazán's works have generally not been included among texts that further culinary nationalism due to what critics perceived as an overreliance on French influences. She argues instead that, as with other nation-building discourses, French or other foreign influences on discursive forms in cookbooks was an "inevitable part of their cultural modernity" and does not preclude considerations of them as nation-building texts. Anderson, *Cooking Up the Nation*, 17.
21. Arjun Appadurai, "How to Make a National Cuisine: Cookbooks in Contemporary India," *Comparative Studies in Society and History* 30, no. 1 (1988): 18–19.
22. See also Eric Storm's "When Did Nationalism Become Banal."
23. Martínez Llopis in Teodoro Bardají, *Índice Culinario*, ed. José María Pisa (Huesca: La Val Onsera, 1993), 13.
24. Emilia Pardo Bazán, *La cocina española antigua*, Biblioteca de la Mujer (Madrid: Sociedad Anónima Renacimiento, 1913), 4, 5; Emilia Pardo Bazán, *La cocina española moderna*, Biblioteca de la Mujer (Madrid: Sociedad Anónima Renacimiento, n.d.), vi.
25. Pardo Bazán, *La cocina española moderna*, 46, 155, 34, 297.
26. Lara Anderson, "The Unity and Diversity of La Olla Podrida: An Autochthonous Model of Spanish Culinary Nationalism," *Journal of Spanish Cultural Studies* 14, no. 4 (2013): 400.
27. Pardo Bazán, *La cocina española antigua*, 10.
28. Pardo Bazán, *La cocina española antigua*, 10, 20. Referring to the recipe for "Migas de nata," Pardo Bazán, *La cocina española antigua*, 22.
29. Pardo Bazán, *La cocina española antigua*, 6.
30. Later criticism by Dionisio Pérez ("Post-Thebussem") insisted that Pardo Bazán colluded in the money-making plans of publishers to have cookbooks in their catalogs that presented French recipes disguised as Spanish. Dionisio Pérez, "(Post-Thebussem)," *Guía del buen comer español: Inventario y loa de la cocina clásica de España y sus regiones* (Madrid: Sucesores de Rivadeneyra, S.A., 1929), 10.
31. Pardo Bazán, *La cocina española antigua*, 6.
32. Pardo Bazán, *La cocina española moderna*, I. Her reference "los hemos mejorado en tercio y quinto" is language specific to Spanish law. See White, *A New Collection of Laws*, 106.
33. Pardo Bazán, *La cocina española moderna*, IV.

34. Pardo Bazán, *La cocina española antigua*, 4.
35. Pardo Bazán, *La cocina española antigua*, 91.
36. Pardo Bazán, *La cocina española antigua*, 11.
37. Pardo Bazán, *La cocina española antigua*, 12. The translation of the *olla podrida* as "hodgepodge stew," which I repeat throughout this study, is Nadeau's. Nadeau, *Food Matters*, 63.
38. Pardo Bazán, *La cocina española antigua*, 12.
39. Pardo Bazán, *La cocina española antigua*, 5, 6.
40. Labanyi, *Gender and Modernization*, 13.
41. The cookbook is not Pardo Bazán's first attempt to participate in the canon creation of her time. Ángeles Ezama Gil identifies the three literary history projects she left incomplete: the *Historia de las letras castellanas*, the *Filósofas y teólogas españolas del renacimiento*, and the *Historia de la literatura mística y ascética*. Of note, Pardo Bazán's Spanish cuisine ties to its former colonies in Latin America. In *CEA*, she requests that readers send her recipes "de toda España y de América" (from all over Spain and from America). Pardo Bazán, *La cocina española antigua*, 5. Additionally, Spanish cuisine "tiene su sello" (has its own stamp) as shown by its extension and evolution in America. She further highlights that in Cuba, Mexico, and Chile national dishes reveal "lo hispánico" (the hispanic) of their origins and the application of Iberian techniques to a new context. Pardo Bazán, *La cocina española antigua*, 6. Despite the collapse of the empire, Spanish cuisine exerts a continuing cultural influence.
42. John Guillory, *Cultural Capital: The Problem of Literary Canon Formation* (Chicago: University of Chicago Press, 1993).
43. Catherine Brown, "The Relics of Menéndez Pidal: Mourning and Melancholia in Hispanomedieval Studies," *La corónica* 24, no. 1 (1995): 18–19.
44. Pardo Bazán, *La cocina española antigua*, 4–5.
45. Regina Bendix, *In Search of Authenticity: The Formation of Folklore Studies* (Madison: University of Wisconsin Press, 1997), 7–8.
46. Antonio Machado y Álvarez, "Introducción," *Folk-Lore: Biblioteca de las tradiciones populares españolas: Tomo I*, (Sevilla: Francisco Álvarez y Ca. Editores, June–Agosto 1883), VIII.
47. Machado y Álvarez, "Introducción," IX–X. For Machado y Álvarez, having and studying popular culture was more important than the communities that created it, despite the innovations represented by his 1881 *Colección de cantes flamencos* and the 1887 *Cantes flamencos y cantares*.
48. Emilia Pardo Bazán, "Discurso leído en la sesión inaugural del Folk-Lore gallego," in *Folklore gallego*, 1884 (Donostia–San Sebastián: Roger Editor/ Biblio Manías, 2000), 10.
49. Pardo Bazán, "Discurso leído," 10. Pardo Bazán uses the term *civilización* in this passage, but her implication is modernization.

50. Neither Pardo Bazán nor Machado y Álvarez view regional folklore as incompatible with their idea of a Spanish nation enriched by its regional diversity. That said, while she emphasizes respecting linguistic irregularities and what she describes as the simple and naive concerns of the uneducated in her work on Galicia (Discurso leído," 11), about cuisine she affirms that the language of Spanish cookbooks should be Castilian Spanish, "castellano castizo." Pardo Bazán, *La cocina española antigua*, 7.
51. Pardo Bazán, *La cocina española antigua*, 5.
52. Pardo Bazán, *La cocina española antigua*, 5.
53. Pardo Bazán, *La cocina española antigua*, 4.
54. Roberta Johnson, *Gender and Nation*, 33.
55. Azorín, *Valencia; Madrid* (Madrid: Alfaguara/Santillana, 1998), 90.
56. Azorín, *Valencia; Madrid*, 22; Johnson, *Gender and Nation*, 31.
57. Pardo Bazán, *La cocina española antigua*, 4.
58. Giard, "Doing-Cooking," 157, 275.
59. Isabel González Turmo, *Comida de rico, comida de pobre: los hábitos alimenticios en el Occidente andaluz (Siglo XX)* (Sevilla: Universidad de Sevilla, 1997), 307.
60. González Turmo, *Comida de rico*, 307.
61. Pardo Bazán, *La cocina española antigua*, 6.
62. Azorín, *Valencia; Madrid*, 22
63. Johnson, *Gender and Nation*, 31.
64. Derek Flitter, *Spanish Romanticism and the Uses of History: Ideology and the Historical Imagination* (London: Legenda, 2006), 130-31.
65. Pardo Bazán, *La cocina española antigua*, 6.
66. Pardo Bazán, *La cocina española antigua*, 4.
67. Flitter, *Spanish Romanticism*, 130.
68. Emilia Pardo Bazán, "[Cartas . . .] (Sobre la huelga, la filología de la cocina, el Diccionario de la Academia)," *Diario de la Marina*, October 22, 1911, in *Cartas de la Condesa en el Diario de la Marina La Habana (1909–1915)*, ed. Cecilia Heydl-Cortínez (Madrid: Pliegos, 2002), 143, 145.
69. Pardo Bazán, "Cartas," 142.
70. Pardo Bazán, "Cartas," 143, 144.
71. Changes include freedom of the press, decentralization, freedoms of association and commerce, the disappearance of consumption taxes, and the abolishment of obligatory military service. The enactment of universal (masculine) suffrage made possible the inclusion of a plurality of political voices in Parliament. At the same time, the working class began to organize through political channels; Marxist socialists formed La Nueva Federación Madrileña 1872, which, in 1887, paved the way for the formation of the Partido Obrero Socialista Español and the socialist Union General de Trabajadores. Benjamin Martin, *The Agony of Modernization: Labor and Industrialization in Spain* (Ithaca, NY: ILR Press, Cornell University, 1990), 96.

72. Pardo Bazán, "Cartas," 144. The officials traveled to Cullera in an attempt to quell the strikes there. The subsequent violence was attributed in part to their heavy-handed attempts to bring order to the town. Six of the individuals held responsible for the killings were sentenced to death, two to life sentences, but international protests and pressure from the Left resulted in the pardon of all alleged perpetrators in early 1912. Vincent Franch i Ferrer, "Los sucesos de Cullera y Sueca," *Historia y vida* 120 (1978), 92–95. The Semana Trágica began with a generalized riot on July 26, provoked by the call-up of mostly working-class reserve soldiers from Barcelona to support the colonial war effort in Morocco. The insurrection, suppressed by August 1, resulted in the burning of religious schools, churches, and convents and the deaths of priests, policemen, and soldiers. Martin, *The Agony of Modernization*, 139.
73. Pardo Bazán, "Cartas," 143.
74. Rural workers often starved or lived in a state of chronic hunger and malnutrition. Gerald Brenan, *The Spanish Labyrinth: An Account of the Social and Political Background of the Spanish Civil War*, 2nd ed. (Cambridge: Cambridge University Press, 1990), 120. And urban workers experienced "malnutrition, disease, overwork, deficient housing, and unhealthy working conditions." Martin, *The Agony of Modernization*, 48. Wages were so insufficient to meet basic nutritional needs that Spanish workers during the first decade of the twentieth century spent two-thirds to three-quarters of their earnings on food, compared to 34 percent in Brussels and 30 percent in Paris. Martin, *The Agony of Modernization*, 51. Additionally, subsistence crises were often at the root of labor conflicts and social protests, among them the general strike of 1917, when the cost of food exceeded wages.
75. Pardo Bazán, "Cartas," 144.
76. Pardo Bazán, "Cartas," 145.
77. Pardo Bazán, "Cartas," 146, 147, 148, 149.
78. Pardo Bazán, "Cartas," 148, 144.
79. Pardo Bazán, "Cartas," 149. In contrast to her position in her "Discurso" in which she insists that "las incorrecciones del lenguaje, las sencillas e ingenuas preocupaciones del vulgo [. . .]" (incorrections of language, the simple and naïve preoccupations of the common people) be preserved, in *CEA* she emphasizes the importance of writing about cuisine in *castellano castizo* (pure Spanish). Pardo Bazán, *La cocina española antigua*, 7. She repeats this concern in *CEM*, while acknowledging that certain culinary terms in French are unavoidable. Pardo Bazán, *La cocina española moderna*, IV.
80. Pardo Bazán, "Discurso leído," 10.
81. Pardo Bazán, *La cocina española moderna*, I, III.
82. Pardo Bazán, *La cocina española moderna*, II, I, VI.
83. Pardo Bazán, *La cocina española moderna*, I.
84. Norbert Elias, *The Civilizing Process: The History of Manners* (New York: Urizen Books, 1995), 3, 5.

85. Noël Valis, *The Culture of* Cursilería: *Bad Taste, Kitsch, and Class in Modern Spain*, (Durham, NC: Duke University Press, 2002), 9, 11. See also Bridget Aldaraca, *El Ángel del Hogar: Galdós and the Ideology of Domesticity in Spain* (Chapel Hill: UNC Press for North Carolina Studies in the Romance Languages and Literatures, 1991), 19; and Zachary Erwin, "Fantasies of Masculinity in Emilia Pardo Bazán's *Memorias de un solterón*," Revista de Estudios Hispánicos 46, no. 3 (2012): 547–68.
86. Pardo Bazán, *La cocina española moderna*, VIII.
87. Pardo Bazán, *La cocina española moderna*, VIII. The frequency and intensity of Pardo Bazán's discussion of the aesthetics of cuisine in *CEM* indicates a preoccupation with the ability of women to comply with this way of making cuisine modern, similar to Íñigo Sánchez Llama's observation of how Pilar Sinués de Marco's domestic guides and conduct manuals "textualize" anxieties about the fragility of the middle class. Íñigo Sánchez Llama, *Galería de escritoras isabelinas: la prensa periódica entre 1833 y 1895* (Madrid: Ediciones Cátedra, 2000), 346.
88. Pardo Bazán, *La cocina española moderna*, 249, 171; Pardo Bazán, *La cocina española antigua*, 90.
89. Pardo Bazán, *La cocina española moderna*, 219.
90. Pardo Bazán, *La cocina española moderna*, II; González Turmo, *Comida de rico, comida de pobre*, 42.
91. Pardo Bazán, *La cocina española moderna*, 95.
92. See González Turmo's *Comida de rico, comida de pobre* (1995) for a study of the nutrition and eating habits of different social classes in Andalucia during the early twentieth century. Pierre Bourdieu discusses the "taste for necessity" characteristic of the working class, distinct from that of the middle class that strives to distance itself from those below and to aspire to items or practices of the privileged. Pierre Bourdieu, *Distinction: A Social Critique of the Judgement of Taste*, trans. Richard Nice (Cambridge, MA: Harvard University Press, 1984), 372.
93. Valis, *The Culture of* Cursilería, 32.
94. Tolliver, *Cigar Smoke and Violet Water*, 15.
95. Emilia Pardo Bazán, *La mujer española y otros escritos*, ed. Guadalupe Gómez-Ferrer (Madrid: Ediciones Cátedra, 1999), 87.
96. The entry for this text in the Biblioteca Nacional's catalogue does not mention a date. Gómez Trueba confirms that Pardo Bazán began the series in 1892.
97. Pardo Bazán, "Mi libro de cocina: La cocina española antigua, la Biblioteca de la Mujer y otros asuntos feministas," *Diario de la Marina*, 30 June 1913, in *Cartas de la Condesa en el Diario de la Marina La Habana (1909–1915)*, ed. Cecilia Heydl-Cortínez (Madrid: Pliegos, 2002), 223.
98. Carmen Bravo-Villasante, *Vida y obra de Emilia Pardo Bazán*, (Madrid: Revista de Occidente, 1962), 280. Alejandro Berreiro was the director of the newspaper *La voz de Galicia*. Bravo-Villasante, *Vida y obra de Emilia Pardo Bazán*, 279.
99. Pardo Bazán, *La cocina española antigua*, 4.

100. Pardo Bazán, "Mi libro de cocina," 222.
101. Pardo Bazán, *La cocina española antigua*, 3, 4.
102. Aldaraca, *El Ángel del Hogar*, 18–19.
103. Pardo Bazán, "Mi libro de cocina," 222.
104. Pardo Bazán, *La cocina española antigua*, 4.
105. Bravo-Villasante, *Vida y obra de Emilia Pardo Bazán*, 281.
106. Pardo Bazán, *La cocina española antigua*, 4.
107. Pardo Bazán, "Mi libro de cocina," 220, 221.
108. Tolliver, *Cigar Smoke and Violet Water*, 33–34.
109. Bravo-Villasante, *Vida y obra de Emilia Pardo Bazán*, 259. Later, Pardo Bazán gifted her own cookbooks to Concha, specifying in a letter to her husband, "Me alegraré de que [Concha] saque de ellos un poco de utilidad" (I will be happy for Concha to find them useful) (from "CARTA NÚMERO 3 de Emilia Pardo Bazán para Unamuno," dated 20.3.1916, held at the Casa Museo Miguel de Unamuno in Salamanca and transcribed by Rubén Rodríguez-Jiménez, Texas Woman's University).
110. Bravo-Villasante, *Vida y obra de Emilia Pardo Bazán*, 281.
111. Tolliver, *Cigar Smoke and Violet Water*, 38.
112. Pardo Bazán, "Mi libro de cocina," 223.
113. Pardo Bazán, *La cocina española antigua*, 4.
114. Tolliver, *Cigar Smoke and Violet Water*, 61. Tolliver quotes Pardo Bazán's letter to Barreiro, which Bravo Villasante reproduces in her 1973 biography. Tolliver, *Cigar Smoke and Violet Water*, 285.
115. Pardo Bazán, *La cocina española antigua*, 4.
116. Emilia Pardo Bazán, "Prólogo," *La cocina práctica* (Santiago de Compostela: Galí, 1905), 9.
117. Manuel María (Picadillo) Puga y Parga, *La cocina práctica*, Decimosexta edición (Santiago de Compostela: Galí, 1981), 9.
118. Emilia Pardo Bazán, "La vida contemporánea," *La ilustración artística*, Número 1285 (1906): 522.
119. Pardo Bazán, *La cocina española antigua*, 7.
120. Emilia Pardo Bazán, "La cocina," *La ilustración artística*, Número 1251 (1905): 810.
121. "La mujer española" (1890) and "La educación del hombre y la de la mujer" (1892).

CHAPTER 2

1. Concepción Núñez Rey, *Carmen de Burgos: Columbine en la Edad de Plata de la literatura española* (Sevilla: Fundación José Manuel Lara, 2005), 10.
2. See studies by Michael Ugarte, Roberta Johnson, Anja Louis, Concepción Núñez Rey, Catherine Davies, and Elizabeth Starcevic. The description of Burgos as an "escritora-ama de casa" appears in María del Carmen Simón Palmer's *Escritoras españolas del siglo XIX: Manual bio-bibliográfico* (Madrid: Castalia,

1991), 130. Burgos describes herself as a "bas bleu" or bluestocking, in *Nueva cocina práctica*, 70.

3. There exists some uncertainty regarding the original publication dates for Burgos's first and third cookbooks as first editions of the books are undated. The Biblioteca Nacional's catalogue dates *La cocina moderna* to 1918, which biographer Nuñéz Rey accepts in her chronology of Burgos's works. The catalogue lists 1927 as the publication date for all the volumes published as part of her *Obras completas*. However, Lynn Scott makes a convincing case for dating the publication of Burgos's *La cocina moderna* to 1906 and her *Nueva cocina práctica* to 1925.

4. Anja Louis, *Women and the Law: Carmen de Burgos, an Early Feminist* (Rochester, UK: Tamesis, Woodbridge, 2005), 7; Lynn Thomson Scott, "Carmen de Burgos: Piecing a Profession, Rewriting Women's Roles" (PhD diss., University of Florida, 1999); Catherine Davies, "The 'Red Lady': Carmen de Burgos (1867–1932)," in *Spanish Women's Writing, 1849–1996* (Atlantic Highlands, NJ: Athlone Press, 1998).

5. Louis, *Women and the Law*; and Johnson, *Gender and Nation*.

6. Anja Louis and Michelle Sharp, introduction to *Multiple Modernities: Carmen de Burgos: Author and Activist* (New York: Routledge, 2017).

7. See also Rocío Rødtjer's study that analyzes Burgos's writing on how women were excluded from sites and discourses of legitimacy. Rocío Rødtjer, *Women and Nationhood in Restoration Spain, 1874–1931: The State as Family* (London: Legenda, 2019), 119. Burgos's second cookbook, *¿Quiere Ud. comer bien?*, contains none of the paratextual materials that distinguish the first and third volumes.

8. Davies, "The 'Red Lady,'" 119, 120.

9. As examples see Rafael Cansinos-Asséns, *La novela de un literato* (1982); Juan Manuel de Prada (quoted in Scott 66); and Federico Utrera, *Memorias de Colombine* (1998). Additionally, the column "Chismes y Cuentos," in the magazine *Madrid Cómico* (1910), made Burgos the focus of ridicule, mocking her physically and insinuating that she submitted a recipe for *tortilla* (omelet) to the magazine instead of a poem or other literary text. Blanca Bravo Cela, *Carmen de Burgos (Colombine): Contra el silencio* (Madrid: Espasa, 2003), 144.

10. Núñez Rey, *Carmen de Burgos*, 163–64.

11. Johnson, *Gender and Nation*, 27–28.

12. Lynn Thomson Scott, "Carmen de Burgos: Piecing a Profession, Rewriting Women's Roles" (PhD diss., University of Florida, 1999), 23.

13. Margarita Nelken, *La condición social de la mujer en España*, 1919 (Madrid: CVS Ediciones, 1975), 52.

14. Jeffrey Zamostny, "Introduction: Kiosk Literature and the Enduring Ephemeral," in *Kiosk Literature of Silver Age Spain: Modernity and Mass Culture*, eds. Jeffrey Zamostny and Susan Larson (Chicago: Intellect, 2017), 3.

15. Michelle Sharp, "Carmen de Burgos: Teaching Women of the Modern Age," in

Kiosk Literature of Silver Age Spain: Modernity and Mass Culture, eds. Jeffrey Zamostny and Susan Larson (Chicago: Intellect, 2017), 313.

16. José Carlos Mainer, *La Edad de Plata (1902–1939). Ensayo de interpretación de un proceso cultural* (Madrid: Cátedra, 1983), 73.
17. Mainer, *La Edad de Plata*, 58.
18. Recall that in 1900 women comprised over 50 percent of the population, and between 1900 and 1920, the number of literate women doubled from 2,395,839 to 4,462,730. Botrel, *Libros*, 309. In a collaboration spanning 1905 to 1928, Sempere published Burgos's *La cocina moderna* and the *Nueva cocina práctica* as part of a series aimed at female readers, the Biblioteca de la mujer, in addition to hardcover editions of Burgos's short stories, novels, and versions of her speeches. Sopena published the 1916 *¿Quiere usted comer bien?* Scott, "Carmen de Burgos," 38, 40, 70.
19. Maite Zubiaurre, "Double Writing / Double Reading Cities, Popular Culture, and Stalkers: Carmen de Burgos' *El Persiguidor*," *Revista Hispánica Moderna* 56, no. 1 (2003), 58.
20. Núñez Rey, *Carmen de Burgos*, 21.
21. Susan Larson, "Conclusion: Kiosk Literature as a Geography of Cultural Objects," in *Kiosk Literature of Silver Age Spain: Modernity and Mass Culture*, eds. Jeffrey Zamostny and Susan Larson (Chicago: Intellect, 2017), 421. See also Walter Benjamin, "The Work of Art in the Age of Mechanical Reproduction," in *Illuminations*, ed. Hannah Arendt (New York: Schocken Books, 1968).
22. Scott, "Carmen de Burgos," 92. Federico Utrera echoes this speculation in *Memorias de Colombine, la primera periodista* (Madrid: HMR Hijos de Muley-Rubio, 1998).
23. Larson, "Conclusion," 424.
24. Chartier, "La sociedad liberal," 275–77.
25. Elizabeth Starcevik, *Carmen de Burgos: Defensora de la mujer* (Almería: Librería–Editorial Cajal, 1976), 47–48.
26. Scott, "Carmen de Burgos," 97.
27. Kate Cairns and Josée Johnston, *Food and Femininity* (London: Bloomsbury Academic, 2015), 26.
28. Scott, "Carmen de Burgos," 56. The book actually carries two titles. The front cover indicates *Nueva cocina práctica* and features a header indicating that it belongs to Burgos's "Obras completas = Serie práctica." Moreover, it features an illustration of a family at a round table and centers two women on the page. The interior pages indicate that the title is *La cocina práctica*.
29. Davies, "The 'Red Lady,'" 121.
30. Louis, *Women and the Law*, 7–8.
31. Louis identifies Burgos's aim to "construct proximity and interaction between the intellectual debates of her time and women's lived experiences" in her journalism, essays, fiction, and activism. Louis, *Women and the Law*, 10. Johnson describes how the domestic problems at the center of Burgos's plots "resonate

with national concerns" and recreate "a national indwelling through the basic institution of civil society, where tradition is firmly rooted in masculine and feminine roles within marriage." In her representation of these masculine and feminine roles, Burgos portrays how sociopolitical factors, rather than biological ones, define the nation. Johnson, *Gender and Nation*, 234–35.

32. Carmen de Burgos Segui, *La cocina moderna* (Valencia: Prometeo Sociedad Editorial, 1906), v–vi.
33. Burgos, *La cocina moderna*, vi.
34. For analysis of the conventional domestic advice and practical manuals that explicitly instruct readers about their roles as submissive and subservient angels in the house see Catherine Jagoe, *Ambiguous Angels: Gender in the Novels of Galdós* (Berkeley: University of California Press, 1994), 32.
35. See Maryellen Bieder, "Woman and the Twentieth-Century Spanish Literary Canon: The Lady Vanishes," *Anales de la literatura española contemporánea* 17, no. 1–3 (1992): 301–24.
36. Zubiaurre, "Double Writing," 62. Zubiaurre describes Burgos's "double writing" as a practice made necessary by the "demands that the androcentric society of her time imposed" on women writers. Zubiaurre, "Double Writing," 58. Additionally, Ugarte argues that Burgos's minor texts do "cultural work" when they attempt to redefine the social order in order to reflect "how a culture thinks about itself." Michael Ugarte, *Madrid 1900: The Capital as Cradle of Literature and Culture* (University Park: Pennsylvania State University Press, 1996), 80. An analysis of "the ways in which the text is disseminated, the strategies it employs to win a specific readership, its construction of a dialogue with the established order" allows for understanding Burgos's cookbooks as one attempt to redefine gender roles in the social order in early twentieth-century Spain. Ugarte, *Madrid 1900*, 80.
37. Zubiaurre, "Double Writing," 62.
38. Burgos, *La cocina moderna*, v.
39. Although the 1925 version of the letter introduces small but meaningful changes from the 1906 version, Burgos does not indicate anywhere that she edited or revised the letter.
40. Burgos, *La cocina moderna*, vi.
41. Burgos, *La cocina moderna*, v.
42. Carmen de Burgos Segui, *Nueva cocina práctica* [*La cocina práctica*] (Valencia: Editorial Sempere, 1925), 5. Italics mine.
43. Burgos, *La cocina moderna*, v.
44. Burgos, *La cocina moderna*, v.
45. Nelken, *La condición social*, 50, 51.
46. Nelken, *La condición social*, 52–53.
47. Burgos, *La cocina moderna*, v–vi.
48. Burgos, *La cocina moderna*, v. Italics mine.
49. Burgos, *La cocina moderna*, vi.

50. Gerda Lerner, *The Creation of a Feminist Consciousness: From the Middle Ages to Eighteen-Seventy* (Oxford: Oxford University Press, 1986), 12.
51. Burgos, *La cocina moderna*, vi.
52. Burgos, *La cocina moderna*, vi; Burgos, *Nueva cocina práctica*, 7. The change in verb choice from "no me opongo" (I do not oppose) to "deseo" (I want) strengthens this sentiment even as Burgos maintains her tempering of the phrase by asserting the priority of women's responsibility to their homes.
53. Burgos, *La cocina moderna*, v.
54. Zubiaurre, "Double Writing," 58.
55. Carmen de Burgos Segui, *La mujer en España: Conferencia pronunciada en la Asociación de la Prensa en Roma el 28 de Abril de 1906* (Valencia: F. Sempere y Compañía, Editores, 1906), 9.
56. Carmen de Burgos Segui, "La base de nuestra regeneración," *El Pueblo* (November 13, 1906), 1. See Núñez Rey on Burgos's writing under this pseudonym. Núñez Rey, *Carmen de Burgos*, 162.
57. Núñez Rey, *Carmen de Burgos*, 162.
58. Burgos quoted in Núñez Rey, *Carmen de Burgos*, 167.
59. Carmen de Burgos Segui, *Misión social de la mujer: Conferencia pronunciada por D.a Carmen de Burgos Seguí el día 18 de febrero de 1911* (Bilbao: Sociedad "El Sitio"; Imp. Jose Rojas Núñez, 1911), 7.
60. Burgos, *Misión social de la mujer*, 7, 9.
61. Burgos, *Misión social de la mujer*, 15.
62. Burgos, *Misión social de la mujer*, 17, 11, 14.
63. Carmen de Burgos Segui, *Influencias recíprocas entre la mujer y la literatura* (Logroño: Imp. y Lib, 1912), 5.
64. Burgos, *Influencias*, 5–6, 6.
65. Burgos, *Influencias*, 19, 7.
66. Carmen de Burgos Segui, *Las artes de la mujer* (Valencia: F. Sempere y Compañía, [1911?]), v.
67. Burgos, *Las artes de la mujer*, v, vi.
68. Burgos, *La cocina moderna*, 7.
69. Burgos, *La cocina moderna*, 7.
70. Valis's definition of *cursilería*. Valis, *The Culture of* Cursilería, 16.
71. Ugarte, *Madrid 1900*, 88.
72. She states that she would renounce working this way if the topic was any other: "De otra cosa tratase, y yo renunciaría á transcribir lo que de su historia hubiese llegado a mi noticia." Burgos, *La cocina moderna*, 7. However, the style is common to her work in general and also characterizes her *La mujer en España*, *Influencias recíprocas*, and even in her 1904 study *La protección y la higiene de los niños*, a criticism of misguided and insufficient legislation meant to protect children and mothers.
73. Burgos, *La cocina moderna*, 7, 8, 9.
74. Burgos, *La cocina moderna*, 9, 10, 11, 12.

75. Burgos, *La cocina moderna*, 11. The Alexandra Burgos mentions is likely Alexandra, Empress consort of Russia, spouse of Nicolas II and granddaughter of Queen Victoria.
76. Burgos, *La cocina moderna*, 11.
77. Burgos, *La cocina moderna*, v; Burgos, *Nueva cocina práctica*, 6.
78. Enders and Radcliff, *Constructing Spanish Womanhood*, 20.
79. Nash, "Un/Contested Identities," 33–34.
80. Nash, "Un/Contested Identities," 29–30.
81. Parkhurst Ferguson, *Accounting for Taste*, 3.
82. See Anderson *Cooking Up the Nation* and Chapter 1 of this book.
83. See Johnson on how Burgos deconstructs biological definitions of marriage, family, and domesticity in favor of social ones in her fiction writing. Johnson, *Gender and Nation*, 228.
84. Burgos, *La cocina moderna*, 12.
85. Geraldine M. Scanlon, *La polémica feminista en la España contemporánea (1868–1974)*, trans. Rafael Mazarrasa (Madrid: Akal, 1986), 17–18.
86. Sarah Stage and Virginia B. Vicenti *Rethinking Home Economics: Women and the History of a Profession* (Ithaca, NY: Cornell University Press, 1997), 3.
87. Burgos, *La cocina moderna*, 12. Since 1870, private initiatives organized by the Asociación para la Enseñanza de la Mujer as part of Krausist Fernando de Castro's Ateneo Artístico y Literario de Señoras existed to prepare women for public-sphere jobs. The Asociación opened the door to creating educational institutions for women's professional development in fields additional to teaching, for example the planned Escuela de Institutrices, the Escuela de Comercio para Señoras, and the Escuela de Correos y Telégrafos. Ultimately unsuccessful, these attempts failed due to the scarcity of jobs available for women. Scanlon, *La polemica feminista*, 34–35.
88. Burgos, *La cocina moderna*, 13.
89. See Blanca Bravo Cela, *Carmen de Burgos (Colombine)*, 45.
90. Carolyn Boyd, *Historia Patria: Politics, History, and National Identity in Spain, 1875–1975* (Princeton, NJ: Princeton University Press, 1997), 43.
91. Johnson, *Gender and Nation*, 15. See Johnson on Krausist-sponsored lectures on women's education in 1869 and Boyd on the politicized nature of any attempts at public education reform. Johnson, *Gender and Nation*, 16; Boyd, *Historia Patria*, xiii–xviii.
92. Burgos, *La cocina moderna*, 12–13.
93. Johnson, *Gender and Modernization*, 19.
94. In titling her essay after Apicius, we see another gesture from Burgos about her own erudition. Works of "recopiladores" (compilers) like Apicius often included in their texts a range of materials, among them the obscure, challenging, or forgotten. The point was to demonstrate intellectual status rather than advance new knowledge, according to Santiago Rubio Fernaz. See also Sally Grainger, "The Myth of Apicius," *Gastronómica* 7, no. 2 (May 2007): 71–77.

95. Sharp, "Carmen de Burgos," 202.
96. Lara Anderson, "Spanish Culinary Autochtony and Culinary Modernity: María Mestayer de Echagüe's *La Cocina Completa* and *Platos Escogidos de La Cocina Vasca*," *Cincinnati Romance Review* 33 (2012): 98–113.
97. Burgos, *Nueva cocina práctica*, 9.
98. Burgos, *Nueva cocina práctica*, 12, 10. She names "Aegis, de Rodas; Nereo, de Quios, y Aphtonetes, de Atenas" (10).
99. Burgos, *Nueva cocina práctica*, 13, 16, 28.
100. Burgos, *Nueva cocina práctica*, 18–20.
101. Burgos, *Nueva cocina práctica*, 20, 23, 24.
102. Burgos, *Nueva cocina práctica*, 24. One amusing cookbook highlights this point clearly: she gives the example of *La cocina en Música* (1738) by J. Lebas that "quería facilitar a las damas el enseñar cantando a las cocineras el medio de hacer los *ragoûts* y las salsas" (wanted to facilitate teaching by having ladies sing to their female cooks how to make ragouts and sauces). Burgos, *Nueva cocina práctica*, 26.
103. Burgos, *Nueva cocina práctica*, 29.
104. Burgos, *Nueva cocina práctica*, 29.
105. Food has long served as a marker of social classification or problems. The sociology of food as a field dates to the 1980s when sociologists began to study food's relationship to social ties, social and cultural differences, and its integration into social organizational forms. Michaela De Soucey, "Food," in *Oxford Bibliographies Online: Sociology*, ed. Lynette Spillman (Oxford: Oxford University Press, 2017 [2012]). See also John-Pierre Poulain on how there is no single sociology of food but multiple sociologies. John-Pierre Poulain, *The Sociology of Food: Eating and the Place of Food in Society* (London: Bloomsbury Academic, 2017), 168.
106. Burgos, *Nueva cocina práctica*, 34.
107. The essay is part of *Notas contemporáneas* (1909).
108. Quotes in Burgos, *Nueva cocina práctica*, 34.
109. See Paul Freedman *Food: This History of Taste* (2007) on how the idea of taste encapsulates the flavors of foods, their production of an artistic effect, the craft and creations of both ordinary and skilled producers, in addition to how expressions of taste are used to define social groups and their practices. Paul Freedman, *Food: This History of Taste* (Berkeley: University of California Press, 2007), 9–11.
110. According to Un Cocinero, "[l]as aldeanas manchegas y extremeñas no corren ya al paso de la corte con sus blancos corderos, sus pichones torcaces, sus tarros de miel, sus orzas de escabeche y la sencilla ambición de que sólo lo suyo sea lo que se coma S.M.: los reyes pueden creer que en todo su reino se come y se bebe lo que en París y como en París" (the village women of La Mancha and Extremadura no longer keep pace with the court with their white lambs,

young squabs, pots of honey, jars of escabeche, and the simple ambition that their products be what His Majesty eats; the monarchs can believe that in all their kingdom one eats and drinks the same as in Paris and how one does in Paris). Quoted in Burgos, *Nueva cocina práctica*, 18; Burgos, *Nueva cocina práctica*, 24.

111. Burgos, *Nueva cocina práctica*, 37.
112. Burgos, *Nueva cocina práctica*, 38.
113. Burgos, *Nueva cocina práctica*, 40.
114. Burgos, *Nueva cocina práctica*, 40–41.
115. Burgos, *Nueva cocina práctica*, 44. See Nadeau, *Food Matters*. Additional literary examples that highlight the social roles of cooking come from *La Lozana Andaluza* and the poetry of Baltasar de Alcázar. Burgos, *Nueva cocina práctica*, 48.
116. Burgos, *Nueva cocina práctica*, 51.
117. Burgos, *Nueva cocina práctica*, 52, 53. Capitalized in Burgos's citation of the "Código de las Partidas."
118. Burgos, *Nueva cocina práctica*, 57.
119. Burgos, *Nueva cocina práctica*, 58, 59.
120. Burgos, *Nueva cocina práctica*, 60.
121. Burgos, *Nueva cocina práctica*, 61.
122. Burgos, *Nueva cocina práctica*, 35. In a subsequent commentary, she tells a humorous story about a prince's banquet, where the *sisa* of fifty hams comprised a majority of the funds budgeted for the event when only one would appear on the banquet table. Burgos, *Nueva cocina práctica*, 36.
123. Burgos, *Nueva cocina práctica*, 35.
124. Burgos, *Nueva cocina práctica*, 62, 61. The passive construction, "es el haber hecho que" (having made that), indicates that the generators of this position toward cooking were not the women themselves. Burgos, *Nueva cocina práctica*, 62.
125. Burgos, *Nueva cocina práctica*, 77–78.
126. Scott analyzes a more direct example of Burgos's defense of her writing and gender, in the prologue she wrote for the 1924 *Obras completas* version of *El arte de seducir* (*Tesoro de la Belleza*). In that essay, Burgos asserts "that it is her obligation to 'deshacer el prejuicio de que la mujer que se instruye, lucha y trabaja, es un ser aparte, y el sentimiento y el cultivo del Arte y la sencillez de la vida'" (dismantle the prejudice that women who acquire education, fight, and work, are separate beings, and to prove that incompatibilities between sentiment and cultivating Art and the simplicity of life do not exist). Burgos quoted in Scott, "Carmen de Burgos," 99.
127. Burgos, *Nueva cocina práctica*, 70–71. This is a different version of the anecdote she also included in *El arte de seducir*.

128. Not until 1978 did the Real Academia admit its first woman member, Carmen Conde.

CHAPTER 3

1. Javier Mardones Alonso, *Bibliografía de la gastronomía vasca (1800–1959): Apuntes y anécdotas sobre los libros y autores* (Victoria-Gasteiz: Departamento de cultura, Diputación Foral de Alava, 1997), 96. Or Gaytán de Ayala. José María de Orbe y Gaytán de Ayala was named the Marqués de Valdespina in 1891.
2. José María Pisa, "Delantal del Editor," *La cocina de ellas* (Huesca: La Val de Onsera, 2002), 8.
3. Mardones Alonso, *Bibliografía de la gastronomía vasca*, 97.
4. Marino Gómez Santos, *Gregorio Marañón* (Barcelona: Plaza and Janés, S.A, 2001), 39–44.
5. Gary D. Keller, *The Significance and Impact of Gregorio Marañón* (New York: Bilingual Press/Editorial Bilingüe Studies in the Literary Analysis of Hispanic Texts, 1977), 1.
6. Keller, *Significance and Impact*, 78, 120. In his 1919 article "Sobre la represión de la mendicidad," Marañón criticized the state's treatment of the poor and infirm. Keller, *Significance and Impact*, 120.
7. Pedro Laín Entralgo, *Gregorio Marañón: Vida, obra y persona* (Madrid: Colección Austral, 1969), 43.
8. Laín Entralgo, *Gregorio Marañón*, 50.
9. Laín Entralgo, *Gregorio Marañón*, 51.
10. Gómez Santos, *Gregorio Marañón*, 335–336, 91–92.
11. They comprise the entire first volume of Laín Entralgo's edition of his *Obras completas*.
12. García del Real's wife, Matilde, is the likely author of *Cocina Española y cocina dietética*, but the Biblioteca Nacional attributes the book to Eduardo. In the "Breve ensayo," Marañón acknowledged the "ilustre autora" (distinguished [female] author). Gregorio Marañón, "Prólogo: Breve ensayo sobre la Cocina española," in *Cocina española y cocina dietética* (Madrid: Sobrinos de la Sucesora de M. Minuesa de los Rios, 1929), 20. See Gómez Santos for additional details about the mentioned prologues.
13. In the collection *Mythologies* (1957), Roland Barthes defines a "contemporary" myth as the "mystification which transforms petit-bourgeois culture into a universal nature." Roland Barthes, *Mythologies*, trans. Annette Lavers (New York: Hill and Wang, 1957), 9–10. Marañón's culinary writing endows Spanish culinary authenticity, and by extension, identity, with a new "modern" meaning consistent with bourgeois values.
14. Margaret R. Greer, Walter Mignolo, and Maureen Quilligan, eds., *Rereading the Black Legend: The Discourses of Religious and Racial Difference in the Renaissance Empires* (Chicago: University of Chicago Press, 2007), 1; Stephen

Jacobson, "The Head and Heart of Spain: New Perspectives on Nationalism and Nationhood," *Social History* 29, no. 3 (2004), 396.
15. Jesús Torrecilla, *La imitación colectiva: Modernidad vs. autenticidad en la literatura española* (Madrid: Editorial Gredos, 1996), 17.
16. Mangien, "Cultura cotidiana," 137.
17. *Casticismo*, or the concept of Spanish racial purity or national character, according to Américo Castro, bonded different parts of Spain. See Eva Woods Peiró "Introduction: Modernity, Race, and Visibility" on how Spain sought to present its racial identity as coherent and contained, whether "raceless" or unproblematically fused. Eva Woods Peiró, "Introduction: Modernity, Race, and Visibility," in *White Gypsies: Race and Stardom in Spanish Musicals* (Minneapolis: University of Minnesota Press, 2012), 3.
18. Mary Nash, "Social Eugenics and Nationalist Race Hygiene in Early Twentieth-Century Spain," *History of European Ideas* 15, no. 4–6 (1992), 742.
19. Labanyi, *Gender and Modernization*, 86. Social hygiene surfaced in the late eighteenth century as a state-directed attempt to improve living conditions and increase the population through reproduction. See Richard Cleminson, *Anarchism, Science and Sex: Eugenics in Eastern Spain, 1900–1937* (London: Peter Lang, 2000). See also the works of Pedro Felipe Monlau i Roca *Higiene del matrimonio o Libro de los casados* (1853) and *Higiene privada* (1846), who prescribed healthy Catholic marriages for a healthy vigorous nation. Monlau quoted in Cleminson, *Anarchism*, 66. I explore the nutritional aspects of these interests in Chapter 4.
20. Michael Richards, "Spanish Psychiatry c.1900–1945: Constitutional Theory, Eugenics, and the Nation," *Bulletin of Spanish Studies* LXXXI, no. 6 (2004), 824.
21. Nash argues that the eugenics movement involved intellectuals from across the political spectrum. Marañón and others consolidated social eugenics as a reform movement in the 1920s and '30s. Nash, "Social Eugenics," 744–45. Richards attributes to Catholics and later ultra-rightists a greater interest in moral hygiene than social justice. Richards, "Spanish Psychiatry," 824.
22. Mermall reading Ortega y Gassett. Thomas Mermall, "Culture and the Essay in Modern Spain," in *The Cambridge Companion to Modern Spanish Culture*, ed. David T. Gies (Cambridge: Cambridge University Press, 1999), 168.
23. David Ringrose, *Spain, Europe and the "Spanish Miracle," 1700–1900* (Cambridge: Cambridge University Press, 1996), 37.
24. Labanyi, *Gender and Modernization*, 90; see also Valis, *The Culture of* Cursilería.
25. Adrian Shubert, *A Social History of Modern Spain* (New York: Routledge, 1990), 83, 190.
26. Gómez Santos, *Gregorio Marañón*, 358, 363.
27. Carr, *Modern Spain*, 126–27.
28. Nash, "Estudio preliminar," 13.

29. Nash, "Estudio preliminar," 40–44.
30. Matilla and Frax, "La doble opresión," 90–94.
31. Nash, "Estudio preliminar," 46.
32. Nash, "Estudio preliminar," 45, 47. Nash cites Joan Gaya in "Les dones al treball i els homes en atur." *Catalunya social* (July 1936), and Francesc Tusquets in *El problema feminista* (1931).
33. Susan Kirkpatrick and Jaqueline Cruz, *Mujer, modernismo y vanguardia en España: 1898–1931* (Madrid: Cátedra, 2003), 9.
34. Nash, "Un/Contested Identities," 32.
35. Montserrat Miller, *Feeding Barcelona, 1714–1975: Public Market Halls, Social Networks, and Consumer Culture* (Baton Rouge: Louisiana State University Press, 2015), 11.
36. Sasha Pack, "Tourism, Modernization, and Difference: A Twentieth-Century Spanish Paradigm," *Sport in Society* 11, no. 6 (2008), 657.
37. Eugenia Afinoguénova, "An Organic Nation: State-Run Tourism, Regionalism, and Food in Spain, 1905–1931," *Journal of Modern History* 86, no. 4 (December 2014), 744–45.
38. Cited in Pack, "Tourism, Modernization, and Difference," 660. Capitalization in original.
39. Benjamin Martin, *The Agony of Modernization: Labor and Industrialization in Spain* (Ithaca, NY: ILR Press, Cornell University, 1990), 275; Pack, "Tourism, Modernization, and Difference," 660. The number of automobiles in Spain increased from 135,000 in 1927 to 250,000 in 1930. Martin, *The Agony of Modernization*, 275. Primo's government made the state the investor in Spain's major public works (highways, electricity, telephones, support for industry), which failed to motivate similar levels of investment by the private sector. Martin, *The Agony of Modernization*, 275.
40. Sasha Pack, *Tourism and Dictatorship: Europe's Peaceful Invasion of Franco's Spain* (New York: Palgrave Macmillan, 2006), 46–47.
41. Luis Castells, "La Bella Easo: 1864–1836," in *Historia de Donostia—San Sebastián*, ed. Miguel Artola (Ayuntamiento de San Sebastián: Editorial Nerea, 2000), 300–352.
42. Castells, "La Bella Easo," 334–35, 352, 355. Industrial development in San Sebastián did not follow the model developed in Bilbao, with its larger factories and industrial enterprises. Instead, most factories employed fewer than one hundred workers, which enabled the city to project an image of community largely without conflict until around the First World War. Basque nationalism presented another facet of dissension along lines of class and resentment of the profile that tourism presented about the city's culture. See Castells, 358–63.
43. Pradera's restaurant preserved traditional *cocina vasca* (Basque cooking) until its close in 2010 after ninety-eight years of service. Mitxel Ezquiaga, "El día que Nicolasa salió en The Times," *El diario vasco* (November 15, 2018). Its last

head chef, José Juan Castillo, credits her cookbook, *La cocina de Nicolasa*, with the codification of traditional Basque cuisine.
44. José Juan Castillo, *Biografía*, 2008, accessed June 1, 2008, http://www.cocinavino.com/ensusalsa/biografia.html. While this website is no longer active in 2022, Castillo, head chef at Casa Nicolasa for twenty-five years until its close in 2010, has published a cookbook, *Las recetas fáciles de José Juan Castillo en el Centenario de Casa Nicolasa* (Legazpi: Zum Edizioak, 2012).
45. The cookbook is divided into sections for caldos; sopas; purés; macarrones; huevos; tortillas; fritos; pescados; salsas; platos de carne; aves y caza; cocidos y potajes; verduras; asados de carne, ave, y caza; fiambres; compotas; helados; dulces; and repostería.
46. The Azcaray family ran the Bilbao restaurant Amparo (1866–1918). Like Casa Nicolasa it served an elite clientele that included members of the nobility and the growing middle class, artists, bankers, and politicians. See Haranburu Altuna on how Basque cuisine arose from the combination of French culinary methods and practices with autochthonous ingredients. Luis Haranburu Altuna, *Historia de la alimentación y de la cocina en el País Vasco* (Alegia, Gipuzkoa: Hiria liburuak, 2000). The railroads that traversed the region ended socioeconomic isolation. Plentiful sources of olive oil, wheat, and Riojan and Navarran wines prompted the creation of emblematic dishes like the *pil-pil* and *verde* sauces and sped the decline in consumption of cider and *txacolí*. A cuisine's codification refers to its representation and reproduction in print. See Parkhurst Ferguson, *Accounting for Taste*.
47. Haranburu Altuna, *Historia de la alimentación*, 264.
48. Leonardi, "Recipes for Reading," 126.
49. Rombauer quoted in Leonardi, "Recipes for Reading," 126.
50. Pisa, "Delantal del Editor," 8; Teodoro Bardají, *La cocina de ellas* (Huesca: Ediciones Nauta, Ediciones La Val de Onsera, 2002), 960.
51. In small towns they jealously hide their recipes, refuse to share them, or only give adulterated versions. Bardají, *La cocina de ellas*, 953.
52. Pérez quoted in Teodoro Bardají, *Índice Culinario*, ed. José María Pisa (Huesca: La Val Onsera, 1993), 10.
53. Adriana de Juaristi, *Cocina* (Madrid: Editorial Caro Raggio, 1928).
54. María Mestayer de Echagüe (Marquesa de Parabere), *La cocina completa* (Madrid: Espasa-Calpe, 1955), 9.
55. Nicolasa Pradera, *La cocina de Nicolasa*, 1933 (Madrid: Estades, 1950), 130, 130, 165.
56. Gregorio Marañón, "Prólogo," *La cocina de Nicolasa*, by Nicolasa Pradera, 1933 (Madrid: Estades, 1950), 7.
57. Marañón, "Prólogo," 14, 15.
58. Vicenta, Ursula, and Sira ran El Amparo, a renowned restaurant in Bilbao. The restaurant closed in 1918 due to Vicenta's death. Mardones Alonso, *Bibliografía de la gastronomía vasca*, 47.

59. Marañón, "Prólogo," 16.
60. Haranburu Altuna, *Historia de la alimentación*, 262.
61. Nelken, *La condición social*, 52.
62. Marañón, "Prólogo," 16.
63. Marañón, "Prólogo," 10.
64. Marañón, "Prólogo," 8.
65. Marañón, "Prólogo," 10. Italics mine.
66. Flitter, *Spanish Romanticism*, 130.
67. Marañón, "Prólogo," 10.
68. Nancy Chodorow, *The Reproduction of Mothering: Psychoanalysis and the Sociology of Gender* (Berkeley: University of California Press, 1978), 14.
69. Nash, "Estudio Preliminar," 15. Nash examines Marañón's *Tres ensayos sobre la vida sexual*, "Texto 3" in *Mujer, familia y trabajo en España*, 92–94.
70. Nerea Aresti, *Médicos, donjuanes y mujeres modernas: Los ideales de feminidad y masculinidad en el primer tercio del siglo XX* (Biscay, Spain: Universidad del País Vasco / Euskal Herriko Unibertsitatea, 2001), 235.
71. Burgos quoted in Aresti, *Médicos, donjuanes y mujeres modernas*, 239. See Burgos, *La mujer moderna y sus derechos*, 27.
72. By contrast, Carmen Moreto y Díaz Prieto, a teacher and collaborator with *Sexualidad*, supported a feminist discourse based on legal equality. Margarita Nelken (1919) advanced an economic feminism, which would allow women to support themselves more equitably as workers. See also Chapter 4 of this book.
73. Aresti, *Médicos, donjuanes y mujeres modernas*, 236. See Nash on how Lucía Sánchez Saornil (an anarchist) and María Cambrills (a socialist) advance theories of women's biological difference consistent with those of Marañón; Carmen Karr de Lasarte also finds it difficult to imagine women without considering maternity. Nash, "Estudio Preliminar," 17–18.
74. Marañón, "Prólogo," 15.
75. Marañón, "Prólogo," 10. The viuda de Uhagón's message for her daughters, that "una buena ama de casa [. . .] debe entender el arte del cocinero para preparar a su esposo y familia el bienestar confortable que le haga preferir la comida sencilla de casa a los mayores festines fuera de ella" (a good housewife [. . .] should understand the arts of the [male] chef to prepare for her husband and family the comfortable well-being that causes him to prefer the simple preparations of his home rather than the noteworthy feasts from outside of it). Uhagón, qtd. in Marañón, "Prólogo," 15, is repeated by Sinués de Marco in *La dama elegante* (1880), by Carmen de Burgos in the "Carta-Prólogo" to her 1906 and 1925 cookbooks, and by Pardo Bazán in her 1913 and 1914 cookbooks.
76. Also significant: Marañón is commenting on Uhagón's *writing*, not her cooking. Uhagón's recipes are her discursive production rather than a racial or genetic legacy, as in the case of Pradera. This is another signal of Marañón's perception of both Uhagón's class and Pradera's.

77. Marañón, "Prólogo," 15.
78. Suffrage was just one aspect of first-wave feminist thought in Spain even as the model of the traditional woman and her homemaking tasks maintained its cultural currency. Nash, "Estudio Preliminar," 40.
79. Samantha Barbas, "Just Like Home: 'Home Cooking' and the Domestication of the American Restaurant," *Gastronomica* 2, no. 4 (2002), 43, 48.
80. Gregorio Marañón, *Gordos y Flacos. Tercera edición, muy revisada* (Madrid: Espasa-Calpe, 1936), 11.
81. Marañón, *Gordos y Flacos*, 12.
82. A biological perspective informed the work of Spanish eugenicists like Marañón; it connected national efficiency to racial fitness. However, nurture was also important as the nation needed social welfare to cultivate a vital, healthy population. Nash, "Social Eugenics," 743.
83. Gregorio Marañón, "Breve ensayo sobre la cocina española," *Cuadernos de Gastronomia*, vols. Once y doce (1995), 13. In *Meditaciones* (1933), similar ideas and identical paragraphs from "Breve ensayo" reappear in three essays: "El cocinero, el higienista y el medico"; "La mala fama de la cocina española y sus causas"; and "La grandeza sensual."
84. Marañón, "Breve ensayo sobre la cocina española," 13.
85. Marañón, "Breve ensayo sobre la cocina española," 13.
86. Marañón, *Gordos y Flacos*, 7.
87. Marañón, "Prólogo," 8, 17.
88. Marañón, "Prólogo," 17.
89. Lara Anderson, *Cooking Up the Nation: Spanish Culinary Texts and Culinary Nationalization in the Late Nineteenth and Early Twentieth Century* (Woodbridge, UK: Tamesis, 2013), 123.
90. Afinoguénova, "Organic Nation," 748.
91. Marañón, "Prólogo," 7, 8.
92. Marañón, "Prólogo," 8–9, 10. See Afinoguénova on how regional foods were mobilized during this period to minimize the regional contradictions and differences that inhibited a sense of national unity and belonging. Afinoguénova, "Organic Nation," 750. In line with her study, Marañón's intentional framing of Pradera's peasant roots is consistent with how tourism officials framed peasant lifestyles as essential ingredients for tourism attractions and, at the same time, essential to "reviving" the nation in ways that discouraged class warfare. Afinoguénova, "Organic Nation," 760, 761.
93. Marañón, "Prólogo," 13, 12.
94. Marañón, "Prólogo," 14.
95. Marañón, "Prólogo," 8.
96. Marañón "Breve ensayo," 19; Marañón, "Prólogo," 8.
97. See Flitter on how Romantic literary theorists and historians re-claimed medieval and Golden Age models as the authentic representation of Spanish identity in the nineteenth century. Flitter, *Spanish Romanticism*, 162.

98. Marañón, "Prólogo," 3, 8.
99. Eugenia Afinoguénova and Jaume Martí-Olivella "Introduction: A Nation under Tourists' Eyes: Tourism and Identity Discourses in Spain," in *Spain Is (Still) Different: Tourism and Discourse in Spanish Identity* (Lanham, MD: Lexington Books, 2008). xii. This state support for tourism first appears in Spain in 1905 in the form of the Comisión Nacional de Turismo.
100. Marañón, "Prólogo," 8.
101. M. Barke and J. Towner, eds. *Tourism in Spain: Critical Issues* (Wallingford: CAB, 1996), 6.
102. Marañón, "Breve ensayo," 16.
103. Ali Bab quoted in Marañón, "Breve ensayo," 16–17. Author of *Gastronomie Pratique* (1907) 'Ali-Bab,' or Henri Babinski, was an engineer whose cookbook was originally published in 1907 and re-edited and expanded throughout the twentieth century.
104. Marañón, "Breve ensayo," 17.
105. Marañón, "Breve ensayo," 17. Foreign guidebooks discouraged visitors from *fondas* (taverns) due to questionable sanitation; they were directed instead to establishments that served French cuisine. Barke and Towner, *Tourism in Spain*, 11.
106. Marañón, "Breve ensayo," 18, 19. In the first years of the Republic, expanding resorts, amenities, and beach cultures attracted two hundred thousand foreigners, mostly British and French. Pack, *Tourism and Dictatorship*, 46–47.
107. Marañón, "Breve ensayo," 18.
108. Bendix, *In Search of Authenticity*, 4. Bendix argues that institutions like universities, or in Spain's case, cultural institutions like the Institución Libre de Enseñanza and Centro de Estudios Históricos, research the "components of an ideal culture" and inculcate these ideas into the economically and politically powerful bourgeoisie. Authenticity becomes a "core ingredient" in shaping the boundaries of the ideal culture; thus, the authentic receives scholarly attention, while the inauthentic is maligned for spoiling or harming the components that structure the ideal culture. Bendix, *In Search of Authenticity*, 4.
109. Marañón, "Breve ensayo," 19. See Afinoguénova, "An Organic Nation" and "De la carta a la papeleta."
110. Köstlin quoted in Bendix, *In Search of Authenticity*, 7.
111. Marañón, "Prólogo," 8.
112. Marañón, "Breve ensayo," 18. This description of Pradera's abilities contrasts with the ridicule ascribed to Spaniards who adopt foreign mannerisms to demonstrate "buen gusto." See Torrecilla on Feijoo. Torrecilla, *La imitación colectiva*, 16.
113. Marañón, "Breve ensayo," 12.
114. Marañón, "Prólogo," 12.
115. Marañón, "Breve ensayo," 18.

116. John K. Walton, "Tourism and Consumption in Urban Spain, 1876–1975" in *Spain Is (Still) Different: Tourism and Discourse in Spanish Identity*, eds. Eugenia Afinoguénova and Jaume Martí-Olivella (Lanham, MD: Lexington Books, 2008), 118.
117. Walton, "Tourism and Consumption," 118.
118. Pack, *Tourism and Dictatorship*, 658. Italics mine.
119. Castells, "La Bella Easo," 351–52.
120. F. J. Sánchez Cantón, *Spain* (Madrid: Patronato Nacional del Turismo, Hauser y Menet, 1930), 119, 120, 20.
121. Robert Davidson, "Observing the City, Mediating the Mountain: Mirador and the 1929 International Exhibition of Barcelona," in *Visualizing Spanish Modernity*, eds. Susan Larson and Eva Woods (New York: Berg, 2005), 229.
122. Maurice Roche, *Mega-Events and Modernity: Olympics and Expos in the Growth of Global Culture* (New York: Routledge, 2000), 45–46.
123. Brad Epps, "Modern Spaces: Building Barcelona," in *Iberian Cities*, ed. Joan Ramon Resina (New York: Routledge, 2001), 172.
124. Marañón, "Breve ensayo," 18.

CHAPTER 4

1. Dolors Llopart, "Cuineres. Creadores i difusores de patrimoni immateria," in *Dona i folklore*, ed. Dolors Llopart i Roser Ros (Barcelona: Tantàgora Serveis Culturals, Departament de Cultura de la Generalitat de Catalunya, 2013), 79.
2. See Anderson, "The Unity and Diversity," on how Spanish cuisine has resisted homogeneity, finding any unity in its regional diversity. In their study of the history of Catalan cuisine, Song and Riera note how the writing of Catalan gastronomy attempts to assert its particularities over other culinary practices of Spain. Lara Anderson, "The Unity and Diversity of La Olla Podrida: An Autochthonous Model of Spanish Culinary Nationalism," *Journal of Spanish Cultural Studies* 14, no. 4 (2013). See also Rebecca Ingram, "Mapping and Mocking: Spanish Cuisine and Ramón Gómez de La Serna's 'El Primer Mapa Gastronómico de España,'" Special Issue "Writing about Food: Culinary Literature in the Hispanic World," *Cincinnati Romance Review* 33 (2012).
3. Charlotte Biltekoff, *Eating Right in America: The Cultural Politics of Food & Health* (Durham, NC: Duke University Press, 2013).
4. H. Rosi Song and Anna Riera, *A Taste of Barcelona: The History of Catalan Cooking and Eating* (Lanham, MD: Rowman & Littlefield, 2019). See also Venetia Johannes's *Nourishing the Nation* (2020), an ethnography of the connections between Catalan foodways and nationalism. She notes specifically the "ideal" of *excursionisme*, or how one becomes acquainted with the Catalan nation through travel and consuming its food specialties. Venetia Johannes, *Nourishing the Nation: Food as National Identity in Catalonia* (New York: Berghahn, 2020), 92.

5. Enrique Perdiguero-Gil and Ramón Castejón-Bolea, "Popularising Right Food and Feeding Practices in Spain (1847–1950): The Handbooks of Domestic Economy," *Dynamis* 30 (2010): 141–65.
6. Perdiguero-Gil and Castejón-Bolea, "Popularising Right Food," 141.
7. Montserrat Duch Plana and Montserrat Palau Vergés, "La socialización de los saberes femeninos: El 'Instituto de Cultura y Biblioteca Popular para la Mujer.'" *Historia Social*, no. 82 (2015): 133–47.
8. Isabel Segura Soriano names this collection of archival materials "Llibres de Actes." They range in date from 1912 to 1935 and carry various titles including "Programa: Curs de 1912–1913," "Resumen-Memoria: Programa 1916–1917," and "Report Documentat." Isabel Segura Soriano, *Memòria d'un espai: Institut de Cultura i Biblioteca Popular de la Dona, 1909–2003* (Barcelona: Ajuntament de Barcelona, Institut d'Educació, 2007), 185. For the sake of consistency, I will refer to them as *Actas* and indicate their years of publication in parentheses.
9. Archives and Institut materials are now held at the Archivo General de la Diputació de Barcelona.
10. Segura Soriano, *Memòria d'un espai*, 18.
11. Robert Davidson, *Jazz Age Barcelona* (Toronto: University of Toronto Press, 2009), 16.
12. Miller, *Feeding Barcelona*, 14.
13. Segura Soriano, *Memòria d'un espai*, 18, 19–20.
14. Álvaro Soto Carmona, *El Trabajo industrial en la España contemporánea, 1874–1936* (Barcelona: Anthropos, 1989), 687, 688.
15. Cited in Soto Carmona, *El Trabajo industrial*, 689.
16. Soto Carmona, *El Trabajo industrial*, 699.
17. Dolors Marín Silvestre, *Francesca Bonnemaison: Educadora de ciutadanes* (Diputació de Barcelona, 2004), 27.
18. See Pérez-Villanueva Tovar on the Escuela del Hogar y Profesional de la Mujer and Magallón Portolés on la Residencia de Señoritas directed by North American scientist Mary Louise Foster. Isabel Pérez-Villanueva Tovar, "La Escuela del Hogar y Profesional de la Mujer y las enseñanzas domésticas (1911–1936)," *Arenal* 22, no. 2 (July-Dec. 2015).
19. Duch Plana and Palau Vergés, "La socialización," 135.
20. Segura Soriano, *Memòria d'un espai*, 16.
21. While treating Madrid rather than Barcelona, the novel *Tea Rooms: Mujeres obreras* (1934) by Luisa Carnés explicitly frames the acquisition of culture as emancipatory for working-class women. See studies of Carnés's work in the collection edited by Iliana Olmedo, *Itinerarios de exilio: la obra narrativa de Luisa Carnés* (2014). Information about the *Escuela* in Institut *Actas*, though highly relevant to this study, was limited to descriptions of its existence, how it was publicized, and comments about disappointment that it was not more popular.

22. See publications under the leadership of Roberta Johnson, including *Antología del pensamiento feminista español* (2012), *A New History of Iberian Feminisms* (2018), and *Major Concepts in Spanish Feminist Theory* (2019).
23. Inmaculada Blasco Herranz, "Citizenship and Female Catholic Militancy in 1920s Spain," trans. Jeremy Roe, *Gender & History* 19, no. 3 (November 2007), 453.
24. Blasco Herranz, "Citizenship," 449, 453.
25. Adolfo Gonázlez Posada, 1899, 8, cited in Maryellen Bieder, "First-Wave Feminisms, 1880–1919," in *A New History of Iberian Feminisms*, eds. Silvia Bermúdez and Roberta Johnson (Toronto: Toronto University Press, 2018), 158.
26. Christine Arkinstall, "Forging a Nation for the Female Sex: Equality, Natural Law, and Citizenship in Spanish Feminist Essays, 1881–1920," in *A New History of Iberian Feminisms*, eds. Silvia Bermúdez and Roberta Johnson (Toronto: Toronto University Press, 2018), 149. Edited by Josefa Pujol de Collado, Gertrudis Gómez de Avellaneda and Dolores Mondserdà de Macià, during the years 1883 and 1884 the magazine was far more "avante-garde" than the Madrid magazine of the same title. Arkinstall, "Forging a Nation," 147.
27. Arkinstall, "Forging a Nation," 151–52.
28. Johnson, *Major Concepts*, 9.
29. González Calbet cited in Maryellen Bieder, "Historical Background: From Wars and Revolution to Constitutional Monarchies; Spain's Sporadic Path to Modernity, 1808–1919," in *A New History of Iberian Feminisms*, eds. Silvia Bermúdez and Roberta Johnson (Toronto: Toronto University Press, 2018), 99.
30. Bieder, "First-Wave Feminisms," 158.
31. Bieder, "Historical Background," 99.
32. Marín Silvestre, *Francesca Bonnemaison*, 20, 23, 24.
33. Marín Silvestre, *Francesca Bonnemaison*, 36; Bieder, "First-Wave Feminisms," 159.
34. Marín Silvestre, *Francesca Bonnemaison*, 32, 33–34, 35.
35. Blasco Herranz, "Citizenship," 442, 448, 449.
36. Blasco Herranz, "Citizenship," 446.
37. Marín Silvestre, *Francesca Bonnemaison*, 30.
38. [*Actas*] Archive of the Institut de Culture i Biblioteca Popular de La Dona, Biblioteca Francesca Bonnemaison, Libros de Actas, 1912–1935. Accessed November 7–20, 2015, 1916–1917, 3; *Actas*, 1914–1915, 3.
39. *Actas*, 1916–1917, 4.
40. *Actas*, 1917–1918, 4.
41. Segura Soriano, *Memòria d'un espai*, 37.
42. Transcript of interview cited by Segura Soriano in Segura Soriano, *Memòria d'un espai*, 16.
43. *Actas*, 1923, 5–10.
44. Duch Plana and Palau Vergés, "La socialización," 136.

45. *Actas*, 1917–1918, 4; *Actas*, 1918–1919, 12.
46. *Actas*, 1923, 20.
47. Segura Soriano, *Memòria d'un espai*, 89, 91.
48. *Actas*, 1922, 56.
49. Carme Martí i Cantí, *El camí de les Aigües* (Barcelona: Institució de les Lletres Catalanes, 2017).
50. Segura Soriano, *Memòria d'un espai*, 92.
51. *Actas*, 1918–1919, 5.
52. Dolors Llopart, "Josep Rondissoni, mestre de cuineres i creador de la tradició de la cuina barcelonina," in *Periferias, Fronteras y Diálogos: Actas del XIII Congreso de Antropología de la Federación de Asociaciones de Antropología del Estado Español*, Tarragona, 2–5 de septiembre de 2014 (Tarragona: Universitat Rovira i Virgili, n.d.). 1865.
53. Manel Guirado, *El llegat de Rondissoni: Història i receptes del xef més influent de la Catalunya del segle XX* (Barcelona: Ara Llibres, 2017), 11–13.
54. After the war, Rondissoni opened a *mantegueria i xarcuteria* (grocery and butcher shop) on the Rambla de Catalunya and continued giving cooking classes in different locales. He also opened several restaurants. His masterwork, *Culinaria*, was published in 1945. He died in 1968. Llopart, "Josep," 1865.
55. *Actas*, 1924, 13.
56. Segura Soriano, *Memòria d'un espai*, 90.
57. Segura Soriano, *Memòria d'un espai*, 90; Jennifer Davis, *Defining Culinary Authority: The Transformation of Cooking in France, 1650–1830* (Baton Rouge: Louisiana State University Press, 2013), 11–12.
58. *Actas*, 1928, 41.
59. *Actas*, 1924, 36–44.
60. *Actas*, 1924, 43. Rondissoni maintained marketing relationships with food manufacturers like Maggi and Benesdorp. Maggi seasoning is a vegetable-based sauce used to enhance the flavor of savory foods and as a substitute for a meat-based broth. It was created in 1886 by Swiss miller Julius Maggi. See Jennifer McGavin, "What Is Maggi Seasoning?," The Spruce Eats, July 19, 2021, https://www.thespruceeats.com/maggi-special-seasoning-from-switzerland-1446943.
61. Classes with this style of formal instruction were also complemented by excursions to markets and manufacturers of different food products, Segura Soriano, *Memòria d'un espai*, 91.
62. *Actas*, 1924, 38, 37, 39.
63. *Actas*, 1924, 49. The cookbooks were published between 1924 and 1931. Written in Catalan, the earliest book, *Classes de Cuina Popular: Curs de 1924–1925*, presents only recipes taught in that class; subsequent editions include the recipes and menus taught in both the "Cuina popular" and "Cuina práctica" classes. The book from 1930 to 1931 also includes dishes taught in a "Cuina de

tardes" (Afternoon cooking) class. There was significant overlap in the menus created for each class, despite stratified publics. Each book is organized by the dates of classes, with class sessions that featured, most often, the preparation of one dish. Indices specify that a week of "Cuina popular" classes taught a complete menu (*Classes de Cuina Popular, 1924–1925*, 305), while a month's "Cuina práctica" classes relayed a menu. In contrast to works like *La cuynera catalana* (1835) that relay recipes in a series of brief sentences, Rondissoni's recipes feature a list of ingredients and quantities, indicate the number of people it will serve, and give several paragraphs of cooking instruction and sometimes an image to demonstrate its ideal appearance when served.

64. Llopart, "Josep," 1861. Llopart also attributes the shifting cuisine of Barcelona to the First World War, which spurred a wave of changes in table customs and household décor. More complicated menus that departed from traditional modest cooking were one attribute of that wave. Llopart, "Josep," 1862–63.
65. Manuel Vázquez Montalbán, "Prólogo. Culinaria: A la medida de la gente inteligente," in *Culinaria*, by Josep Rondissoni, 1945 (Barcelona: Bon Ton, Antonio Bosch, [s.a.]), 3, 4, 6.
66. Davis, *Defining Culinary Authority*, 73.
67. Davis, *Defining Culinary Authority*, 73.
68. Parkhurst Fergurson, *Accounting for Taste*, 17.
69. Duch Plana and Palau Vergés, "La socialización," 133.
70. *Actas*, 1916–1917, 4.
71. *Actas*, 1914–1915, 3.
72. Marín Silvestre, *Francesca Bonnemaison*, 25, 35.
73. Notable examples include Mari Pepa Colomer, the first Catalan woman aviator (164–65), the first Spanish state-registered draftswoman Leonor Ferrer Girabau (167–68), Carme Karr Alfonsetti, the feminist writer who directed *Feminal* between 1907 and 1917 and founder of La Llar (173). For a comprehensive list, see Segura Soriano's "Resums biogràfics," 159–83.
74. *Actas*, 1918–1919, 24, 27.
75. Segura Soriano, *Memòria d'un espai*, 95.
76. Segura Soriano, *Memòria d'un espai*, 96. *Actas* 1927, 5. The Institut was initially supported as part of the Mancomunitat's Consell de Pedagogia to formally educate workers. Marín Silvestre, *Francesca Bonnemaison*, 29. Conflict over the use of Catalan at the Institut—in its name, as the language for instruction and its *Actas*—set leadership at odds with Primo's Civil Government, as did their decision in 1924 to abstain from attending a children's festival in honor of the king and queen. This decision resulted in the cancellation of the yearly subvention the Institut had received until that point from the Generalitat de Catalunya. Segura Soriano, *Memòria d'un espai*, 87.
77. *Actas*, 1916–1917, 4; *Actas*, 1926.
78. Segura Soriano, *Memòria d'un espai*, 92. Despite the mention of classes for

obreras, Segura Soriano writes that this sponsorship was part of a wide-ranging advertising campaign geared toward middle-class women to convince them of the benefits of cooking with gas rather than charcoal.

79. Miller, *Feeding Barcelona*, 103–4. Miller also identifies these manufactured ingredients: the aforementioned Maggi drops, Opson rice flour, canned salmon, and French mustard, among others.
80. *Ménage: Revista del arte de la cocina y pastelería moderns*, Año 2, Núm 12, January 1932, 23; *Ménage*, Año 1, March 2, 1931, 14.
81. *Ménage*, Año 4, Núm 37, February 1934, 40–41; *Ménage*, Año 4, 27.
82. Megan Elias, *Stir It Up: Home Economics in American Culture* (Philadelphia: University of Pennsylvania Press, 2008), 2.
83. Segura Soriano, *Memòria d'un espai*, 97.
84. *Actas*, 1918–1919, 31.
85. *Actas*, 1927–1928, 36.
86. Duch Plana and Palau Vergés, "La socialización," 139.
87. Segura Soriano, *Memòria d'un espai*, 97.
88. Segura Soriano, *Memòria d'un espai*, 97, 98.
89. Segura Soriano, *Memòria d'un espai*, 100, 101.
90. *Actas*, 1932, 25.
91. Vázquez Montalbán, "Prólogo," 3.
92. Born of the progressive era in the US context, ideas of community-based citizenship were organized around ideas of "community welfare" (encompassing needs like health, recreation, education), which could be fulfilled through private or public social agencies. Julie A. Reuben, "Beyond Politics: Community Civics and the Redefinition of Citizenship in the Progressive Era," *History of Education Quarterly* 37, no. 4 (1997), 405. Citizenship was framed as a "life process" rather than exclusively legal status or politics and entailed responsibilities in the public and private spheres. Reuben, "Beyond Politics," 415–16.
93. Biltekoff, *Eating Right*, 7.
94. Biltekoff, *Eating Right*, 20.
95. Stage and Vincenti, *Rethinking Home Economics*, 3.
96. Richard Cleminson and Teresa Fuentes Peris, "'La Mala Vida': Source and Focus of Degeneration, Degeneracy and Decline," *Journal of Spanish Cultural Studies* 10, no. 4 (2009), 385.
97. Song and Riera, *A Taste of Barcelona*; Miller, *Feeding Barcelona*.
98. Cleminson and Fuentes Peris, "'La Mala Vida,'" 386, 387, 385.
99. Rafael Salillas, *El Delincuente español (Hampa)* (Madrid: Librería de Victoriano Suárez, 1898), IX–X; Andrés Galera Gómez, *Ciencia y delincuencia: El determinismo antropológico en la España del siglo XIX* (Madrid: CSIC, 1991), 68–75.
100. Cleminson quoting Pick. Cleminson, *Anarchism*, 387.
101. Joshua Goode, *Impurity of Blood: Defining Race in Spain, 1870–1930* (Baton Rouge: Louisiana State University Press, 2009), 15–16.

102. Goode, *Impurity of Blood*, 143.
103. Goode, *Impurity of Blood*, 157–58. Influenced by Italian criminologists Ceasare Lombroso and his student Enrico Ferri, Salillas adapted Italian and French ideas of criminology to a uniquely Spanish context. Goode, *Impurity of Blood*, 158. Throughout his career he worked from within the Ministry of Grace and Justice and also with the Krausist Institución Libre de Enseñanza as part of Franciso Giner de los Ríos's school to study the "science" of penal law. Goode *Impurity of Blood*, 161. He wanted to understand the differences between criminals in different nations—how the "biological development of a nation" contributed to more or less violent crime. Goode, *Impurity of Blood*, 163.
104. Goode, *Impurity of Blood*, 163.
105. Salillas, *Delincuente*, XII.
106. Galera Gómez, *Ciencia y delincuencia*, 70.
107. Goode, *Impurity of Blood*, 163, 256. Also by Salillas, see *La casa como célula social* (1908). Goode notes that Salillas went on to influence the thinking of Spanish eugenicists José María Albiñana (associated with the pre-fascist Partido Nacionalista Español) and liberal and progressive Gregorio Marañón.
108. Josep Cunill de Bosch, *La Cuina Catalana, 1923* (Barcelona: Parsifal Edicions, 1996), 23. Miller's translation.
109. *La Cuina Catalana* and the *Llibre de la cuina catalana* by Ferran Agulló were two of the Catalan nationalist cookbooks that Song and Riera identify as codifications of a popular body of Catalan dishes.
110. Biltekoff, *Eating Right*, 28–29. See Megan Elias on the thought of home economics theorist Ellen Richards: "Where eugenics bred the perfect individual, euthenics would supply the ideal environment. This particular vision for the movement did not catch on, but the central idea that social problems, including the drudgery of the housewife, could be solved through scientific research did endure." Elias, *Stir It Up*, 11.
111. Elias, *Stir It Up*, 11.
112. Scanlon, *La polémica feminista*, 18.
113. Sarah Stage, "Introduction Home Economics: What's in a Name?" *Rethinking Home Economics: Women and the History of a Profession* (Ithaca, NY: Cornell University Press, 1997), 1; Elias, *Stir It Up*, 2.
114. Elias, *Stir It Up*, 2, 1.
115. Elias, *Stir It Up*, 12. Simultaneously with the development of home economics as a field of academic inquiry, corporate producers of household goods established themselves as authorities on the domestic. Elias argues that this alternative discourse weakened the legitimacy that women had established for home economics, diluting the emancipatory project of women's control of the domestic environment. Elias, *Stir It Up*, 2. Products won over the intellectual movement and we see this same dynamic in the ideological shifts that occur in the Institut in the 1930s.
116. Perdiguero-Gil and Castejón-Bolea, "Popularising Right," 155.

117. Magdalena Cambrea, "Curset D'Economìa Domèstica," Barcelona: Institut de Cultura i Biblioteca Popular de la Dona, 1916–1917 i 1917–1918, 2.
118. Perdiguero-Gil and Castejón-Bolea, "Popularising Right Food," 155.
119. Segura Soriano, *Memòria d'un espai*, 50.
120. Sensat quoted in Segura Soriano, *Memòria d'un espai*, 51.
121. Segura Soriano, *Memòria d'un espai*, 51.
122. Rosa Sensat, *Cómo se enseña la economía doméstica* (Madrid: Publicaciones de la Revista de Pedagogía; Serie Metodológica, 1927), 6, 15.
123. Sensat, *Cómo se enseña*, 14–15, 12, 14.
124. Sensat, *Cómo se enseña*, 6, 9.
125. Sensat, *Cómo se enseña*, 14–15.
126. Sensat, *Cómo se enseña*, 9.
127. Sensat, *Cómo se enseña*, 32.
128. Elias, *Stir It Up*, 2.
129. Williams-Forson, "Foreword," ix–xi.
130. Miller, *Feeding Barcelona*, 103.
131. Johnson, *Major Concepts*, 16.
132. Lara Anderson, *Control and Resistance: Food Discourse in Franco Spain* (Toronto: Toronto University Press, 2020), 22.

CONCLUSION

1. Graham and Labanyi, "Introduction," 2.
2. Graham and Labanyi, "Introduction," 3.
3. Anderson, *Control and Resistance*, 3.
4. Suzanne Dunai, "Food Politics in Postwar Spain: Eating and Everyday Life During the Early Franco Dictatorship, 1939–1952" (PhD diss., University of California San Diego, 2019), 1.
5. Dunai, "Food Politics," 1.
6. Meah, "Gender," 88.
7. Warren Belasco, *Food: The Key Concepts* (Oxford: Berg, 2008), 15–16.
8. Graham and Labanyi, "Introduction," 15.
9. See Laura Schwartz's work on these issues in Britain in *Feminism and the Servant Problem: Class and Domestic Labour in the Women's Suffrage Movement* (Cambridge: Cambridge University Press, 2019).
10. Another model is the University of Barcelona's Campus de Alimentación de Torribera, created to "potenciar un sector emergente," that of nutrition, and bring together a range of experts in fields like health, agri-business and nutrition, and social policy. http://www.ub.edu/campusalimentacio/es/campus_projecte.html.
11. Graham and Labanyi, "Introduction," 18.
12. See also Afinoguénova, "De la carta a la papeleta" and Ingram "From the Mediterranean Diet to Gastronationalism: Cultural Studies and Spanish Foodways," in *Routledge Companion to Twentieth and Twenty-First Century Spain: Ideas,*

Practices, Imaginings, eds. L. Elena Delgado and Eduardo Ledesma (Oxfordshire: Routledge, forthcoming, 2023).

13. Dawn Johnston, Lisa Stowe, and Gwendolyn Blue, "Food Culture in Spain," *Canadian Association for Food Studies Newsletter*, May 2007, 1. See also "Culinary Tourism in Córdoba (Spain)," among other studies, by Tomás López-Guzmán and Sandra Sánchez-Cañizares, who frame gastronomy as the tourist attraction that foments economic development.
14. N. Michelle Murray, *Home Away from Home: Immigrant Narratives, Domesticity, and Coloniality in Contemporary Spanish Culture* (Chapel Hill: UNC Press for Department of Romance Studies, University of North Carolina, 2018), 14.
15. As this book goes to press, the Spanish Congreso de Diputados voted to ratify on June 9, 2022, the "Convenio sobre las trabajadoras y los trabajadores domésticos, 2011 (núm. 189)," an important step forward in recognizing problematic aspects of Spanish law affecting domestic workers. After Italy, Spain employs the highest number of domestic workers in Europe (3 percent of the labor force); more than 95 percent are women and and 43 percent are foreign-born. Yet, they lack access to key labor protections such as unemployment benefits. Elena de Sus, "Una victoria histórica para las trabajadoras del hogar," *CTXT: Contexto y acción*, no. 285 (junio 2022). https://ctxt.es/es/20220601/Politica/39938/trabajadoras-domesticas-convenido-OIT-igualdad-derechos-Elena-de-Sus.
16. Cairns and Johnston, *Food and Femininity*, 111.
17. Alice Julier, "Critiquing Hegemony, Creating Food, Crafting Justice: Cultivating and Activist Feminist Food Studies," in *Feminist Food Studies: Intersectional Perspectives*, eds. Barbara Parker, Jennifer Brady, Elaine Power, and Susan Belyea (Toronto: Women's Press, 2019), 14.

BIBLIOGRAPHY

Abarca, Meredith. *Voices in the Kitchen: Views of Food and the World from Working-Class Mexican and Mexican American Women*. College Station: Texas A&M University Press, 2006.

[*Actas*]. Archive of the Institut de Cultura i Biblioteca Popular de La Dona, Biblioteca Francesca Bonnemaison. Libros de Actas, 1912–1935. Accessed November 7–20, 2015.

Afinoguénova, Eugenia, and Jaume Martí-Olivella. "Introduction: A Nation under Tourists' Eyes: Tourism and Identity Discourses in Spain." In *Spain Is (Still) Different: Tourism and Discourse in Spanish Identity*, xi–xxxviii. Lanham, MD: Lexington Books, 2008.

Afinoguénova, Eugenia. "An Organic Nation: State-Run Tourism, Regionalism, and Food in Spain, 1905–1931." *Journal of Modern History* 86, no. 4 (December 2014): 743–79.

———. "De la carta a la papeleta: el 'menú del día' entre la dictadura y la democracia en España, 1964–1981." *Bulletin of Spanish Studies* 97, no. 4 (2020): 515–38.

Agulló, Ferran. *Llibre de la cuina catalana*. 1933. Barcelona: Alta Fulla, 1978.

Aldaraca, Bridget. *El Ángel del Hogar: Galdós and the Ideology of Domesticity in Spain*. Chapel Hill: UNC Press for North Carolina Studies in the Romance Languages and Literatures, 1991.

Álvarez Junco, José. "Rural and Urban Popular Cultures." In *Spanish Cultural Studies: An Introduction*, edited by Helen Graham, and Jo Labanyi, 82–89. Oxford: Oxford University Press, 1995.

Anderson, Benedict. *Imagined Communities*. London: Verso, 1991.

Anderson, Lara, and Rebecca Ingram. "Introduction. Transhispanic Food Cultural Studies: Defining the Subfield." *Bulletin of Spanish Studies* 97, no. 4 (2020): 471–83.

Anderson, Lara. *Control and Resistance: Food Discourse in Franco Spain*. Toronto: Toronto University Press, 2020.

———. "Spanish Culinary Autochtony and Culinary Modernity: María Mestayer de Echagüe's *La Cocina Completa* and *Platos Escogidos de La Cocina Vasca*." *Cincinnati Romance Review* 33 (2012): 98–113.

———. "The Unity and Diversity of La Olla Podrida: An Autochthonous Model of Spanish Culinary Nationalism." *Journal of Spanish Cultural Studies* 14, no. 4 (2013): 400–414.

———. *Cooking Up the Nation: Spanish Culinary Texts and Culinary Nationalization in the Late Nineteenth and Early Twentieth Century*. Woodbridge, UK: Tamesis, 2013.

Appadurai, Arjun. "How to Make a National Cuisine: Cookbooks in Contemporary India." *Comparative Studies in Society and History* 30, no. 1 (1988): 3–24.

———. "Disjuncture and Difference in the Global Cultural Economy." *Theory, Culture and Society* 7 (1990): 295–310.

Aresti, Nerea. *Médicos, donjuanes y mujeres modernas: Los ideales de feminidad y masculinidad en el primer tercio del siglo XX*. Biscay, Spain: Universidad del País Vasco / Euskal Herriko Unibertsitatea, 2001.

Arkinstall, Christine. "Forging a Nation for the Female Sex: Equality, Natural Law, and Citizenship in Spanish Feminist Essays, 1881–1920." In *A New History of Iberian Feminisms*, edited by Silvia Bermúdez and Roberta Johnson, 147–57. Toronto: Toronto University Press, 2018.

———. *Spanish Female Writers and the Freethinking Press*. Toronto: University of Toronto Press, 2014.

Avakian, Arlene Voski, and Barbara Haber. *From Betty Crocker to Feminist Food Studies: Critical Perspectives on Women and Food*. Amherst: University of Massachusetts Press, 2005.

Azorín. *Valencia; Madrid*. Madrid: Alfaguara/Santillana, 1998.

Bak-Geller Corona, Sarah. "The Cookbook in Mexico: A Founding Document of the Modern Nation." In *The Emergence of National Food: The Dynamics of Food and Nationalism*, edited by Atsuko Ichijo, Venetia Johannes, and Ronald Ranta, 28–38. London: Bloomsbury Academic, 2019.

Balfour, Sebastian. "The Loss of Empire, Regenerationism, and the Forging of a Myth of National Identity." In *Spanish Cultural Studies: An Introduction*, edited by Helen Graham and Jo Labanyi, 25–31. Oxford: Oxford University Press, 1995.

Barbas, Samantha. "Just Like Home: 'Home Cooking' and the Domestication of the American Restaurant." *Gastronomica* 2, no. 4 (2002): 43–52.

Bardají, Teodoro. *Índice Culinario*. Edited by José María Pisa. Huesca: La Val Onsera, 1993.

———. *La cocina de ellas*. Huesca: Ediciones Nauta, Ediciones La Val de Onsera, 2002.

Barke, M., and J. Towner, eds. *Tourism in Spain: Critical Issues*. Wallingford: CAB, 1996.

Barthes, Roland. *Mythologies*. Translated by Annette Lavers. New York: Hill and Wang, 1957.
Belasco, Warren. *Food: The Key Concepts*. Oxford: Berg, 2008.
Bendix, Regina. *In Search of Authenticity: The Formation of Folklore Studies*. Madison: University of Wisconsin Press, 1997.
Benjamin, Walter. "The Work of Art in the Age of Mechanical Reproduction." In *Illuminations*, edited by Hannah Arendt, 217–51. New York: Schocken Books, 1968.
Bieder, Maryellen. "First-Wave Feminisms, 1880–1919." In *A New History of Iberian Feminisms*, edited by Silvia Bermúdez and Roberta Johnson, 158–81. Toronto: Toronto University Press, 2018.
———. "Women and the Twentieth-Century Spanish Literary Canon: The Lady Vanishes." *Anales de la literatura española contemporánea* 17, no. 1–3 (1992): 301–24.
———. "Historical Background: From Wars and Revolution to Constitutional Monarchies; Spain's Sporadic Path to Modernity, 1808–1919." In *A New History of Iberian Feminisms*, edited by Silvia Bermúdez and Roberta Johnson, 93–110. Toronto: Toronto University Press, 2018.
Biltekoff, Charlotte. *Eating Right in America: The Cultural Politics of Food and Health*. Durham, NC: Duke University Press, 2013.
Blasco Herranz, Inmaculada. "Citizenship and Female Catholic Militancy in 1920s Spain." Translated by Jeremy Roe. *Gender & History* 19, no. 3 (November 2007): 441–66.
Botrel, Jean-François. "La novela por entregas." In *Creación y público en la literatura española*, edited by Jean-François Botrel and S. Salaün, 111–55. Barcelona: Editorial Castalia, 1974.
———. *Libros, Prensa y Lectura en la España del siglo XIX*. Madrid: Pirámide, 1993.
Bourdieu, Pierre. *Distinction: A Social Critique of the Judgement of Taste*. Translated by Richard Nice. Cambridge, MA: Harvard University Press, 1984.
———. *The Logic of Practice*. Translated by Richard Nice. Stanford, CA: Stanford University Press, 1980.
Boyd, Carolyn. *Historia Patria: Politics, History, and National Identity in Spain, 1875–1975*. Princeton, NJ: Princeton University Press, 1997.
Bravo Cela, Blanca. *Carmen de Burgos (Colombine): Contra el silencio*. Madrid: Espasa, 2003.
Bravo-Villasante, Carmen. *Vida y obra de Emilia Pardo Bazán*. Madrid: Revista de Occidente, 1962.
Brenan, Gerald. *The Spanish Labyrinth: An Account of the Social and Political Background of the Spanish Civil War*. 2nd ed. Cambridge: Cambridge University Press, 1990.
Brown, Catherine. "The Relics of Menéndez Pidal: Mourning and Melancholia in Hispanomedieval Studies." *La corónica* 24, no. 1 (1995): 15–41.
Burgos Segui, Carmen de. *Influencias recíprocas entre la mujer y la literatura*. Logroño: Imp. y Lib, 1912.

———. "La base de nuestra regeneración." *El Pueblo*, November 13, 1906.
———. *La cocina moderna*. Valencia: Prometeo Sociedad Editorial, 1906.
———. *La mujer en España: Conferencia pronunciada en la Asociación de la Prensa en Roma el 28 de Abril de 1906*. Valencia: F. Sempere y Compañía, Editores, 1906.
———. *La mujer moderna y sus derechos*. 1927. Edited by Pilar Ballarín. Madrid: Editorial Biblioteca Nueva, 2007.
———. *La Protección y la Higiene de los Niños: Boceto de Estudio*. Valencia: Imprenta de Manuel Alufre, 1904.
———. *Misión social de la mujer: Conferencia pronunciada por D.a Carmen de Burgos Seguí el día 18 de febrero de 1911*. Bilbao: Sociedad "El Sitio"; Imp. Jose Rojas Núñez, 1911.
———. *Nueva cocina práctica [La cocina práctica]*. Valencia: Editorial Sempere, 1925.
———. *¿Quiere usted comer bien?* Barcelona: Sopena, 1916.
Butrón, Inés. *Comer en España: De la cocina de subsistencia a la cocina de vanguardia*. Gijón, Asturias: Ediciones Trea, 2020.
Cairns, Kate, and Josée Johnston. *Food and Femininity*. London: Bloomsbury Academic, 2015.
Cambrea, Magdalena. "Curset D'Economìa Domèstica." Barcelona: Institut de Cultura i Biblioteca Popular de la Dona, 1916-1917 i 1917-1918.
Cansinos-Asséns, Rafael. *La novela de un literato*. Madrid: Alianza Editorial, 1982.
Carnés, Luisa. *Tea Rooms: Mujeres obreras*. 1934. Gijón, Asturias: Hoja de Lata, 2016.
Carr, Raymond. "Liberalism and Reaction." In *Spain: A History*, edited by Raymond Carr, 205-42. Oxford: Oxford University Press, 2001.
———. *Modern Spain 1875-1980*. Oxford: Oxford University Press, 2001.
———. *Spain: 1808-1939*. Edited by Alan Bullock, and F. W. D. Deakin. Oxford: Clarendon Press, 1966.
Castells, Luis. "La Bella Easo: 1864-1836." In *Historia de Donostia—San Sebastián*, edited by Miguel Artola, 283-385. Ayuntamiento de San Sebastián: Editorial Nerea, 2000.
Castillo, José Juan. *Biografía*, 2008. Accessed June 1, 2008. http://www.cocinavino.com/ensusalsa/biografia.html.
———. *Las recetas fáciles de José Juan Castillo en el Centenario de Casa Nicolasa*. Legazpi: Zum Edizioak, 2012.
Certeau, Michel de. *The Practice of Everyday Life*. Translated by Steven Rendall. Berkeley: University of California Press, 1984.
Chartier, Roger. "La sociedad liberal: Rupturas y herencias." In *Orígenes culturales de la sociedad liberal (España siglo XIX)*, edited by Jesús A. Martínez, 273-86. Madrid: Biblioteca Nueva, 2003.
ChefBNE. "ChefBNE." Accessed October 14, 2020. http://chefbne.bne.es.

Chodorow, Nancy. *The Reproduction of Mothering: Psychoanalysis and the Sociology of Gender*. Berkeley: University of California Press, 1978.

Clèmessy, Nelly. *Emilia Pardo Bazán como novelista: De la teoría a la práctica*. Translated by Irene Gambra. Madrid: Fundación universitaria española, 1981.

Cleminson, Richard, and Teresa Fuentes Peris. "'La Mala Vida': Source and Focus of Degeneration, Degeneracy and Decline." *Journal of Spanish Cultural Studies* 10, no. 4 (2009): 385–97.

Cleminson, Richard. *Anarchism, Science and Sex: Eugenics in Eastern Spain, 1900–1937*. London: Peter Lang, 2000.

Climent-Espino, Rafael, and Ana Gómez Bravo, eds. *Food, Texts, and Cultures in Latin America and Spain*. Nashville, TN: Vanderbilt University Press, 2020.

Counihan, Carol. *The Anthropology of Food and Body: Gender, Meaning, and Power*. New York: Routledge, 1999.

Cruz, Jesus. *Gentlemen, Bourgeois, and Revolutionaries: Political Change and Cultural Persistence among the Spanish Dominant Groups, 1750–1850*. Cambridge: Cambridge University Press, 1996.

Cunill de Bosch, Josep. *La Cuina Catalana*. 1923. Barcelona: Parsifal Edicions, 1996.

Cuynera catalana, 1835, 1851. Valladolid: Maxtor Editorial, 2010.

Davidson, Robert. *Jazz Age Barcelona*. Toronto: University of Toronto Press, 2009.

———. "Observing the City, Mediating the Mountain: Mirador and the 1929 International Exhibition of Barcelona." In *Visualizing Spanish Modernity*, edited by Susan Larson, and Eva Woods, 228–44. New York: Berg, 2005.

———. "Terroir and Catalonia." *Journal of Catalan Studies* (2007): 39–53.

Davies, Catherine. "The 'Red Lady': Carmen de Burgos (1867–1932)." In *Spanish Women's Writing, 1849–1996*, 117–36. Atlantic Highlands, NJ: Athlone Press, 1998.

Davis, Jennifer. *Defining Culinary Authority: The Transformation of Cooking in France, 1650–1830*. Baton Rouge: Louisiana State University Press, 2013.

De Soucey, Michaela. "Food." In *Oxford Bibliographies Online: Sociology*, edited by Lynette Spillman. Oxford: Oxford University Press, 2017 [2012].

Duch Plana, Montserrat, and Montserrat Palau Vergés. "La socialización de los saberes femeninos: El 'Instituto de Cultura y Biblioteca Popular para la Mujer.'" *Historia Social*, no. 82 (2015): 133–47.

Dunai, Suzanne. "Food Politics in Postwar Spain: Eating and Everyday Life During the Early Franco Dictatorship, 1939–1952." PhD diss., University of California San Diego, 2019.

Eça de Queirós, José María. "Cocina arqueológica." In *Notas comtermporáneas*, 1909, translated by Andrés González Blanco. Madrid: Sucesores de Rivadeneyra, [n.d].

Elias, Megan. *Stir It Up: Home Economics in American Culture*. Philadelphia: University of Pennsylvania Press, 2008.

Elias, Norbert. *The Civilizing Process: The History of Manners*. New York: Urizen Books, 1995.

Enders, Victoria Lorée, and Pamela Beth Radcliff, eds. *Constructing Spanish Womanhood: Female Identity in Modern Spain*. Albany: State University of New York Press, 1999.
Epps, Brad. "Modern Spaces: Building Barcelona." In *Iberian Cities*, edited by Joan Ramon Resina, 148–97. New York: Routledge, 2001.
Erwin, Zachary. "Fantasies of Masculinity in Emilia Pardo Bazán's *Memorias de un solterón*." *Revista de Estudios Hispánicos* 46, no. 3 (2012): 547–68.
Ezama Gil, Ángeles. "Una escritora con vocación de historiadora de la literatura: el canon de escritura femenina de Emilia Pardo Bazán." *Voz y Letra* 17, no. 2 (2006): 89–106.
Ezquiaga, Mitxel. "El día que Nicolasa salió en The Times." *El diario vasco*, November 15, 2018. https://www.diariovasco.com/gipuzkoa/nicolasa-pradera-thetimes-20181115194954-nt.html.
Faus Sevilla, Pilar. *Emilia Pardo Bazán: Su época, su vida, su obra*. A Coruña: Fundación Pedro Barrié de la Maza, 2003.
Flitter, Derek. *Spanish Romanticism and the Uses of History: Ideology and the Historical Imagination*. London: Legenda, 2006.
Folguera Crespo, Pilar. "Revolución y restauración. La emergencia de los primeros ideales emancipadores (1868–1931)." In *Historia de las mujeres en España*, edited by Elisa Garrido, 451–92. Madrid: Editorial Síntesis, 1997.
Fox, Inman. *La invención de España: Nacionalismo liberal e identidad nacional*. Madrid: Ediciones Cátedra, 1997.
Franch i Ferrer, Vincent. "Los sucesos de Cullera y Sueca." *Historia y vida* 120 (1978): 92–95.
Freedman, Paul. *Food: This History of Taste*. Berkeley: University of California Press, 2007.
Galera Gómez, Andrés. *Ciencia y delincuencia: El determinismo antropológico en la España del siglo XIX*. Madrid: CSIC, 1991.
García, Marco Antonio. "Propósitos filológicos de la colección 'Clásicos Castellanos' de la editorial La Lectura." In *X Congreso de la Asociación Internacional de Hispanistas*. Barcelona: Centro Virtual Cervantes, [n.d.].
García del Real, Eduardo (Matilde). *Cocina española y cocina dietética*. "Prólogo" by Gregorio Marañón. Madrid: Sobrinos de la Sucesora de M. Minuesa de los Ríos, 1929.
"Un Gastrónomo Jubilado." *La gran economía de las familias: Arte de arreglar y componer lo sobrante de las comidas de un día para otro*. [. . .] Madrid: Imprenta de F.Lopez Vizcaino, 1869.
Giard, Luce. "Doing-Cooking." In *The Practice of Everyday Life, Volume 2: Living & Cooking*, 145–248. Minneapolis: University of Minnesota Press, 1998.
Gold, Hazel. "Del foro al fogón: Narrativas culturales en el discurso culinario de Emilia Pardo Bazán." In *La literatura de Emilia Pardo Bazán*, 313–23. A Coruña: Casa Museo Emilia Pardo Bazán, Fundación Caixa, 2009.
Gómez Bravo, Ana. *Comida y Cultura en el Mundo Hispánico*. Sheffield, UK: Equinox, 2017.

———. *The Converso Cookbook: Strom Center for Jewish Studies.* Seattle: University of Washington, 2014. Accessed 15 December 2020, http:jewishstudies.washington.edu/converso-cookbook-home.

———. "Food, Blood, and a Jewish Raza in Fifteenth-Century Spain." In *Food, Texts, and Cultures in Latin America and Spain*, 39–75. Nashville, TN: Vanderbilt University Press, 2020.

Gómez Santos, Marino. *Gregorio Marañón.* Barcelona: Plaza and Janés, S.A, 2001.

González Turmo, Isabel. *Comida de rico, comida de pobre: Los hábitos alimenticios en el Occidente andaluz (Siglo XX).* Sevilla: Universidad de Sevilla, 1997.

Good, Kate. "Women and Huevos: Matters of Food, Religion, and Gender in Emilia Pardo Bazán's 'Los huevos arrefalfados.'" *Decimonónica* 14, no. 1 (2017): 1–15.

Goode, Joshua. *Impurity of Blood: Defining Race in Spain, 1870–1930.* Baton Rouge: Louisiana State University Press, 2009.

Goody, Jack. "The Recipe, the Prescription and the Experiment." In *The Domestication of the Savage Mind*, 129–45. Cambridge: Cambridge University Press, 1977.

Graham, Helen, and Jo Labanyi. "Introduction. Culture and Modernity: The Case of Spain." *Spanish Cultural Studies: An Introduction. The Struggle for Modernity*, 1–24. Oxford: Oxford University Press, 1995.

Grainger, Sally. "The Myth of Apicius." *Gastronómica* 7, no. 2 (May 2007): 71–77.

Greer, Margaret R., Walter Mignolo, and Maureen Quilligan, eds. *Rereading the Black Legend: The Discourses of Religious and Racial Difference in the Renaissance Empires.* Chicago: University of Chicago Press, 2007.

Guillory, John. *Cultural Capital: The Problem of Literary Canon Formation.* Chicago: University of Chicago Press, 1993.

Guirado, Manel. *El llegat de Rondisonni: Història i receptes del xef més influent de la Catalunya del segle XX.* Barcelona: Ara Llibres, 2017.

Haranburu Altuna, Luis. *Historia de la alimentación y de la cocina en el País Vasco.* Alegia, Gipuzkoa: Hiria liburuak, 2000.

Heydl-Cortínez, Cecilia, ed. *Cartas de la Condesa en el Diario de la Marina La Habana (1909–1915).* Madrid: Pliegos, 2002.

Hobsbawm, Eric and Terence Ranger, eds. *The Invention of Tradition.* Cambridge: Cambridge University Press, 1983.

Holguín, Sandie. *Creating Spaniards: Culture and National Identity in Republican Spain.* Madison: University of Wisconsin Press, 2002.

Ingram, Rebecca. "Mapping and Mocking: Spanish Cuisine and Ramón Gómez de La Serna's 'El Primer Mapa Gastronómico de España.'" In "Writing About Food: Culinary Literature in the Hispanic World." Special Issue of *Cincinnati Romance Review* 33 (2012): 78–97.

———. "Popular Tradition and Bourgeois Elegance in Emilia Pardo Bazán's *Cocina Española*." *Bulletin of Hispanic Studies* 91, no. 3 (2014): 261–74.

———. "*Escritora-ama de casa?*: The Political Tactics of Carmen de Burgos' Culinary Writing." *Bulletin of Spanish Studies* 94, no. 7 (2017): 1145–57.
———. "Bringing the *escuela* to the *despensa*: Regenerationist Politics in Carmen de Burgos's Cookbooks." In *Multiple Modernities: Carmen de Burgos, Author and Activist*, edited by Anja Louis and Michelle Sharp, 180–96. New York: Routledge, 2017.
———. "From the Mediterranean Diet to Gastronationalism: Cultural Studies and Spanish Foodways." In *Routledge Companion to Twentieth and Twenty-First Century Spain: Ideas, Practices, Imaginings*, edited by L. Elena Delgado and Eduardo Ledesma. Oxfordshire: Routledge, forthcoming 2023.
Inness, Sherrie, ed. *Cooking Lessons: The Politics and Gender of Food*. Lanham, MD: Rowman and Littlefield Publishers, 2001.
———. *Secret Ingredients: Race, Gender and Class at the Dinner Table*. New York: Palgrave, 2006.
Jagoe, Catherine. *Ambiguous Angels: Gender in the Novels of Galdós*. Berkeley: University of California Press, 1994.
Johannes, Venetia. *Nourishing the Nation: Food as National Identity in Catalonia*. New York: Berghahn, 2020.
Johnson, Roberta. *Gender and Nation in the Spanish Modernist Novel*. Nashville, TN: Vanderbilt University Press, 2003.
———. *Major Concepts in Spanish Feminist Theory*. Albany: State University of New York Press, 2019.
Johnston, Dawn, Lisa Stowe, and Gwendolyn Blue. "Food Culture in Spain." *Canadian Association for Food Studies Newsletter*, May 2007.
Juaristi, Adriana de. *Cocina*. Madrid: Editorial Caro Raggio, 1928.
Juderías, Julián. *La leyenda negra. Estudios acerca del concepto de España en el extranjero*. [N.p.]: Editorial Nacional, 1967.
Julier, Alice. "Critiquing Hegemony, Creating Food, Crafting Justice: Cultivating and Activist Feminist Food Studies." In *Feminist Food Studies: Intersectional Perspectives*, edited by Barbara Parker, Jennifer Brady, Elaine Power, and Susan Belyea, 13–32. Toronto: Women's Press, 2019.
Keller, Gary D. *The Significance and Impact of Gregorio Marañón*. New York: Bilingual Press / Editorial Bilingüe Studies in the Literary Analysis of Hispanic Texts, 1977.
Kirkpatrick, Susan and Jaqueline Cruz. *Mujer, modernismo y vanguardia en España: 1898–1931*. Madrid: Cátedra, 2003.
Labanyi, Jo. *Gender and Modernization in the Spanish Realist Novel*. Oxford: Oxford University Press, 2000.
Laín Entralgo, Pedro. *Gregorio Marañón: Vida, obra y persona*. Madrid: Colección Austral, 1969.
Larson, Susan. "Conclusion: Kiosk Literature as a Geography of Cultural Objects." In *Kiosk Literature of Silver Age Spain: Modernity and Mass Culture*, edited by Jeffrey Zamostny, and Susan Larson, 421–27. Chicago: Intellect, 2017.

Laudan, Rachel. "Foodways and Ways of Talking about Food," *Rachel Laudan: A Historian's Take on Food and Food Politics* (blog), February 16, 2017, https://www.rachellaudan.com/2017/02/19542.html.

Leavitt, Sarah A. *From Catharine Beecher to Martha Stewart: A Cultural History of Domestic Advice*. Chapel Hill: University of North Carolina Press, 2002.

Leonardi, Susan. "Recipes for Reading: Pasta Salad, Lobster à La Riseholme, Key Lime Pie." In *Cooking by the Book: Food in Literature and Culture*, edited by Mary Anne Schofield, 126–37. Toledo, OH: Bowling Green State University Popular Press, 1989.

Lerner, Gerda. *The Creation of a Feminist Consciousness: From the Middle Ages to Eighteen-Seventy*. Oxford: Oxford University Press, 1986.

Llopart, Dolors. "Cuineres. Creadores i difusors de patrimoni immateria." In *Dona i folklore*, edited by Dolors Llopart i Roser Ros, 77–82. Barcelona: Tantàgora Serveis Culturals, Departament de Cultura de la Generalitat de Catalunya, 2013.

———. "Josep Rondissoni, mestre de cuineres i creador de la tradició de la cuina barcelonina." In *Periferias, Fronteras y Diálogos: Actas del XIII Congreso de Antropología de la Federación de Asociaciones de Antropología del Estado Español*, Tarragona, 2–5 de septiembre de 2014, 1860–68. Tarragona: Universitat Rovira i Virgili, n.d.

Llopis, Martínez. "Prólogo." *Índice Culinario*, by Teodoro Bardají, 1915. Edited by José María Pisa. Huesca: La Val de Onsera.

López Sánchez, José María. *Heterodoxos Españoles: El Centro de Estudios Históricos, 1910–1936*. Madrid: CSIC, 2006.

López-Guzmán, Tomás, and Sandra Sánchez-Cañizares. "Culinary Tourism in Córdoba (Spain)." *British Food Journal* 114, no. 2 (February 2012): 168–79.

Louis, Anja, and Michelle Sharp. Introduction to *Multiple Modernities: Carmen de Burgos: Author and Activist*, 1–13. New York: Routledge, 2017.

Louis, Anja. *Women and the Law: Carmen de Burgos, an Early Feminist*. Rochester, UK: Tamesis, Woodbridge, 2005.

Loureiro, Angel G. "Spanish Nationalism and the Ghost of Empire." *Journal of Spanish Cultural Studies* 4, no. 1 (2003): 65–76.

Luján, Nestor. *Historia de la gastronomía*. Barcelona: Folio, 1997.

Lyons, Martyn. "New Readers in the Nineteenth Century: Women, Children, Workers." In *A History of Reading in the West*, edited by Guglielmo Cavallo and Roger Chartier, 313–44. Amherst: University of Massachusetts Press, 1999.

Machado y Álvarez, Antonio. "Introducción." *Folk-Lore: Biblioteca de las tradiciones populares españolas: Tomo I*, V–XIII. Sevilla: Francisco Álvarez y Ca. Editores, June-Agosto 1883.

Magallón Portolés, Carmen. "El laboratorio Foster de la Residencia de Señoritas. Las relaciones de la JAE con el International Institute for Girls in Spain, y la formación de las jóvenes científicas españolas." *Asclepio: Revista de Historia de la Medicina y de la Ciencia* V–IX, no. 2 (July 2007): 37–62.

Mainer, José Carlos. "De historiografía literaria española: El fundamento liberal." *Estudios de historia de España. Homenaje a Manuel Tuñón de Lara*, 471. Madrid: Universidad Internacional Menéndez y Pelayo, 1981.
———. *La Edad de Plata (1902-1939). Ensayo de interpretación de un proceso cultural*. Madrid: Cátedra, 1983.
Mangien, Brigitte. "Cultura cotidiana: Ciudad y campo." In *Los felices años veinte: España, crisis y modernidad*, edited by Carlos Serrano and Serge Salaün, 135–39. Madrid: Marcial Pons Ediciones de Historia, 2006.
Mangini González, Shirley. *Las modernas de Madrid: Las grandes intelectuales españolas de la vanguardia*. Barcelona: Ediciones Península, 2001.
Marañón, Gregorio. "Breve ensayo sobre la cocina española." *Cuadernos de Gastronomía* vols. Once y doce (1995): 13–23.
———. *Gordos y Flacos. Tercera edición, muy revisada*. Madrid: Espasa-Calpe, 1936.
———. *Meditaciones*. Santiago de Chile: Editorial Cultura, 1937.
———. "Prólogo: Breve ensayo sobre la Cocina española." In *Cocina española y cocina dietética*. Madrid: Sobrinos de la Sucesora de M. Minuesa de los Rios, 1929.
———. "Prólogo." *La cocina de Nicolasa*, by Nicolasa Pradera, 1933, 7–18. Madrid: Estades, 1950.
Mardones Alonso, Javier. *Bibliografía de la gastronomía vasca (1800-1959): Apuntes y anécdotas sobre los libros y autores*. Victoria-Gasteiz: Departamento de cultura, Diputación Foral de Alava, 1997.
Marín Silvestre, Dolors. *Francesca Bonnemaison: Educadora de ciutadanes*. Barcelona: Diputació de Barcelona, 2004.
Martí i Cantí, Carme. *El camí de les Aigües*. Barcelona: Institució de les Lletres Catalanes, 2017.
Martí-López, Elisa. *Borrowed Words: Translation, Imitation, and the Making of the Nineteenth-Century Novel in Spain*. Lewisburg, PA: Bucknell University Press, 2002.
Martin, Benjamin. *The Agony of Modernization: Labor and Industrialization in Spain*. Ithaca, NY: ILR Press, Cornell University, 1990.
Martínez Llopis, Manuel. *Historia de la Gastronomía Española*. Madrid: Editora Nacional, 1981.
Martínez Veiga, Ubaldo. *Mujer, trabajo y domicilio: Los orígenes de la discriminación*. Barcelona: Icaria, 1995.
Matilla, María Jesús, and Esperanza Frax. "La doble opresión. Las mujeres de las clases populares entre el XIX y el XX." In *Las mujeres y el 98. Dirección General de la Mujer*, 87–126. Madrid: Comunidad de Madrid, 1999.
McFeely, Mary Drake. *Can She Bake a Cherry Pie?: American Women and the Kitchen in the Twentieth Century*. Amherst: University of Massachusetts Press, 2000.

Meah, Angela. "Gender." In *Food Words: Essays in Culinary Culture*, edited by Peter Jackson, 88–95. London: Bloomsbury, 2013.
Ménage: Revista del arte de la cocina y pastelería moderns. Año 1, March 2, 1931.
Ménage: Revista del arte de la cocina y pastelería moderns. Año 2, Núm 12, January 1932.
Ménage: Revista del arte de la cocina y pastelería moderns. Año 4, Núm 37, February 1934.
Menús de Guerra: Cuina de Avantguarda i Supervivència. Barcelona: Museu d'Història de Catalunya, Agencia Catalana del Patrimoni Cultural, Fundació Antigues Caixes Catalanes, 2019.
Mermall, Thomas. "Culture and the Essay in Modern Spain." In *The Cambridge Companion to Modern Spanish Culture*, edited by David T. Gies, 163–72. Cambridge: Cambridge University Press, 1999.
Mestayer de Echagüe, María (Marquesa de Parabere). *La cocina completa*. Madrid: Espasa-Calpe, 1955.
Miller, Montserrat. *Feeding Barcelona, 1714–1975: Public Market Halls, Social Networks, and Consumer Culture*. Baton Rouge: Louisiana State University Press, 2015.
Monlau, Pedro Felipe. *Nociones de higiene domestica y gobierno de la casa: Para uso de las escuelas de primera enseñanza de niñas*. Madrid: Impr. de Hernando y Comp, 1897.
Moreno, María Paz. *De la página al plato: El libro de cocina en España*. Gijón, Asturias: Trea, 2012.
———. "*La cocina española antigua* de Emilia Pardo Bazán: Dulce venganza en intencionalidad múltiple en un recetario ilustrado." *La Tribuna: Cuaderno de estudios de la Casa-Museo Emilia Pardo Bazán*, no. 4 (2006): 243–51.
———. *Madrid: A Culinary History*. Lanham: Rowman and Littlefield, 2018.
———. "Writing about Food: Culinary Literature in the Hispanic World." *Cincinnati Romance Review* 33 (2012): 78–97.
Moyano Andrés, Isabel. "La cocina escrita." *Exposición: La cocina en su tinta*. Madrid: Biblioteca Nacional de España, 22 Dec. 2010–13 Mar. 2011. http://www.bne.es/es/LaBNE/Publicaciones/CatalogosExposiciones/la-cocina-en-su-tinta.html.
Muro, Ángel. *Conferencias Culinarias: Primera serie (Abril)*. Madrid: Imprenta de Fortanet, 1890.
———. *El Practicón*. Barcelona: Tusquets Editores, SA, 1894.
Murray, N. Michelle. *Home Away from Home: Immigrant Narratives, Domesticity, and Coloniality in Contemporary Spanish Culture*. Chapel Hill: UNC Press for Department of Romance Studies, University of North Carolina, 2018.
Nadeau, Carolyn. *Food Matters: Alonso Quijano's Diet and the Discourse of Food in Early Modern Spain*. Toronto: University of Toronto Press, 2016.
Nash, Mary. "Estudio preliminar." In *Mujer, familia y trabajo en España 1875–1936*, 7–60. Barcelona: Grupo A, Anthropos, 1983.
———. *Mujer y movimiento obrero en España*. Barcelona: Fontamara, 1981.

———. "Social Eugenics and Nationalist Race Hygiene in Early Twentieth-Century Spain." *History of European Ideas* 15, no.4-6 (1992): 741–48.

———. "Un/Contested Identities: Motherhood, Sex Reform and the Modernization of Gender Identity in Early Twentieth-Century Spain." In *Constructing Spanish Womanhood: Female Identity in Modern Spain*, edited by Victoria Lorée Enders and Pamela Beth Radcliff, 25–50. Albany: State University of New York Press, 1999.

Nelken, Margarita. *La condición social de la mujer en España*. 1919. Madrid: CVS Ediciones, 1975.

"Nieves." *Ramillete del ama de casa*. Barcelona: Luis Gili, 1912.

Núñez Rey, Concepción. *Carmen de Burgos: Columbine en la Edad de Plata de la literatura española*. Sevilla: Fundación José Manuel Lara, 2005.

Olmedo, Iliana. *Itinerarios de exilio: la obra narrativa de Luisa Carnés*. Sevilla: Renacimiento, 2014.

Ong, Walter J. *Orality and Literacy: The Technologizing of the Word*. New York: Routledge, 2002.

Ortiz García, Carmen. "Comida e identidad: Cocina nacional y cocinas regionales en España," In *Alimentación y cultura: Actas del Congreso Internacional*, vol 1, 301–24. Museo Nacional de Antropología. España. Huesca: La Val de Onsera, 1998.

Pack, Sasha. *Tourism and Dictatorship: Europe's Peaceful Invasion of Franco's Spain*. London: Palgrave Macmillan, 2006.

———. "Tourism, Modernization, and Difference: A Twentieth-Century Spanish Paradigm." *Sport in Society* 11, no. 6 (2008): 657–72.

Parasecoli, Fabio. "Food, Cultural Studies and Popular Culture." In *Routledge International Handbook of Food Studies*, edited by Ken Albala, 274–81. London: Taylor and Francis, 2012.

Pardo Bazán, Emilia. "CARTA NÚMERO 3 de Emilia Pardo Bazán Para Unamuno." Dated 20.3.1916, Casa Museo Miguel de Unamuno in Salamanca. Transcribed by Rubén Rodríguez-Jiménez, Texas Woman's University. Microsoft Word file.

———. "[Cartas . . .] (Sobre la huelga, la filología de la cocina, el Diccionario de la Academia)." *Diario de la Marina*, October 22, 1911. In *Cartas de la Condesa en el Diario de la Marina La Habana (1909-1915)*, edited by Cecilia Heydl-Cortínez, 143–49. Madrid: Pliegos, 2002.

———. "Condesa de Pardo Bazán (Día 3 de diciembre de 1916)." In *Conferencias dadas en la Escuela del hogar y profesional de la mujer: Curso de 1916-1918*, 85–103. Madrid: Imprenta de Cleto Vallinas, 1919.

———. "Discurso leído en la sesión inaugural del Folk-Lore gallego," In *Folklore gallego*, 1884. Donostia-San Sebastián: Roger Editor/ Biblio Manías, 2000.

———. "La cocina." *La ilustración artística*, Número 1251 (1905): 810.

———. *La cocina española antigua*. Biblioteca de la Mujer. Madrid: Sociedad Anónima Renacimiento, 1913.

———. *La cocina española moderna*. Biblioteca de la Mujer. Madrid: Sociedad Anónima Renacimiento, n.d.

———. "La vida contemporánea." *La ilustración artística*, Número 1285 (1906): 522.

———. *La mujer española y otros escritos*. Edited by Guadalupe Gómez-Ferrer. Madrid: Ediciones Cátedra, 1999.

———. "Mi libro de cocina: *La cocina española antigua*, la Biblioteca de la Mujer y otros asuntos feministas." *Diario de la Marina*, 30 June 1913. In *Cartas de la Condesa en el Diario de la Marina La Habana (1909-1915)*, edited by Cecilia Heydl-Cortínez, 220-26. Madrid: Pliegos, 2002.

———. "Prólogo." *La cocina práctica*. Santiago de Compostela: Galí, 1905.

Pardo de Figueroa, Mariano ("Thebussem"). *La mesa moderna: Cartas sobre el comedor y la cocina Cambiadas entre El Doctor Thebussem y Un Cocinero de S.M.* Fac. 1888. Barcelona: Parsifal Ediciones, 1997.

Parker, Barbara, Jennifer Brady, Elaine Power, and Susan Belyea. "Introduction: This Is What Feminist Food Studies Looks Like." In *Feminist Food Studies: Intersectional Perspectives*, edited by Barbara Parker, Jennifer Brady, Elaine Power, and Susan Belyea, 1-12. Toronto: Women's Press, 2019.

Parkhurst Ferguson, Priscilla. *Accounting for Taste: The Triumph of French Cuisine*. Chicago: University of Chicago Press, 2006.

Perdiguero-Gil, Enrique, and Ramón Castejón-Bolea. "Popularising Right Food and Feeding Practices in Spain (1847-1950): The Handbooks of Domestic Economy." *Dynamis* 30 (2010): 141-65.

Pérez, Dionisio. "(Post-Thebussem)." *Guía del buen comer español: Inventario y loa de la cocina clásica de España y sus regiones*. Madrid: Sucesores de Rivadeneyra, SA, 1929.

Pérez Galdós, Benito. "Observaciones sobre la novela contemporánea en España," 1870. In *Ensayos de Crítical Literaria*, edited by Laureano Bonet, 123-39. Barcelona: Ediciones Península, 1990.

Pérez Samper, M.d l Á. "Los recetarios de las mujeres y para mujeres. Sobre la conservación y transmisión de los saberes domésticos en la época moderna." *Cuadernos de Historia Moderna* 19 (1997): 121-54.

Pérez-Villanueva Tovar, Isabel. "La Escuela del Hogar y Profesional de la Mujer y las enseñanzas domésticas (1911-1936)." *Arenal*, 22, no. 2 (July-Dec. 2015): 313-35.

Perinat, Adolfo, and Ma Isabel Marrades. *Mujer, prensa y sociedad en España. 1800-1939*. Madrid: Centro de Investigaciones Sociológicas, 1980.

Pisa, José María. "Delantal del Editor." In *La cocina de ellas*, 7-8. Huesca: La Val de Onsera, 2002.

Poulain, Jean-Pierre. *The Sociology of Food: Eating and the Place of Food in Society*. London: Bloomsbury Academic, 2017.

Pradera, Nicolasa. *La cocina de Nicolasa*. 1933. Madrid: Estades, 1950.

Puga y Parga. Manuel María (Picadillo). *La cocina práctica*. Decimosexta edición. Santiago de Compostela: Galí, 1981.

Ray, Krishnendu. *The Ethnic Restaurateur*. London: Bloomsbury, 2015.
Reuben, Julie A. "Beyond Politics: Community Civics and the Redefinition of Citizenship in the Progressive Era." *History of Education Quarterly* 37, no. 4 (1997): 399-420.
Richards, Michael. "Spanish Psychiatry c. 1900-1945: Constitutional Theory, Eugenics, and the Nation." *Bulletin of Spanish Studies* 81, no. 6 (2004): 823-48.
Ringrose, David. *Spain, Europe and the "Spanish Miracle," 1700-1900*. Cambridge: Cambridge University Press, 1996.
Roche, Maurice. *Mega-Events and Modernity: Olympics and Expos in the Growth of Global Culture*. London: Routledge, 2000.
Rødtjer, Rocío. *Women and Nationhood in Restoration Spain, 1874-1931: The State as Family*. London: Legenda, 2019.
Rondissoni, Josep. *Classes de Cuina Popular, Curs de 1924-1925*. Barcelona: Institut de Cultura i Biblioteca Popular de la Dona, Imprempta Altés, [s.a.].
Ruiz-Ocaña Dueñas, Eduardo. *La obra periodística de Emilia Pardo Bazán en* La ilustración artística *de Barcelona (1895-1916)*. Madrid: Fundación Universitaria Española, 2004.
Salillas, Rafael. *El Delincuente español (Hampa)*. Madrid: Librería de Victoriano Suárez, 1898.
———. *La casa como célula social*. 1908. Congreso de Zaragoza de la Asociación para el Progreso de las Ciencias. Vol. 5, Sección 4, Ciencias Sociales, 53-95. Eduardo Arias, 1909.
Sánchez Cantón, F. J. *Spain*. Madrid: Patronato Nacional del Turismo, Hauser y Menet, 1930.
Sánchez Llama, Íñigo. *Galería de escritoras isabelinas: La prensa periódica entre 1833 y 1895*. Madrid: Ediciones Cátedra, 2000.
Scanlon, Geraldine M. *La polémica feminista en la España contemporánea (1868-1974)*. Translated by Rafael Mazarrasa. Madrid: Akal, 1986.
Schwarz, Laura. *Feminism and the Servant Problem: Class and Domestic Labor in the Women's Suffrage Movement*. Cambridge: Cambridge University Press, 2019.
Scott, Lynn Thomson. "Carmen de Burgos: Piecing a Profession, Rewriting Women's Roles." PhD diss., University of Florida, 1999.
Segura Soriano, Isabel. *Memòria d'un espai: Institut de Cultura i Biblioteca Popular de la Dona, 1909-2003*. Barcelona: Ajuntament de Barcelona, Institut d'Educació, 2007.
Sensat, Rosa. *Cómo se enseña la economía doméstica*. Madrid: Publicaciones de la Revista de Pedagogía; Serie Metodológica, 1927.
———. *Per a l'escola secundària en projecte de l'Institut de Cultura i Biblioteca Popular per la Dona (1922-1923)*. Barcelona: Institut de Cultura i Biblioteca Popular de la Dona [s.a].
Shapiro, Laura. *Something from the Oven: Reinventing Dinner in 1950s America*. New York: Viking, 2004.

Sharp, Michelle. "Carmen de Burgos: Teaching Women of the Modern Age." In *Kiosk Literature of Silver Age Spain: Modernity and Mass Culture*, edited by Jeffrey Zamostny, and Susan Larson, 311–28. Chicago: Intellect, 2017.

Shubert, Adrian. *A Social History of Modern Spain*. London: Routledge, 1990.

Simón Palmer, María del Carmen. *Escritoras españolas del siglo XIX: Manual bio-bibliográfico*. Madrid: Castalia, 1991.

Simón Palmer, María del Carmen. *Bibliografía de la gastronomía española: Notas para su realización*. Madrid: Ediciones Velazquez, 1977.

Sinovas Maté, Juliana. *Cartas de la condesa en el Diario de la Marina de La Habana, Cuba (1909–1921)*. Newark: Juan de la Cuesta, 2006.

Sinués de Marco, María Pilar. *La dama elegante: Manual práctico y completísimo del buen tono y del buen orden doméstico*. Madrid: Librería de A. de San Martin, 1880.

Song, H. Rosi, and Anna Riera. *A Taste of Barcelona: The History of Catalan Cooking and Eating*. Lanham, MD: Rowman and Littlefield, 2019.

Soto Carmona, Álvaro. *El Trabajo industrial en la España contemporánea, 1874–1936*. Barcelona: Anthropos, 1989.

Stage, Sarah, and Virginia B. Vicenti. *Rethinking Home Economics: Women and the History of a Profession*. Ithaca, NY: Cornell University Press, 1997.

Stage, Sarah. "Introduction Home Economics: What's in a Name?" In *Rethinking Home Economics: Women and the History of a Profession*, 1–13. Ithaca, NY: Cornell University Press, 1997.

Starcevik, Elizabeth. *Carmen de Burgos: Defensora de la mujer*. Almería: Librería-Editorial Cajal, 1976.

Storm, Eric. "The Nationalization of the Domestic Sphere." *Nations and Nationalism* 23, no. 1 (January 2017): 173–93.

———. "When Did Nationalism Become Banal? The Nationalization of the Domestic Sphere in Spain." *European History Quarterly* 15, no. 2 (2020): 204–25.

Theophano, Janet. *Eat My Words: Reading Women's Lives through the Cookbooks They Wrote*. New York: Palgrave, 2002.

Tolliver, Joyce. *Cigar Smoke and Violet Water: Gendered Discourse in the Stories of Emilia Pardo Bazán*. Lewisburg, PA: Bucknell University Press, 1998.

Torrecilla, Jesús. *La imitación colectiva: Modernidad vs. autenticidad en la literatura española*. Madrid: Editorial Gredos, 1996.

———. "'My Distinguished Friend and Colleague Tula': Emilia Pardo Bazán and Literary-Feminist Polemics." In *Recovering Spain's Feminist Tradition*, edited by Lisa Vollendorf, 217–37. New York: Modern Language Association, 2001.

Trigo, Abril. "General Introduction." In *The Latin American Cultural Studies Reader*, edited by Ana Del Sarto, Alicia Riós, and Abril Trigo, 1–14. Durham, NC: Duke University Press, 2004.

Ugarte, Michael. *Madrid 1900: The Capital as Cradle of Literature and Culture*. University Park: Pennsylvania State University Press, 1996.

Utrera, Federico. *Memorias de Colombine, la primera periodista*. Madrid: HMR Hijos de Muley-Rubio, 1998.
Valis, Noël. *The Culture of Cursilería: Bad Taste, Kitsch, and Class in Modern Spain*. Durham, NC: Duke University Press, 2002.
Vázquez Montalbán, Manuel. "Prólogo. Culinaria: A la medida de la gente inteligente." In *Culinaria*, by Josep Rondissoni, 1945, 3–7. Barcelona: Bon Ton, Antonio Bosch, [s.a.].
Walton, J. K., and J. Smith. "The First Century of Beach Tourism in Spain: San Sebastián and the Playas Del Norte from the 1830s to the 1930s." In *Tourism in Spain: Critical Issues*, edited by Michael Barke, John Towner, and Michael T. Newton, 35–61. Wallingford: CAB, 1996.
Walton, John K. "Tourism and Consumption in Urban Spain, 1876–1975" in *Spain Is (Still) Different: Tourism and Discourse in Spanish Identity*, 107–28. Lanham, MD: Lexington Books, 2008.
Wenzer, Jacob. "Foodscapes." In *Food Words: Essays in Culinary Culture*, edited by Peter Jackson and CONANX Group, 83–85. London: Bloomsbury, 2013.
White, Joseph M. *A New Collection of Laws, Charters, and Local Ordinances of the Governments of Great Britain, France and Spain, Relating to the Concessions of Land*, Vol. I. Philadelphia: T. & J. W. Johnson, 1839.
Williams-Forson, Psyche. Foreword to *Feminist Food Studies: Intersectional Perspectives*, edited by Barbara Parker, Jennifer Brady, Elaine Power, and Susan Belyea, ix–xii. Toronto: Women's Press, 2019.
Woods Peiró, Eva. "Introduction: Modernity, Race, and Visibility." In *White Gypsies: Race and Stardom in Spanish Musicals*, 1–30. Minneapolis: University of Minnesota Press, 2012.
Zamostny, Jeffrey. "Introduction: Kiosk Literature and the Enduring Ephemeral." In *Kiosk Literature of Silver Age Spain: Modernity and Mass Culture*, edited by Jeffrey Zamostny and Susan Larson, 3–27. Chicago: Intellect, 2017.
Zubiaurre, Maite. *Cultures of the Erotic in Spain, 1898–1939*. Nashville, TN: Vanderbilt University Press, 2012.
———. "Double Writing/ Double Reading Cities, Popular Culture, and Stalkers: Carmen de Burgos' *El Persiguidor*." *Revista Hispánica Moderna* 56, no. 1 (2003): 57–70.

INDEX

Page numbers in *italic* indicate figures.

Abarca, Meredith, 5
Afinoguénova, Eugenia, 9, 99, 101, 171n92
Agulló, Ferran, 179n109
Alfonso XIII, 6, 78–79, 81, 86
Ali-Bab, 102–3, 172n103. *See also* Babinski, Henry
Anderson, Lara
    Cooking up the Nation, 10, 153n20
    culinary nationalism, 16, 99
    Franco's regime, 138, 142
    "Introduction. Transhispanic Food Cultural Studies," 10, 151n53
    on Parabere, 66
    unifying diverse foodscapes, 19–20
    "Unity and Diversity La Olla Podrida, The," 173n2
angel of the house, 4, 9, 82–83, 115–16, 138
Appadurai, Arjun, 19
Arkinstall, Christine, 10, 115, 175n26
Avakian, Arlene, 4
Azcaray, Sira, and Ursula Azcaray, 85, 88–89, 169n46, 169n58
Azorín, 10, 25, 47

Babinski, Henry, 172n103. *See also* Ali-Bab
Badia, Maria, 109–10, 120

Bak-Geller, Sarah, 19
Barbas, Samantha, 94
Barcelona
    bourgeois taste, 124–25
    consumer culture, 81
    cooking style, 141
    degeneracy, 130
    Eixample, 112
    feminism, 115–16
    high society, 122
    industrial working class, 17, 109
    modernization, 7, 109–12, 119, 129, 137–38, 140
    1929 Exhibition, 107, 113
    Semana Trágica, 29, 114, 156n72
    unrest, 112
    women in the workforce, 113–14, 140
Bardají, Teodoro, 86, 151n47
Barreiro, Alejandro, 37–39, 158n114
Barthes, Roland, 166n13
Bendix, Regina, 104, 172n108
Bieder, Maryellen, 10
Biltekoff, Charlotte, 110, 130, 178n92
Blanco, Alda, 10
Blasco Herranz, Inmaculada, 117
Bonnemaison, Francesca, 111, 114, 116–17, 126, 128–29
Bourdieu, Pierre, 4, 157n92
Bravo-Villasante, Carmen, 38

Burgos, Carmen de
  alternative model of femininity, 50, 52–53, 56–57, 59–60, 76, 139
  aristocratic women, 61–62, 67
  bluestocking, 44, 159n2
  "Carta-Prólogo," 50, 52–53, 56–57, 170n75
  circulation of writing, 49
  classical world, 67, 69
  cocina moderna, La (*LCM*), 44, 50, 61, 146, 159n3, 160n18, 162n52
  cooking and the public sphere, 55–56, 63, 140
  cooking and writing, 54–55
  double writing, 53–54, 161n36
  education, 59–60, 63–65
  erudite, 45, 54, 60–61, 67–68, 76, 140, 163n94
  "escritora-ama de casa" (writer-homemaker), 44, 140
  feminism, 44–45, 50, 58–60, 63, 76, 115, 139, 141
  fiction, 44–45, 47, 50, 53, 163n83
  gendered critical dismissal, 44–46, 48–49, 74, 76, 159n9, 165n126
  good taste, 72–73
  Influencias recíprocas entre la mujer y la literatura, 58–59
  kiosk literature, 46–47
  as middle-class, 46
  Misión social de la mujer, 58–59
  modernizing reforms, 47, 65
  mujer en España, La, 58, 63, 162n55, 162n72
  mujer moderna y sus derechos, La, 11, 44–45, 48, 61
  Nueva cocina práctica (*NCP*), 44, 50, 65, 159n3
  nueva mujer moderna, 60
  nutrition, 52, 57, 64–65
  paella recipe, 48–49, 74–75
  paratext, 11, 45, 58, 66, 75, 85, 140, 159n7
  questioning women's roles, 54–56, 63–64, 161n31, 161n36
  ¿Quiere usted comer bien?, 44, 50, 159n7, 160n18
  in twenty-first century, 146
  women readers, 47, 64, 76, 140
  women's foodwork and modernization, 45, 68, 73, 75
  women's lived experience, 45, 50, 75, 160n31

Cairns, Kate, 49
Carnés, Luisa, 174n21
Carr, Raymond, 6, 82
Castells, Luis, 106
casticismo, 30, 101–4, 108, 167n17
Castillo, José Juan, 169nn43–44
Castejón-Bolea, Ramón, 111
Charnon-Deutsch, Lou, 10
ChefBNE, 145
Chodorow, Nancy, 92
Cleminson, Richard, 131
Climent-Espino, Rafael, 10
cocinas ambulantes, 65, 143
cocinera, 9, 26, 40–41, 43, 72, 96–97, 120, 124
cocinero, 9, 32, 67, 86, 96
consumer culture, 81–82, 110, 146
Counihan, Carol, 5
Cruz, Jesús, 7, 81, 107
Cunill de Bosch, Josep, 132

Davidson, Robert, 107, 112
Davies, Catherine, 50
Davis, Jennifer, 123, 125
democracy, 2, 6, 28, 43, 81–55, 108, 139–40, 146
degeneracy, 12, 72, 112, 130–33, 136–38, 142–43
Doménech, Ignacio, 77, 140, 151n47

domesticity
  conventional understandings of, 52, 60, 74, 94, 111, 138
  feminist understandings of, 4–5, 115, 134, 139–41, 143, 163n83
  ideology of, 2, 7, 52–53, 56–57, 82, 89, 114, 119
  politicization of, 64
  site of nostalgia, 55
Don Quijote, 10, 22, 62, 70–71
Duch Plana, Montserrat, 111, 119
Dunai, Suzanne, 9, 142

Epps, Brad, 107
Elias, Megan, 128, 179n110
Elias, Norbert, 32
Enders, Victoria, 63

Flitter, Derek, 28, 91
Freedman, Paul, 164n109
Fuentes Peris, Teresa, 131

Galera Gómez, Andrés, 131
Generation of '98 thinkers, 16, 25
Giard, Luce, 4, 26
Gold, Hazel, 16
Gómez Bravo, Ana, 9–10, 145
González Turmo, Isabel, 9, 157n92
Good, Kate, 16
good taste / buen gusto, 72–73, 136, 172n113
Goody, Jack, 4
Graham, Helen, 142, 144

Haber, Barbara, 4
Haranburu Altuna, Luis, 85
home economics
  degeneracy, 145, 133, 179n110
  feminist/progressive, 78, 137–38, 179n115
  scientific, 26, 130, 134–35, 142
  transnational, 124, 130, 133
  US context, 147, 140

illiteracy, 18, 43, 111
Institut de Cultura i Biblioteca Popular de la Dona
  bringing culture to women, 114, 119, 130, 135
  Catholic, 111, 127
  Catholic feminism, 117
  combating degeneracy, 112, 130, 136
  community based citizenship, 129
  cooking right, 12, 119, 129–30, 136
  crossing class barriers, 109–11, 119, 125, 137
  "Cuina popular" / "Cocina popular," 120, 122, 176n63
  "Cuina pràctica"/ "Cocina práctica," 119, 121–22, 176n63
  curriculum, 111, 117, 119–20, 134
  emancipatory ethos, 111, 135
  feminism, 112, 115, 128–29, 134, 137
  focus on employment, 114, 117–18, 125–26, 128
  gendered culinary authority, 123
  home economics, 12, 110, 130, 133–35, 137, 140, 142
  modern culinary identity, 111, 124
  neglect of family life, 128
  photographs of, *121, 122, 134*
  progressive programs, 117, 119, 128, 136–37
  reading and writing classes, 120
  shift to students as consumers, 127–29, 137
  sliding scale tuition, 117
  small modernization, 116, 126
  stratification of class, 125–26
  transnational cooking style, 119, 123, 125, 137
  working class, 112, 117
  working-class women, 109, 117, 119, 124–26, 129, 134, 140

Johannes, Venetia, 173n4
Johnson, Roberta
   alleged absence of women intellectuals, 10
   on Burgos, 53, 160n31, 163n83
   Gender and Nation, 25
   Krausism and education, 163n91
   Major Concepts in Spanish Feminist Theory, 138, 175n22
Johnston, Josée, 49
Juaristi, Adriana de, 86–87
Juderías, Julián, 80

kiosk literature, 8, 11, 46–48
Krausist, 18, 23, 65, 163n87, 179n103

Labanyi, Jo
   "cultural jamboree," 144
   Franco's regime, 142
   intellectual elitism, 142
   modern cultural practices, 107
   writing the nation, 17, 153n19
Laín Entralgo, 166n11
Larson, Susan, 48
Laudan, Rachel, 5
Leonardi, Susan, 3, 85
Lerner, Gerda, 57
Llopart, Dolors, 177n64
Lombroso, Cesare, 179n103
Luján, Néstor, 85
Luna, Gabriel, 72. *See also* Burgos, Carmen de

Machado y Álvarez, Antonio, 18, 23, 154n47, 155n50
Maggi seasoning, 123, 127, 176n60, 178n79
Mangien, Brigitte, 7
Marañón, Gregorio
   Agrupación al servicio de la República, 79, 82
   authenticity, 11, 79–80, 98, 101, 103–4, 106–8, 140
   Basque cooking and traditions, 88, 91, 98–101, 105, 107
   "Breve ensayo," 79, 95–96, 101–2, 166n12
   cuisine as sensual practice, 70, 97, 107
   discursive construction of Pradera, 12, 79, 88–89, 92, 94–95, 98, 104, 107
   election, 79
   erasure of women's progress, 93
   essentialism, 63, 90–92
   essentialization of Pradera, 88–90, 92, 101, 108
   eugenics, 95
   Gordos y Flacos, 79, 95, 97
   hygiene, 95–98
   imprisonment, 78
   leyenda negra, 80, 101–4
   normative middle class, 88–89
   political writings, 78–79
   "Prólogo"/"Prologue," 11, 77, 85, 88–101
   as prologuist, 79
   relation to feminism, 92
   sanitization of social unrest, 11, 107–8
   tourism, 11, 79–80, 84, 100–104, 106, 108, 140, 171n92
   weight and human potential, 96
Mardones Alonso, Javier, 85
Marín Silvestre, Dolors, 116–17
Martí i Cantí, Carme, 120
Martínez Llopis, Manuel, 85
McFeely, Mary Drake, 148n10
Menéndez Pidal, Ramón, 18, 23
Menéndez y Pelayo, Marcelino, 8, 18, 78, 152n14
Mesteyer de Echagüe, María, 66, 100. *See also* Parabere, Marquesa de
Miller, Montserrat
   Catalan nationalism, 131

historian, 9
manufactured ingredients, 127, 178n79
market halls, 110, 113
women, 83–84, 137
Monlau, Pedro Felipe, 8, 63, 167n19
Moreno, María Paz, 2, 10, 15
Muro, Ángel, 9, 24, 38, 69, 151n47
Murray, N. Michelle, 146

Nadeau, Carolyn, 9, 145, 154n37, 165n115
Nash, Mary, 167n21, 168n32, 170n69
Nelken, Margarita, 7, 46, 55–56, 90, 114, 116, 170n72
new woman / new modern woman / *nueva mujer moderna*, 7, 60, 83, 90, 136
Nordau, Max, 47, 131

Ortega y Gasset, José, 78, 81, 142

Pack, Sasha, 106
Palau Vergés, Montserrat, 111, 119
Parabere, Marquesa de, 66, 86–101. See also Mesteyer de Echagüe, María
Pardo Bazán, Emilia
　advertisement, *14*
　aesthetics of food, 33, 141, 157n87
　ambivalent feminism, 16, 39–41, 43
　aristocracy, 33, 46, 88
　Biblioteca de la Mujer, 15, 31, 35–36, 39
　"Cartas de la condesa," 28, 42
　cocina española antigua, La (CEA), 15, 24–26, 28–29, 31, 34, 39, 154n41, 156n79
　cocina española moderna, La (CEM), 15–16, 20, 31, 38, 42, 156n79, 157n87
　"Condesa de Pardo Bazán," 1
　culinary nationalism, 21, 153n20
　cynicism, 16, 39, 42–43, 139
　feminism, 1–2, 10, 15, 35–36, 39, 42, 139
　folklore, 23–24, 31, 155n50
　French versus Spanish cuisine, 20–21, 153n30, 156n79
　health of the nation, 133
　imagined readers, 16, 18, 27–32, 36, 39, 41–42, 140–41
　kiosk literature, 47
　literary nationalism, 18, 21
　middle-class women, 18, 31, 34–35, 37–38, 41, 139–40
　"Mi libro de cocina," 35–37, 39
　nation building, 1, 16, 18, 42, 133
　protests, 17, 29–31, 42, 156n72
　public intellectual, 2, 37, 139
　pueblo as imaginary/idealized subject, 27–31, 42–43
　relationship to readers, 36–39, 86
　Spanish national cuisine, 18, 141, 154n41
　Spanish national identity, 18–19, 32, 35
　traditional cooking, 20, 22–27, 31, 34
　working class, 16–17, 31, 139–40, 143
Parkhurst Ferguson, Priscilla, 19, 63
Perdiguero-Gil, Enrique, 111
Pérez, Dionisio, 86, 99, 153n30
Pérez Galdós, Benito, 21, 47, 78
Pérez Samper, Maria de los Ángeles, 8
Picadillo, 16, 19, 24, 38, 40, 86, 151n47. See also Puga y Parga, Manuel María
Pradera, Nicolasa
　authorial modesty, 85–87
　Basque cuisine, 11, 85, 88, 99–100, 107, 168n43

Pradera, Nicolasa (*continued*)
  Casa Nicolasa/Nicolasa, 11, 77–78, 85, 168–69n43
  cocina de Nicolasa, La, 25, 77, 85
  entrepreneur, 84, 89
  erasure by Marañón, 11, 79, 85, 88–89, 92, 94–95, 107–8, 140
  French culinary training, 105
  happy cook, 85, 108
  middle class, 89
  national breakdown, 11, 107–8
  parenthetical comments, 87–88
  popular cuisine, 90, 104
  portraits, 78
  shared cooking tradition, 88
  tourism, 77, 80, 84, 99–100, 104, 106
protests, 17, 29–31, 42, 82, 112, 156n72, 156n74
Puga y Parga, Manuel María, 16, 151n47. *See also* Picadillo

Radcliff, Pamela, 63
recipes as social network, 40–41
Reuben, Julie, 112, 129
Richards, Ellen, 179n110
Richards, Michael, 167n21
Riera, Anna, 10, 110, 131, 144, 173n2
Ringrose, David, 81
Rondissoni, Josep
  as chef and professor, 26, 109
  cookbooks and recipes, 112, 132, 137, 177n63
  cooking classes, 126, 121–30, 141
  marketing relationships, 176n60

Salillas, Rafael, 130–32, 138, 179n103, 179n107
Sánchez Cantón, Francisco Javier, 106
San Sebastián, 77–78, 84–85, 100, 105–6, 168n42

Scanlon, Geraldine M., 116
Segura Soriano, Isabel
  Biblioteca Francesca Bonnemaison, 143
  "Cuina popular," 120
  cultural norms, 128–29
  industry sponsorships, 178n78
  "Llibres de Actes," 174n8
  "Resums biogràfics," 177n73
  scientific thinking and male supervision, 122
Semana Trágica, 6, 17, 29, 114, 156n72
Sempere, Francisco, 47, 52–56, 58, 61
Sensat, Rosa, 111–12, 130, 134–36
Sharp, Michelle, 47, 66
Shubert, Adrian, 7, 81
Simón Palmer, María del Carmen, 9, 48
Sinués de Marco, Maria del Pilar, 9, 61, 157n87, 170n75
social hygiene, 81, 95, 167n19
Song, H. Rosi, 10, 110, 131, 144, 173n2, 179n109
Sopena, Ramón, 47, 160n18
Soto Carmona, Álvaro, 113
Spanish Civil War, 1, 6, 109, 111, 116, 119
Stage, Sarah, 64
Starcevic, Elizabeth, 44
Storm, Eric, 9
suffrage, 17, 46, 58, 115, 155n71, 171n78

Tolliver, Joyce, 39, 158n114
traitorous onions, 41

Ugarte, Michael, 53, 61, 66, 161n36
Uhagón, Dolores Vedia de, 24, 88, 93–94, 170nn75–76
Unamuno, Miguel de, 10, 25–26, 38, 46–47, 80, 158n109

Valis, Noël, 33–34, 107
Valle-Inclán, Ramón del, 10, 47, 80
Vázquez Montalbán, Manuel, 124, 129
Vincenti, Virginia, 64

Walton, John K., 106
Wheaton, Barbara Ketcham, 4
Williams-Forson, Psyche, 4

Zubiaurre, Maite, 10, 53, 80, 161n36

www.ingramcontent.com/pod-product-compliance
Lightning Source LLC
Chambersburg PA
CBHW030652230426
43665CB00011B/1056